HOW SWEET IT IS

A SONGWRITER'S REFLECTIONS ON MUSIC, MOTOWN, AND THE MYSTERY OF THE MUSE

LAMONT DOZIER

with Scott B. Bomar

How Sweet It Is:
A Songwriter's Reflections on Music, Motown, and the Mystery
of the Muse

Cover design by Randall Leddy
Cover photo by Lisa Margolis
All interior photos from the collection of the author except for
the following:
Photo on page P4, lower photo on P11, lower photo on P13,
lower photos on P14, and lower photo on P15 via Getty Images.
Lower photo on page P6 courtesy of Walt Disney Television/©
ABC/Getty Images.

Library of Congress Cataloging-in-Publication Data available
upon request.
Hardback ISBN: 9781947026315
Hardback with CD ISBN: 9781947026667

Published by BMG
www.bmg.com

CONTENTS

Introduction

TRYING TO GET AROUND MYSELF

"I know you're in there, motherfucker!"

Somebody was pounding on the door. Ferociously. I opened my eyes. It was dark, but I could see well enough to know my surroundings weren't familiar.

"Is that bitch in there with you?"

Oh, right. The motel. I rubbed my eyes and tried to shake off the grogginess. I was in the little no-tell motel down the street from Motown's headquarters at 2648 West Grand Boulevard in Detroit. It was the kind of place where you wanted to hurry up and get your key from the check-in desk before you saw someone you knew. I'd been there a time or two when I walked in and spotted somebody I recognized waiting in line. I just backed out before they saw me.

Bang! Bang! Bang! The door was vibrating in its frame. "You better open up this goddamn door, Lamont!"

It was my main squeeze. And she was pissed. My first wife and I had split up several months earlier, and I had been dating around a little bit. I wasn't living with anyone at the time, but the very angry woman on the other side of that door certainly would have called herself my girlfriend. And it sounded like she wanted me to let her in! The problem was I was in there with another girl. And I could see in that girl's eyes that she was starting to get real nervous about what the main squeeze was going to do to her if she got past the one-and-three-quarters-inch of wood that stood between them.

"Get dressed," I whispered to the girl in bed beside me. "You're gonna have to slip out the bathroom window and quietly escape around back. This woman's out for blood. I'll call you later." She silently gathered up her things and tiptoed to the bathroom in the dark.

"Are you gonna open this door, asshole, or am I gonna have to find a way to break it down?"

How did she know where I was? Somebody must've seen me. I grabbed the bathrobe that was resting across a chair next to the bed, slipped it on, and crept up to the peephole. I looked out and saw lights flickering on in other rooms. She was making all kinds of noise out there, and people were starting to peek out their curtains to see if it was someone who was after them. Unfortunately, this time it was someone who was after me.

I looked back toward the bathroom. My friend had made her exit and was slowly lowering the window back down from outside. Thank God we were on the first floor. I crept back over to the bedside table and flicked the switch on the lamp. I quickly scanned the room for a stray bra, shoe, or any other telltale sign of my recent companion. All clear!

"It's about damn time," my girl shouted when she saw the light come on. I paused for a few moments, squinted my eyes as if I'd just woken up, slid off the security chain, took a deep breath, and began to open the door. She pushed it open and forced her way past me. "Where's the bitch at? I know she's in here!" I feigned a yawn. "I don't know what you're talking about, baby," I muttered. "I'm just getting some rest after a long night at the studio. I had a little too much to drink, so I decided not to drive home." She put her hands on her hips. "Oh, that is some bullshit," she yelled. "Ain't nobody come here to get no rest!" She scooped my pants off the floor and flung them toward me. I dodged them just before the keys in the pocket clanked against the window, making a huge racket. By this point, everyone in the motel was awake. Hell, the way she was carrying on, everyone in the neighborhood might've been awake. She kept on screaming and yelling while I tried desperately to get her to quiet down.

"I ain't no fool, Lamont. I know you had some girl up in here with you."

"Baby, please. I was just trying to get some sleep."

"You're a liar, and you know it. You better just admit it now."

"Baby, please stop."

"Oh, I'm gonna stop alright. I'm gonna stop that bitch when I find out who she is, and you better be damn sure I'm gonna stop your ass from runnin' around on me."

"Baby, please stop. I'm begging you, please. You're waking up the whole place. Just stop. Stop! In the name of love."

You know those movie scenes where you hear a record scratch and everything comes to a screeching halt? That's what happened in my head at that moment. It was like the whole world suddenly stood still as my own words rang in my ears. *Stop! In the name of love.*

"Baby," I said, "Did you hear that?"

"Hear what?"

"That cash register. Stop in the name of love? If that's not a hit song title, I don't know what is!"

"Oh, shut up, Lamont. You're not gonna distract me with that shit."

It was silent for a moment. "That *is* actually pretty good," she finally said, allowing herself a little smirk. "Stop in the name of love, I mean."

Somehow or another she finally calmed down, and we went back to my apartment. I got a few hours of sleep before I had to get up and head over to work at Hitsville, which was what we called the headquarters from which Berry Gordy ran his Motown, Tamla, and associated record labels. When I arrived that morning, my partner Brian Holland was sitting at the piano in our office playing a melody I hadn't heard before. "What's that, man?" I asked as I set my briefcase down next to the desk. "Oh, it's just a thing I've been working on," he said. "Kind of a rough idea." I leaned against the wall. "Play that again," I said. He started from the top. I began to sing, "Stop, in the name of love." Brian nodded his head. "Before you hurt my heart," I continued. "I like that," he said. "*Something* like that," I responded. That's not quite it yet, but it's close. Play that first chord again." Brian hit the keys as I sang, "Stop!" I reached over and grabbed his hand to stop him from playing the next chord. "That's what it needs," I said. "We've got to really emphasize that word." I sat down on the bench. "And maybe it's 'break' my heart instead of 'hurt' my heart," I continued. Within a few minutes, we'd created a roadmap for the whole song.

When Brian's brother Eddie arrived later, we gave him the framework we'd created, and he finished up the lyrics. We recorded it with The Supremes, and in March of 1965, it became their fourth consecutive single penned by the team of Brian

Holland, Lamont Dozier, and Eddie Holland to reach number one on the *Billboard* pop chart.

That's how it worked in those days. We were living our lives, writing what we knew, and working at a feverish pace to crank out the hit songs to keep the Sound of Young America chugging along. The team of Holland-Dozier-Holland only lasted for about a decade, but we made history together. The three of us wrote—and Brian and I produced—ten number-one pop hits for The Supremes alone. In addition to "Stop! In the Name of Love" there was "Where Did Our Love Go," "Baby Love," "Come See About Me," "Back in My Arms Again," "I Hear a Symphony," "You Can't Hurry Love," "You Keep Me Hangin' On," "Love is Here and Now You're Gone," and "The Happening." There were plenty of others, including "My World Is Empty Without You" and "Reflections" that were big hits that fell just shy of the top of the chart.

And then there was The Four Tops, with whom we found nearly as much success as we did with The Supremes: "Baby I Need Your Loving," "I Can't Help Myself (Sugar Pie Honey Bunch)," "It's The Same Old Song," "Shake Me, Wake Me (When It's Over)," "Reach Out I'll Be There," "Standing in the Shadows of Love," "Bernadette," and "7 Rooms of Gloom" are just the tip of the iceberg.

Of course there were plenty of other Motown artists who found success with our songs, including Marvin Gaye ("Can I Get a Witness," "You're a Wonderful One," "How Sweet It Is [To Be Loved by You]"), Martha and the Vandellas ("Heat Wave," "Quicksand," "In My Lonely Room," "Nowhere to Run," "Jimmy Mack"), The Miracles ("Mickey's Monkey"), The Marvelettes ("Strange I Know," "Come and Get These Memories"), Jr. Walker & The All Stars ("[I'm A] Road Runner"), The Elgins ("Heaven Must Have Sent You"), and many more.

After we left Motown and established our own Hot Wax and Invictus labels, the hits kept coming. The Glass House scored with "Crumbs Off the Table," The Chairman of the Board hit with "Give Me Just a Little More Time," and Freda Payne found success with "Band of Gold." At the same time, rock artists began covering songs from our Motown days and turning them into even bigger hits than before. "Don't Do It" by The Band, "Take Me in Your Arms (Rock Me a Little While)" by the Doobie Brothers, and "This Old Heart of Mine" by Rod Stewart are just a few of many examples.

What Eddie and Brian and I were able to accomplish together in a relatively short period of time still amazes me. It was like the three of us were meant to come together at a certain time and in a certain place to create something special. It was preordained and simply too deep and too spiritual to be a mere coincidence.

Nothing, of course, lasts forever. There were ugly lawsuits with Motown and Berry Gordy. There were legal fights between me and the Holland brothers, too. Accusations have been made, and things have been said over the years that have hurt me. I'm sure I probably hurt others, too. But I look back on it now, and I see all those guys as my brothers. Brothers fight, but when you create something like we created, it pulls you together in a lifelong bond that can't ever be fully broken. In the end, it really is all about the music.

There's much more to my story than just the remarkable run with Brian and Eddie. As an artist, I found success with singles like "Why Can't We Be Lovers," "Trying to Hold On to My Woman," "Fish Ain't Bitin,'" "Let Me Start Tonite," and "Goin' Back to My Roots." I produced records for Aretha Franklin, Dionne Warwick, James Ingram, and others. Then, in the 1980s, I had a songwriting resurgence working both on my own and with various co-writers. Alison Moyet hit the charts with "Invisible"; Peabo Bryson and Regina Belle scored a hit with their version of my song "Without You"; I collaborated with Simply Red's Mick Hucknall on their Top 10 single "You've Got It"; Eric Clapton cut two of my then-new songs on his *August* album; and Phil Collins and I won a Grammy and a Golden Globe—and even nabbed an Oscar nomination—for our song "Two Hearts."

But it didn't stop there. I still write every day. If Motown had never happened and I'd become an electrician, lawyer, or banker, I would have still come home every night after work to sit at the piano. I do it because I *have* to do it. Music is like oxygen to me. I need it to survive. I can't go a day without fooling with the piano, and it's hard for me to even sit around and enjoy a football game or other leisure activity because I'm always itching to create. I was put on this earth to make music. That's the job I was given. And if I'm not doing my job, then why am I sitting around taking up space?

From the time I was young I was looking for something greater. I wanted inner peace, but that's not something that comes easily. I guess that's why I started writing songs. I wanted to try to search for solutions to the problems of this world. I wanted to stare in the face of the big questions about life and love—shared love, painful love, unrequited love, perfect love, God's love, and every other kind of love—to try to connect with others and make sense of things. Sometimes it seems we humans are going nowhere in terms of finding a meaningful life. We're making the same dumb mistakes now we were making 100 years ago, but that hasn't ever stopped me from exploring solutions through music.

For me, a song has to mean something. If it doesn't touch me in an emotional place—whether that be joy, sadness, desire, humor, tenderness, or what have you—then I'll just set it aside. It's not that song's time yet. A song has a life of its own, and it takes the time it's going to take to blossom. Sometimes it's frustrating, but they come when they want to come. Some take fifteen minutes, and some take years. I'm blessed enough to know when I'm on the right track and when I'm not, but those instincts have largely been honed from a lot of experience. Burt Bacharach once told me that it can take months or years to get the right feeling or the right point across. You've got to have patience. That's the price you pay to be a good songwriter. If you just write whatever garbage pops out on your first try, then you're doing an injustice to the music that you're supposed to respect.

There's actually a song I've been writing for thirty years called "Trying to Get Around Myself." It's still not right, but I've been chipping away at it. The focus—what it's saying—isn't quite what it's supposed to be. It could be because I'm not at the right point yet in my life, but when it comes—when the right words, the right meaning, and the right feeling come together—I'll know it.

The title itself is a pretty good description of the process. Every time I'm writing a song, I'm putting in the work and applying my craft, but I'm ultimately trying to get around myself to receive the song as it should be. Sometimes when I'm writing, I'm looking for one chord in my mind, and then my finger might fall on a wrong note that changes the whole melody. I'll think, *Wow, that's the direction I'm supposed to be going.* There are no accidents in creativity. That's the muse at work. Something or somebody is there sitting over your shoulder.

It's kind of a paradox, isn't it? You discipline yourself and do the work so you can be open to receive what the muse sends you and know when to get out of the way—and how to get around yourself. The bulk of the time goes into the search, looking for the direction or looking for the chords that are going to speak for the idea, but then something greater takes over. Songwriting is equal parts sweat equity, time commitment, and courting the mystery of the muse.

What's been given to me is a blessing. God gave me a gift. I have no formal training, but I have these special feelings, and I have a good ear. I definitely put in the work and the time, but I can't take all the credit. What comes out of the craft is bigger than me. That's the work of the Master Muse, which is what I call God. I've had some mystical experiences over the years that range from the mind-boggling to the spine-tingling. As a songwriter, I believe I have to be open to the spiritual realm. Not everything can be explained with the mind, so to touch people's hearts with my music I have to put myself in a position to tap into the spiritual stuff—to channel the things that get to the essence of what it means to be human and to function in a world that's spiritually connected in ways we can't even imagine. The Bible says that life on earth is like seeing through a glass darkly. It says that we can only know reality "in part," but that one day in the next life we'll see God face-to-face, and we'll know all things fully. I'm always trying to tap into that. I want to see through that glass as much as I can *now*. And the way to connect with that larger reality for me is music.

Throughout this book I'll share little nuggets and observations about songwriting that I've learned and applied over the years. There might be something that you'll find helpful if you're a writer yourself. I've put these concepts in bold so they'll stand out in the story, but I also included them in a list at the end of the book for those who might want to go back and revisit some of the concepts. This isn't an exhaustive list of "songwriting rules" so much as a set of guiding principles that I've tried and tested over many decades.

Of course there's talent and luck and timing and all kinds of things that make up success. No matter what your endeavor is, you have to reach for that success if you expect to find it. This book is the story of how I began reaching for it before I really knew what I was trying to grasp, and where that journey has led me today. It's not only about how I've tried to get around myself as a songwriter, but also how I've had to get around myself as a person to continue to pursue my dreams.

I've always been a very private person, so writing a memoir doesn't come naturally. I'm pretty shy and introspective in terms of how I process my emotions. I usually channel my feelings into music or lyrical ideas rather than articulating them into sentences and paragraphs. Writing a memoir is a new frontier for me. But I also feel like it's important to reflect on my own experiences and share my thoughts about creativity because it might be an encouragement to someone else.

Another challenge of sharing my memories about the past— particularly the Motown years—is that not everyone remembers things the same way. I'm sure Berry, Eddie, Brian, Smokey Robinson, Diana Ross, or Duke Fakir of The Four Tops might have varying recollections of the details of some of the things we experienced together. The mind works in funny ways, but this is my story from my perspective as I recall it.

Thinking back over my seventy-eight years of life has brought up some painful memories as well as some really joyful moments. I've revisited some mistakes, missteps, struggles, triumphs, and successes. I believe, however, that I've reached a place of balance in my life. Where I once sacrificed personal relationships for my career, I now understand the importance of priorities. I had a couple of brief marriages in my younger years that didn't last very long, but my third wife, Barbara, and I met in 1976 and have been together well over four decades now.

Barbara knows me better than anyone, and we're a real team. She understands my obsession with music, but she's also helped me learn how to keep our marriage strong. We've been through some ups and downs together, but each season has only strengthened our love. The man who once hid out in a no-tell motel seems like a whole other person to me today. I'm not that guy anymore, and what I value today is much different than what I grasped at as a younger man.

In the same way, I didn't always have the kind of relationships I wish I could have with my children from earlier relationships. When Barbara gave birth to our son Beau in 1979, I pledged to be the right kind of father. Beau, our other son, Paris, and our daughter, Desiree, have brought unspeakable love and light into my life as they've helped me grow as a person.

At this point, I've been inducted into the Songwriters Hall of Fame and the Rock & Roll Hall of Fame, but success, titles, and accolades don't mean as much to me now as my four loves: the craft of songwriting, the Master Muse, my wife, and my children. Fortunately I've learned to treasure and enjoy each along a sometimes rocky pathway. I've known good times and bad, but everything happens for a reason. As I look back, I can honestly say, *How sweet it is!*

Chapter One

GOING BACK TO MY ROOTS

I was born in Detroit, but my family roots are in the South. Both my mother's people and my father's people were part of the first Great Migration of more than a million and a half African Americans who left the South between 1916 and 1940 in search of better jobs, better opportunities, and fewer racial prejudices in places like Chicago, New York, Philadelphia, Pittsburgh, and St. Louis. Detroit, in particular, experienced a significant influx of Southern migrants—both white and black—who flocked to the auto industry factories to work for Ford, General Motors, Dodge, Packard, and Chrysler.

My first family members to settle in Detroit were my mother's parents, Rossie and Melvalean Waters. They were from Alabama, but were already living in Detroit when my mom, Ethel Jeannette

Waters, was born in 1926. My grandfather used to brag that the singer and actress Ethel Waters was his third cousin. That was his pride and joy to know that he was part of a star's bloodline, so that's why he gave my mother the same name. I don't know exactly what brought my mom's folks to Michigan, but I know my grandfather only completed the second grade. There really weren't a lot of opportunities for a black man in Alabama at that time, so I suspect it was the common hope for a better life and better job prospects that drew them north. My grandmother was about sixteen when my mom was born. It would be more than three years before she and Rossie actually married, in 1929. After that, they had three more daughters, my aunts Angela, Jennie, and Eula.

Next came my dad's people, Georgia natives Charlie and Zelma Dozier. Zelma was of mixed race, born in 1903 to a black father and a white mother. Can you imagine a white woman marrying a black man in the South at the turn of the twentieth century? It was unheard of! My great-grandmother's family completely disowned her, but she and her husband remained in Georgia anyway. Some of the stories I used to hear about how they were treated were heartbreaking, but they stayed together and stayed in Atlanta. That was their home, and they weren't going to be intimidated into leaving.

I guess it would have been pretty hard to shock anyone in a racially mixed family in that era, so I suspect nobody batted an eye when Zelma and Charlie got together at a pretty young age. People got married much younger back then anyway. My father's brother, Charles, was two years older than him, but my grandparents were still just teenagers when my dad, Willie Lee Dozier, came along in 1919. My Aunt Carrie arrived a few short years later. During the 1930s, with the Depression making everyone's life more difficult, Charlie, Zelma, and their three children left Georgia and headed for Michigan.

Before Detroit earned a reputation as the Motor City, it was the Stove Capital of the World. Thanks to Michigan's iron ore resources, stove production was a big business going all the way back to the 1870s. It was actually the stoves, and not the cars, that brought my dad's family to Detroit from Atlanta. My grandfather went to work in the Detroit-Michigan Stove Company factory, which built Garland Stoves. For years there was a monstrous fifteen ton, twenty-five foot high wooden replica of a Garland Stove that sat outside the company's headquarters on Jefferson Boulevard. I later found out the thing had been built for the 1893 World's Fair in Chicago, then brought back to Detroit and put on display. I remember driving by that huge stove as a kid and just being mesmerized by it. I was the kind of child who loved to imagine the details of historical events. I was fascinated by human potential and what motivated people to strive for greatness. I was a daydreamer who thought about how I might be able to do something great myself one day. There was just something in me, a natural curiosity about the world, that I guess was pretty unique for someone that age.

I was never told how my parents, Willie and Ethel, met and fell in love. I don't even know if they actually fell in love or not. What I do know is they slipped across the state line and got married in Toledo, Ohio, on November 15, 1940. My father and mother listed their ages on the marriage license application as twenty-two and twenty-one, respectively. In reality, he was twenty-one, and she was just fourteen. Why would an out-of-work laborer and a teenage girl sneak into a neighboring state to get married on a chilly November day? I was born exactly seven months later on June 16, 1941, so I'll let you do the math!

Before I was born, my father would build little knick-knack shelves to display collectibles and that sort of thing. He'd sell them to help bring in a little extra money, and he always had a project table in the corner where he would work on his shelves and jot down little notes and ideas that would come to him. He was sitting there one Sunday night in 1941, working on a new shelf, while my mother, eight months pregnant, was in the kitchen cleaning up the dinner dishes. They had the radio on when the announcer said, "Who knows what evil lurks in the hearts of men? The Shadow knows!" It was the opening of my dad's favorite radio program, *The Shadow.* He listened every week to escape into the adventures of the main character, whose name was Lamont Cranston.

Something about that name caught his ear that evening. "Lamont," he muttered aloud. "Hmm, Lamont … Lamont." He reached for his notepad that already had a list of a dozen names that had each been crossed out. He wrote "Lamont" and looked at it for a moment. Then he wrote "Dozier" next to it. "That's it," he shouted. "I've got it, Ethel!" My mother turned off the sink and came into the room, brushing her hair off her forehead with the back of her wrist. "What have you got, Willie?" He stood up and put his hands on her bulging stomach. "I've got our son's name. Lamont Dozier. It sounds like somebody important, don't it?" She gave him a half smile. "How do you know it's going to be a boy?" He broke into a broad grin. "Oh, it's going to be a boy alright. He's going to be Lamont Dozier, and he's going to do great things. That much I know."

Not too long after I was born, my mother got pregnant again with my brother, Reggie. He and I were the oldest of the siblings and the only boys. Then came my sisters, Laretta, Zel, and Norma. Zel was short for Zelmalean, which my folks got by combining the names of each of their mothers, Zelma and Melvalean. People don't use that method of coming up with names very often these days, but it was kind of a common thing back then.

We grew up on the east side of Detroit in a neighborhood called Black Bottom. They originally called it that because of the fertile soil in the area, but by the time we were living there, it had a double meaning. Though originally settled by European immigrants, by the 1940s Black Bottom was a predominantly black neighborhood—specifically the black folks who were living at the *bottom* of the social ranking. We were all poor, and our neighborhood was considered what people would later call a "ghetto" area.

We rented a house on Congress Street that must have been more than a hundred years old at the time. It was a shabby, rundown kind of place that badly needed painting and a bunch of repairs that the landlord was never going to address. I have no idea how many families might have lived in that house before us, but the owners kept renting it out to poor people. While it might have been a drafty ramshackle old place, at least we had a little space. There were three bedrooms: one for my folks, one for my three sisters, and one for me and Reggie. There was a big table in the kitchen that was a family gathering place. My mother was a great cook, and she worked hard to keep the house clean. She took pride in her own home, but keeping it neat was always an uphill battle.

We lived downstairs, and the family that lived above us would throw their trash out the windows. The house was pretty well rat-infested anyway, but that trash would attract more of them. My parents would get so frustrated. I can remember they'd take turns going up and banging on our upstairs neighbors' door. "What are you people doing? Don't you see what a mess you're making? You've got to be more considerate!" But then the neighbors would just do it again. The only opponents we had to fight harder than the neighbors were those damn rats. I remember my mother waking us up in the middle of the night, kicking rats off the bed.

She'd turn on the light, and there'd be rats scurrying everywhere. It drove her crazy because she was a good housekeeper, and she didn't want her kids to have to be exposed to that kind of thing. To this day I can't stand the thought of rats.

My mother bore most of the responsibility of raising us. My dad had been drafted into the army during World War II when I was just a baby. There was some sort of accident where he fell off a truck and injured his back and neck. He was discharged and returned home with chronic pain, which made it difficult for him to hold a job. I don't know if it was the physical pain of his injury, or the inner pain of feeling like he was letting down his family, but he wasn't really the same after he got back. He was often emotionally disengaged and started turning to the bottle to self-medicate. Of course that only made things worse. As his drinking got heavier, my mom had to do more to keep the family functioning. Over time, my dad became an absentee father, and my mother practically became a single mom.

Since my dad often had a hard time finding or keeping a job, my mom worked to earn a living as far back as I can remember. Because she was so good at it, she found plenty of work cleaning houses and cooking for other families out in the suburbs. It was hard on her to come home and do all that for our family after she'd already been doing it all day for other people. I remember when I was about three years old, my mother would give me and Reggie a bath on Saturday, get us all cleaned up, put fresh clothes on us, and then set us out on the porch while she finished cooking and cleaning the house. Keeping us out of her hair was probably the only way she'd ever get it done!

If my mother needed to go to the store or run an errand, she'd have to bring us along with her. Though we lived in a city famous for manufacturing cars, that wasn't a luxury our family could afford. We had to ride the bus or the streetcars that were common in Detroit then. One winter day when I was about three years old and Reggie was two, we were coming back from the grocery store on a streetcar with my mother. She was juggling her shopping bags and had the two of us sitting next to her on the bench, all bundled up in our winter jackets. At one of the stops, a large woman with matted hair boarded the car and sat across from us. She was dirty and was carrying several bags. I didn't know what homelessness was at that age, but I'd heard people use the term "bag lady." Being as young as I was, I was a little scared by her appearance. She kept staring at us, which made me even more frightened. Suddenly, she pointed straight at me and locked eyes with my mother. "Are those your children?" My mom shifted in her seat, nodded her head, and offered an uneasy smile. "That boy there, the one with the big head. He's going to make you really proud one day, and he's going to take you out of poverty." The woman's eyes got wide. Then the street car suddenly stopped. She gathered up her bags, got off the car, and disappeared into the gray winter afternoon.

Though it was a bizarre encounter, my mother never forgot what that woman said. She considered it a prediction or prophecy that I was going to do something significant one day. When people are living in the ghetto with very little money and even less optimism for the future, they're eager to get a good word or a glimmer of hope for something better around the bend. There was a lot of palm reading and that kind of thing going on in Black Bottom. People were just trying to get a handle on what their future might bring, and they wanted to hear that something good was ahead. They wanted to believe that things were going to get better.

I already mentioned that I was a daydreamer as a kid, but I was also a people watcher. A big part of my daydreaming was focused on why people do things the way they do. I was always looking for little lessons that I could apply to my own life. I sensed that there was a way out of the ghetto, and I was determined to crack the code on how I might make my escape one day. Man, I was like a little sociologist from the time I was small. I used to love to go down to the Grand Trunk railroad tracks in Black Bottom. I would lie on one of the slopes of tall grass on either side of the rail lines and watch the passenger trains go by. I'd see the people in there being served food and drinks and living the good life. We used to call them the swells. They looked like they didn't have a care in the world. I'd fantasize about those rich people coming through the Detroit ghetto on their way to New York City and just get lost in my imagination about what their lives must be like.

Around the same time, I started getting interested in celebrities. I attended Barstow Elementary School, which is long gone now, but it was well known for its playground where world heavyweight champion boxer Joe Louis used to train. My mother and father would tell stories about how he'd be out running around the Barstow playground. They'd talk about how he was a champion and how he was changing things for black people in America with his fame. I remember really meditating on those words, *famous* and *champion*. Why were some people famous? What made them famous? How did somebody get to be a champion? I started getting this feeling inside. It was a sense of wanting something more. Something greater.

You might think that analyzing fame or watching the swells live the "good life" on those passing trains would discourage me, but it didn't. In fact, it gave me a sense of determination. I didn't feel bad or ashamed that we didn't have much, but I did have a drive to get out of my circumstances and find something better. The poverty we lived in gave me the strength to dream. The experience taught me what I did and didn't want to take from my parents' lives when I became an adult.

When my mother had to work on Saturdays, she'd drop me and my siblings off at the Rupert Theater for the triple feature from eleven in the morning until six in the evening. I was obsessed with the movies because they were yet another window into a world that was very different from mine. There were some horrible things you'd see in the neighborhood. People would get stabbed or shot for one reason or another. People would be drinking too much, and you'd see these awful car wrecks and shit. When I'd go to the movies, all I'd see were all these wonderful things about how people lived, and I'd be sitting up there daydreaming away. The movies themselves were like a dream of how people might live. They were a teacher to me in terms of putting thoughts and dreams in my head to want something better than life in the ghetto. But going to the movies also served a practical purpose. We'd save our ticket stubs because if we had so many, we could trade them in for dishes or plates. All our plates came from the Rupert Theater. My mother would say, "Don't forget to save your ticket stubs. I just need two more to get that serving bowl."

While I knew I wanted something different for myself from a material standpoint, there were some great values I learned from my mother and father that I planted deep in my heart in my younger years. One of those important life lessons I learned early on was the value of honesty. When I was about seven or eight years old, my dad was still building those knick-knack shelves. One day he ran out of glue, and he gave me some money to go down to the hobby shop to get some more for him. I felt like an important young man as I pulled open the door to the shop with actual cash in my pocket. I took my time walking up and down the aisles in search of that familiar-looking bottle. I enjoyed turning the money over in my pocket and imagining what it would be like to have enough to buy anything I wanted in the store. When I finally located the glue I realized they had a whole bunch of bottles of it. Maybe because he was emotionally distant, I was always looking for ways to get my father's approval. I thought, *Boy, wouldn't Dad be happy if I came home with two bottles of glue? I could give him an extra one as a gift.* So I slipped one bottle in my pocket and took the other up to the counter where I had to stand on my tip toes to hand the shop owner the money.

When I pushed my way through the hobby shop door and back onto the sidewalk, the sun seemed a little brighter, and the sky looked a little bluer. I couldn't wait to get home and show my dad what a great thing I'd done for him. I had a little strut in my step as I strolled back to the house. I didn't know for sure what he would say, but I knew I'd be the hero of the day.

When I walked in the house, my father was sitting at the kitchen table reading the paper. I slid onto the chair directly across from him. He didn't look up. "Did you get that glue, boy?" I set the little paper bag on the table. "Yes, sir," I nodded. "And I also got a little surprise for you." He closed the newspaper, folded it in half and set it on the table next to him. "Oh, yeah? What's that?" I reached into my pocket, pulled out the second bottle of glue, and set it on the table. I tried to stay cool, but I couldn't stop a broad grin from spreading across my face. My dad arched his eyebrow. "If you've got the glue, then what's in here?" He had already grabbed the little bag, unfolded the top, and was peering inside by the time he finished his sentence. "What the hell is this, Lamont?" I chuckled nervously. "I got you an extra one, Pop!" He stood up so fast, his chair fell backward, making a loud crack as it hit the floor. "An extra one? Goddammit, boy, did you steal this glue?" I felt my face get hot. I thought I was doing a good thing. I thought my dad would be happy that I was looking out for him. This was not how I pictured the moment unfolding.

The next thing I knew I was back on the sidewalk, practically running to keep up with my dad's long strides. "You've really done it now," he growled as he dragged me back to the store with the stolen bottle of glue in one hand and my upper arm gripped tightly in the other. "You know better than that, Lamont. What were you thinking, stealing from people? That's how criminals behave!" As I later found out, the shop owner and my father were good friends. And they decided to teach me a lesson that day.

"Good afternoon, James," my dad said to the store owner as he marched me through the front door. I'm sure he must have winked to his buddy as he said, "It seems we've got a criminal on our hands here. I guess you probably recognize this young man who was in here earlier. He paid for one bottle of glue but took two, and he's come back to return what he stole." James clucked his tongue and shook his head. "Well, what should we do with him, Willie?" My dad shrugged. "I don't think we have any choice but to call the police." James nodded in agreement. "Yeah, he's definitely going to have to do some jail time." Boy, they really did a number on me. I was crying and hollering. "No, I'm sorry! I'm sorry! I didn't mean to! Please don't send me to jail!" The two of them milked it for a little while until James finally came out from behind the counter and knelt down so our eyes met. "Well, son, since you brought it back, I think we can let you off with a warning this time. But you have to promise that you're never going to do this kind of thing again." Tears were still streaming down my face, but now they were tears of relief. "Yes, sir," I told him. "You'll never have any problem from me ever again."

That experience taught me an important life lesson that also became an important songwriting lesson: *Don't take something that belongs to someone else unless you have their permission.* **In life, if you steal, there's usually a cost to pay. And that goes for songs, too. Sometimes I'll be at the**

piano, and a melody or song concept will come spilling out so quickly that I get a little nervous. Was that an original idea? Was that something I heard recently that got stuck in my head? Before I can ever consider a song finished, I have to make sure that I'm not unintentionally lifting someone else's idea. I've been known to play new songs for several different people to ask if it sounds familiar. Even after all these years I use a lot of caution to make sure that my ideas are my own. Maybe it's an abundance of caution, but it's a good habit to be in as a writer.

In 1988 Steve Winwood had a big hit with a song called "Roll with It." It spent about a month at number one on the US pop chart and even earned a couple of Grammy nominations. The only problem was it sounded a whole lot like a song called "(I'm a) Road Runner" that the Holland Brothers and I wrote and produced for Jr. Walker & The All Stars in the mid-1960s. Once the lawyers got involved, there was no question that "(I'm a) Road Runner" had been infringed. It didn't get nasty or anything, and we settled it out of court, but if you look at the writing credits on "Roll with It" today you'll notice that the names Holland, Dozier, and Holland have been added.

I'm not suggesting that Steve Winwood is an out-and-out thief. I'm sure he's a good man. It might well have been an unintentional thing where our song was in his subconscious and just came out when he was writing "Roll with It." Maybe he was even attempting to pay tribute to "(I'm a) Road Runner" and his intentions were good. Just like when I thought I was doing a good thing by taking that glue, lifting melodies or song ideas doesn't necessarily mean the person doing it has bad intentions. That's why I always encourage young writers to be very careful to make sure that they're not using something that actually belongs to someone else. Even if you have the best of intentions, it can create problems down the road.

Probably the best example of this principle is when hip-hop artists sample portions of older recordings in new songs. When the sampling phenomenon first began, I didn't know what to make of it. Hip-hop music was new at that time, and I didn't really "get" it yet. I had put out a solo album called *Black Bach* in 1974 that wound up being sampled more times that I can count by artists ranging from folks I'd never heard of to some big names like OutKast, The Notorious B.I.G. featuring 2Pac, Nas, Meek Mill, T.I., and Missy Elliott. When I first became aware of sampling, I got kind of upset that people were nicking my songs.

Over time, however, I came to see it as newer artists paying homage to what came before, and now I welcome it. When we came along at Motown, some of the older guard among the great American songwriters turned up their noses at us because they didn't understand the pop music of my generation. Great songs stand the test of time, but the way songs are delivered will change with the decades. That was true in the time of those who came before, it's true for me, and it will be true for those who come after me. The reality is that hip-hop has come to dominate the music industry today. I might have been a little late to the party, but I now have tremendous respect for talented rappers. I've always been a fan of an artist in any genre who can create a signature sound with unique phrasing, and there are so many examples of that in hip-hop. I look at a guy like Kendrick Lamar, who has also sampled some of my stuff, and I'm just amazed by his skills.

These days I get really excited when someone samples one of my songs. But they need permission to do it. I still believe you can't simply take something that somebody else created without their consent. For me, it's not about the money. I can think of many times that independent hip-hop artists with very small budgets have approached us to use one of my old songs in a sample. We've approved a lot of those uses because we appreciate people going through the proper channels and seeking the appropriate permissions. That's the right way to do it.

As a songwriter, I recognize that we all draw on our influences. We channel much of the music that we soak up and, as they say, there's nothing new under the sun. But we also have an artistic responsibility to insert enough of our fresh ideas and original concepts that we're not taking something that doesn't belong to us. I always tell young writers that you can't be too careful. The bottom line is, I don't steal, and I don't *want* to steal any music, even if it's not intentional.

That lesson from my dad has served me well for many years. He was far from perfect, but his influence would shape me—for good and for bad—as I began to wake up to the power of music.

Chapter Two

NOWHERE TO RUN

Though my father's employment status would fluctuate, he did land a job working at a gas station for a while. He wasn't making much, but when he'd get paid on Friday, he'd go out and drink up half the money with his buddies. Then he'd blow most of the rest on himself by picking up some new clothes or going to the movies. My dad was crazy about movies and loved Robert Mitchum in particular. He practically idolized him. We might not have enough food, but my dad was going to get to his Robert Mitchum movies. Other times he'd blow most of his paycheck on a pack of records. If there was anything left at all, he'd give it to my mother, who was really suffering to try make ends meet. I could see the frustration and disappointment on my mom's face, but I was too young to really make sense of it all. What I did understand is that I liked the sounds I was hearing from those 78 rpm records my dad would bring home.

Some of the earliest music I remember hearing as a kid was the stuff my dad loved. He was a fan of Billy Eckstine, Nat King Cole, Frank Sinatra, Al Hibbler, and that kind of thing. Those old discs were made of shellac and were really fragile. If me or one of my siblings broke one, my dad would have a fit. He'd start screaming and carrying on as if we'd personally wounded him. He really prized those records, but that was part of the problem. He was out drinking up his paycheck and spending money on records when he should have been buying bread or a bag of beans. He was neglecting his family, but I still have to give him some credit for introducing me to music.

My dad actually had a pretty good singing voice, but his brother Clifford had a remarkable natural talent for playing piano. Uncle Clifford couldn't read a note of music, but he had an ear. If he heard a song once, he could play it for you. I used to love to listen to him play what they called boogie-woogie style on the piano over at my grandmother's house. His fingers would fly across those keys, and he'd make up little jingles and funny songs that were really entertaining to me as a kid.

One of the good memories I have of my father is the time he took me to the Paradise Theater in Black Bottom. Located over on Woodward Avenue, the Paradise was Detroit's version of the Apollo Theater in Harlem. Though you hear a lot of talk about the Harlem Renaissance, there was a larger rebirth of African-American arts going on in the country's major cities as all these folks were moving out of the South into urban areas. Music, in particular, was an increasingly important form of black self-expression in those days. All the important black artists would come through the Paradise Theater: Dizzy Gillespie, Sarah Vaughan, Erskine Hawkins, Louis Armstrong, Lionel Hampton, Cab Calloway, Louis Jordan, Dinah Washington, and on and on. It was a poor area, but whenever we got word that a famous performer was coming to town, everybody would scrape together their extra pennies and save up for the big show. I don't know why he took me instead of my mother or one of his friends, but my father took me to a Cavalcade of Stars show at the Paradise when I was five or six years old—just the two of us. The bill featured Billy Eckstine, Count Basie, Nat King Cole, Sarah Vaughan, and Ella Fitzgerald.

As my father and I made our way up to the nosebleed section, I could feel the electricity in the room. Some of the folks there had probably saved up for months just to be at the show, and everybody was feeling *good*. When the performers came on stage, I loved what I was hearing, but I was just as taken with the audience response. As an avowed people-watcher who was always trying to figure out what made people act the way they act, I was soaking up the reactions of the folks who were seated all around us. They were clapping their hands and stomping their feet. Some were laughing from pure joy, while others got so carried away that there were tears streaming down their faces. Maybe we were all poor and we all had our problems, but in that moment everyone was just having a great time. The audience members were just as entertaining to me as the entertainers on the stage.

During one of the intermissions, I turned to my father. "I'd like to make people feel like this one day," I told him. He cocked his head to the side. "Feel like what, Lamont?" I pointed back and forth in a semi-circle to the people sitting all around us. "Like *this*," I said. "Happy." He nodded his head and smiled, but I don't think he quite got what I was talking about. Seeing how music could get down inside people and move them planted a seed inside me. It was a power that I didn't understand, but it was something I knew I wanted to tap into.

Not long after, we got some new neighbors in the apartment upstairs above our place. They had some kind of small church service on Thursday evenings with fifteen or twenty people up there. They'd start singing and then get to dancing and shouting and playing tambourines. They were feelin' the Spirit, man! That used to drive my father crazy. He'd be beating on the ceiling with a broom handle and yelling, "You holy rollers need to quiet down. A man can't think with all that racket!" For me it was just another piece of the puzzle. I knew those folks were responding to the music, and they were feeling it deep in their bones. The power of music moved their souls.

It was the same kind of thing I would see on Sunday mornings. My mother's mother, who I called Granny, was the choir director for a congregation called The Spiritual Israel Church and Its Army over on Hastings Street, which was the center of Black Bottom. It was a predominantly black denomination founded in Alabama in the early 1900s, but the whole church moved up to Detroit in the 1920s. That might be another clue about how my grandparents ended up moving from Alabama, but I don't know for certain. What I do know is that we had to go to church every week. It was a good-sized congregation with about five or six hundred people at the morning service. My mother and my grandmother made sure I was there in my Sunday best ready to soak up some inspiration. They also made sure I was in the children's choir since I was the choir director's grandson. My eyes—and my ears—were definitely open to what was going on around me. Little did I know that my musical world was about to get even wider.

By the late 1940s my dad's drinking had really gotten out of control. Half the time he wasn't around at all, but when he was around, you never knew what kind of mood he might be in. He'd slap my mother around from time to time, which made me feel completely helpless. I hated to see him do her like that when she poured so much of herself into keeping the family afloat. He didn't whip my sisters, but it wasn't uncommon for him to get drunk and beat the shit out of me and my brother Reggie for nothing. I guess he felt like it was OK for the boys to get his wrath for some reason. He'd get to feeling down about one thing or another and then he'd take it out on us. It was a pretty bad situation. Sometimes if my mother had to go to a church meeting or something and needed him to look after us, my dad would just end up knocking me and Reggie around, and then he'd still take off and leave us alone in the house.

Sometimes when my father was drunk, he would mouth off about different things. I remember one time there was a story in the newspaper about the singer Teresa Brewer, who had a big hit with "Music! Music! Music!" She'd grown up in Ohio or some place, and the article mentioned that she'd become so successful that she was able to buy her folks a new home. "Look at this," my father roared to nobody in particular. "Why couldn't I have a kid like this where I don't have to work? This singer bought a house for her parents. That's what I need!" His words stayed with me, and I tried to find out some more about who Teresa Brewer was and how she was able to accomplish great things. I filed that information away. Another piece of the puzzle.

Despite my hurt over my father's behavior, I had a feeling that he wasn't totally to blame for his situation. He was out of work by that time, and I suspect he felt overwhelmed and worthless. He didn't have the skills to deal with his feelings, so he had to try to find a way to cope with the negative things life threw at him. He thought alcohol was the answer, but it only deepened his problems. It got to the point where he let the bottle do his thinking for him. He was not a model husband and father, but watching him deal with his demons actually strengthened me. He set an example of what *not* to do, and I decided from a young age that I would be a very different kind of man one day.

Eventually my mother reached her breaking point. She was fed up with my dad's behavior and something had to change. I was playing in my bedroom one day when she came in, put her hands on her hips, and let out a long sigh. She looked tired. "Lamont," she said matter-of-factly, "you need to get all your clothes and things together and put 'em in a bag. We're going to stay with Granny." That was about all that was said about it. Maybe the reason it took my mom so long to leave my father was because she didn't have any place to go with five children. Eventually it got bad enough to where that problem couldn't hold her back. My middle sister, Zel, and I went to my grandmother's place. Reggie and my sister Laretta went to live with my father's mother. Norma, the baby, was taken in by my Aunt Jennie. I know it broke my mother's heart to split up the family, but she had no choice. She took every job she could get to work toward reuniting us as a family in our own place.

In the meantime, my grandparents had something at their house that we didn't have at our place in Black Bottom: a piano. My Aunt Eula, who also lived there, was studying to be a concert pianist. She used to put me on her lap as she played "Clair de Lune" and all these beautiful melodies on that old upright. I felt safe on that piano bench with Aunt Eula, soaking up Mozart, Schubert, Chopin, and especially Bach. I was so taken with the way Bach formed his chords, which just transported me to another world. When I was on that piano bench, nobody was getting drunk and ranting. Nobody was yelling. I was at peace. I'd been drawn to the ways music affected others, but now the music was affecting me on an entirely new level. It was like the notes were wafting into my ears, reaching down to the deepest places inside me, and soaking into my very soul.

Aunt Eula took piano lessons from a stern teacher named Professor Shaw. I was so fascinated by that piano that sometimes I'd watch through the window or stand just around the corner of the door frame so I could eavesdrop and maybe learn something about how to make music of my own. I wouldn't give away my position because I was frightened of Shaw. Eula wanted to be a touring classical pianist, so perfection was the standard. If she made a mistake he would whack her on the fingers with a ruler and she'd burst into tears.

One day I was playing by the front door just as Professor Shaw arrived to give Aunt Eula a lesson. Granny opened the door, and he was standing there before I could make my escape. My grandmother knew how much I enjoyed hearing my aunt play and said, "Lamont, would you like to take some lessons from Mr. Shaw?" My heart stopped. I'm sure my eyes must have gotten as big as saucers. I was horrified at the thought of this guy whacking me on the hands. *If this is what you have to do to play music, I thought, I don't want to have nothin' to do with it!* I suddenly realized that Granny and Professor Shaw were waiting for a response. "No, no, no" I yelled as I ran out the door. I don't know if Granny came looking for me or not, but I hid out for a couple of hours until I was good and sure that Mr. Shaw was long gone.

Not long after, I started sneaking in and messing around on that piano when nobody else was around. I developed my own style without anyone whacking my hands, and before long, I was obsessed with picking out little melodies and figuring out how notes and chords fit together. To this day, I don't read music. I always wanted to learn, but hit records and success started happening before I ever got the chance to learn music properly.

After my mother and father split up I was primarily raised by women. My mother, aunts, and grandmother were important influences, but it was through living at my grandmother's home that I began to get special insight into the concerns that many women have. My grandmother ran a beauty salon out of the house, and one of my jobs was keeping it clean and sweeping the hair up off the floor. My grandmother was a real helper to the women who came to her to get their hair done. She'd listen to their problems and give them advice on various problems they might be facing. She was as much a counselor as she was a beautician. Her customers were used to me being in there, so they didn't think anything about speaking freely and openly about their lives. For a people-watcher who was curious about what other people did, it was amazing to get a front-row seat to hear what people were really thinking and feeling.

I'd hear the women telling these stories and I'd think about why they were laughing. Or why they were crying. I saw a lot of women shed tears because they'd been mistreated by a husband or boyfriend. I began to realize that a lot of men don't live up to what they should be as lovers, caretakers, or fathers. I remember thinking, *Why can't people treat one another better? Why can't we all be good to each other?* As I soaked up the experiences of those women in the beauty shop, they each contributed to raising me and helping me think about what it means to treat people right. Though I didn't have the words to articulate it as a kid, I became an advocate for women in my grandmother's salon. I wanted to find a way to make them feel better. I wanted to speak directly to them. I wanted to stop their tears.

Little did I know it, but I was learning about perspective. That's a great reminder for people who want to write songs. *First, you need to have a point of view that informs what you want to say.* I've carried that thought through my professional life and have—more often than

not—written songs with women in mind. I know who my audience is. I know who I'm trying to reach and how I want to make them feel. Those early seeds planted in my heart ultimately made me a hopeless romantic who had strong feelings of respect and tenderness for women. I wanted to write songs that said the things women wanted to hear. Through my lyrics I wanted to express the feelings that many women had but were maybe afraid to articulate for themselves. If the songs could say it for them, perhaps it would be a vicarious form of expression. It became part of my mission statement as a creative person.

If you're a songwriter, you'll have your own thoughts about who your audience is and what values you want to transmit through your lyrics. Nobody else can decide that for you, but if you want to be a great writer, it's crucial that you understand your own perspective and how you can best communicate it. Another way of saying it is, you need to have an answer when you look in the mirror and ask, "Who am I?"

Of course it would take some time before my creative impulses would have the opportunity to flower. In those days we were just trying to make our way through life. Though my grandmother could have gotten a job as a hairdresser at someone else's salon, she always believed in the idea that you can't get rich working for somebody else. She taught me to have an entrepreneurial spirit and figure out a way to make my own way and do things for myself. So, when I wasn't sweeping up the floor at her salon, I'd carry my little red wagon up to the A&P or Kroger grocery store and ask the customers if they needed help taking their groceries to the car. I'd get tips that I'd use for extra money to go to the movies.

I loved going to the movies at that age as much as I'd loved it when we used to go to the Rupert Theater over in Black Bottom. When we were living with my grandmother, I'd go over to the

Rialto, which was a much nicer theater with a balcony. It almost didn't matter what film was playing, I just loved being there and letting my mind get lost in other worlds. I'd sit on the front row so I could look up and just be immersed in the action on the screen as if I was one of the characters in the story. As a dreamer, it was just another way of making myself believe I could accomplish something. I was collecting ideas about how people operated and how the world worked. It was important to me to have that time to escape. Most of the money I earned, however, was added to what everybody else was doing to chip in to get the meals on the table as my mother struggled to reunite all us and get our family back on its feet.

It wasn't an easy time, but I never thought it was bad to be poor. Going through challenges helps you learn about life and how to deal with adversity. Life is a school, and when school is challenging, you learn even more. That's why I wasn't bothered by getting a package from the Goodfellows at Christmas time. The Old Newsboys' Goodfellow Fund of Detroit had these little events around the holidays where we could go see Santa Claus. While we were there, we'd get a ticket to go pick up a box that had some clothes and a toy in it. I remember being on the playground in the school yard one time after the Christmas break. A group of older boys came up to me, and one of them nodded, "Oh, I see you've got your new shoes on." I just smiled, "Oh, yeah. Pretty nice, huh?" The boys burst out laughing. I was confused at first. I thought they were praising me about my Goodfellows outfit, but then I realized they were making fun of me. My ears grew hot, but I kept smiling. I wasn't going to let them see they'd hurt me.

That doesn't mean I decided not to care about how I was treated. I've always been a sensitive person, and I probably carried that hurt with me further into adulthood than I should have. Maybe it was because of my father's love for clothes and shoes, or maybe it was those boys on the playground, but when I began to have success, I decided I needed a different suit for every day of the week. I guess that was rooted in my childhood. Today I have closets filled with clothes that still have the tags on them. It's completely insane. I'll say this: having plenty is a lot more fun than not having enough, but in the times when we're lacking material things, those trials shape our character and help make us who we become. Looking back, I'm glad things happened the way they did. If I'd been born with a silver spoon in my mouth, things wouldn't have turned out the same way. It was watching other people—especially the "haves"—that motivated me. A lot of those people probably turned out to be spoiled brats because they didn't have the hunger or the motivation to push themselves. They didn't have to go through the humiliation of being teased or not having a good pair of shoes that didn't have holes in them. Experiencing those things gives you fortitude to become something greater.

Yet another childhood challenge came during the time we were living with my grandmother. I was playing with my Aunt Eula in the street one day when I slipped off her back and busted my knee cap on the asphalt. I landed right on some broken glass and there was blood everywhere. Shards of glass were sticking out of my knee, and I was screaming my head off. Eula scooped me and up and rushed me into my grandmother's shop. They wrapped up the knee to stop the bleeding and rushed me to the Detroit Receiving Hospital. We saw a white doctor who didn't give our family the impression he could be bothered to give a damn about this little black kid with a busted knee. He sewed me up, but he didn't clean the wound properly. He actually left bits of glass and dirt and all kinds of shit in there.

It took about three weeks before blood poisoning set in. My mother took me back to the hospital, and we ended up seeing the head physician. "Who did this to your little boy," he asked my mother. "This is not acceptable!" This man was a dedicated doctor who didn't see race. He just cared about doing the right thing, and he was really pissed about the carelessness of the other doctor. "My God," he said. "We've gotta cut this kid's leg off. He's got blood poisoning and it's moving fast. He could die if we don't take care of this quickly." My mother was crying, "Oh, no. No. Please don't take my baby's leg!" When he saw my mother's reaction I think he felt really bad for her. "There's one other thing we can try first," he told her. "The medical community has recently begun using penicillin to treat infections, but it's still in experimental stages. We can try it, but there are no guarantees." My mother agreed, and that's what saved my leg. I still had to have surgery on it after that, so it was a real ordeal. "When he's older," the doctor told my mother, "he's going to have problems with that knee." Well, now I'm older, and I can tell you: he was right about that!

These various challenges were building my character and shaping me into who I would become in the future. Another important awakening was just around the corner.

Chapter Three

BERNADETTE

A key step in my creative awakening was discovering girls. There was a girl named Rosetta at Barstow Elementary, where I went back when my folks were still together. I thought she was really cute. To me, she was Venus de Milo with arms. We were probably about seven years old, so who knows what in the hell made her stand out to me at that young age. But I guess beauty is in the eye of the beholder!

After we moved in with my grandmother, I started going to Harris Elementary. That's where I encountered a little Italian girl who changed a lot of my thinking about beauty. I was around nine or ten years old and was sitting at my desk on my first day of class when I looked up and saw her. She had this long hair flowing down her back, and I thought she was just beautiful.

Her name was Bernadette, and she gave me a feeling I never felt before about anybody. Not even Rosetta could have topped that feeling.

Maybe she decided to be nice to me because I was the new kid, but Bernadette invited me over to her house after classes one day. Her family stayed right across the street from the school. Her father had a vegetable truck, and he used to fix fresh spaghetti that he'd hang over a line just like they did in the old country. I remember eating dinner with their family and thinking how nice it was that she had a mom and dad to sit down to dinner with. I decided right away that I was madly in love with Bernadette. We never really became boyfriend and girlfriend. I think maybe she kind of liked me in that way, but she really thought of me more as a friend. She had eyes for this other guy in our class named Jimmy. Later on I wrote a song called "Jimmy's Shoes" that was about wishing I could switch places with him. Though we became very good friends, I longed for Bernadette to love me the way I loved her. Puppy love already feels so dramatic when you're young, but I was a sensitive kid, and I felt my emotions very deeply. I had it so bad for Bernadette, I could hardly think straight.

When you have that feeling of first love, you guard it in your heart. It's a sacred thing. The feeling is unexplainable, but it's still there for me, even today. Sure, it's watered down a bit over the years, but when I close my eyes, I can still tap into it. Bernadette was my first muse, and she stayed my muse for a lot of years. Even when I got to Motown, when I thought about what love was supposed to feel like, I'd always come back to her. But it's not even about Bernadette; it's about that *feeling*. That's what I've been writing about for years.

That's another important principle that songwriters must understand. *If you want to write songs that move people, you have to write from a place that moves you.* **You need to find an emotional connection to your subject. If it doesn't**

resonate with you, it's probably not going to resonate with someone else, either. In that respect, all songwriting is personal. It requires tapping in to your deepest longings, and sometimes that can put you in a vulnerable place. But that's what it's all about. Life has to be lived before you can get to the heart of what you're trying to say in a song. That doesn't mean I never sat down and wrote a song that wasn't a little calculated, but I can tell you those aren't my best songs. The ones that have stood the test of time are the ones that tapped into my own feelings and emotions. You've got to be willing to put your own heart on the line if you want to touch the hearts of your listeners.

Experiencing feelings of love makes your heart tender. And sometimes a tender heart makes you see things you didn't see before. Around the time I was starting to understand the concept of romance, I also ran head first into another concept from which I'd somehow been protected up to that point: prejudice. Most of the kids in my class at Harris Elementary were white, which was different than it had been at my old school when we lived in Black Bottom. There was a girl in my new class named Annette who was having a birthday party at her house. I didn't know it, but invitations were sent to all the students except for me.

On the day of her party, all my friends—including Bernadette—were headed over to Annette's house. "Come on, Lamont," Bernadette said, "you should come with us." I didn't know any better, so I headed over to the party with five or six of my buddies. We climbed the front steps, and my friend Jimmy rang the bell. We could hear the laughter coming from inside the house, and I knew it was going to be a lot of fun. After a moment, a man that I assume was Annette's father answered the door. He had a big smile on his face. "Hey every…." He trailed off abruptly. It was as if someone suddenly turned the volume of his voice all the way down against his will. The man took a step backward and his smile instantly melted away. He let out a nervous laugh. Locking eyes with Jimmy he motioned toward me with a single eyebrow. "He can't come in here," the man said flatly. I turned around to see if anyone was behind me. *I wonder who he's talking about,* I thought. Suddenly I realized everyone was looking at me. Jimmy glanced down and kicked at nothing in particular before looking back up at the grown man blocking the doorway. "Is there something wrong with him?" Before he could get the words out, Bernadette spoke up. "If there's a problem with him, then there's a problem with all of us." The man opened his mouth, but before he could say anything I interjected, "No, guys. You all go on ahead. I don't want to spoil anyone's good time." I turned, jogged down the steps alone, and headed down the sidewalk toward my grandmother's house.

I learned about the harsh reality of racism that day. Sure, that doctor who didn't sew up my leg properly might have paid more attention if I'd been a little white boy, but this was the first time I really ran into something so blatant and ugly. Before that happened, my friends and I used to go Christmas caroling in the rich white neighborhoods, and we made some pretty good tips. We never ran into any racial problems, but I guess it was the holidays, and everybody was in another mood. People overlook that kind of thing at that time of year.

What happened at Annette's house didn't make me mad. It made me want to make things better. I wanted to find a way to express myself with words and music that could make people both feel the power of love and also bring them together in unity. That moment sowed a seed in me to want to write, not just for black people or for white people, but for all people. I instinctively knew that humans are the same on the inside and that Annette's father was wrong. Instead of letting it get me down or making me want to get revenge, it spurred me to want to change the world. There was a veil of lies that was deceiving people about race, and I thought maybe I could pull it down with music. It made me want to answer ugliness with beauty. I just had to figure out how to do it.

Around the time I was twelve, the city of Detroit opened up the Jeffries Housing Projects. It consisted of eight towers that were each fourteen stories tall and provided an opportunity for a lot of working-class families to make a fresh start. That included my mother, who had to wait about a year after applying before she was accepted. When she got in, my mom was finally able to reunite all of us in her own place. That meant another move and another new school. I started at Edgar Allan Poe Elementary, which is where I ended up writing my first song.

My homeroom class was English, which was taught by a woman named Edith Burke. One day she gave the class an assignment to write a poem. She said that songs are poems, too, so we could create our lyrics however we wanted. A lot of the boys thought it was more macho to write a song than a poem, so they came up with simple rhymes that mimicked the doo-wop music we were hearing on the radio in those days. But I had been brought up on Frank Sinatra and Nat King Cole. I knew that lyrics could be more sophisticated, and I wanted my words to really mean something. I worked on my assignment every free moment until the morning it was due. I called it "A Song."

I wish I could remember the lyrics, but I do remember the message. It was about people coming together to make the world a better place. If we could figure out how to do it, there wouldn't be wars. There wouldn't be hatred. There would only be kindness. My poem was political, and it was spiritual. It really articulated this vision of people coming together, and Ms. Burke thought it was poignant. She attached "A Song" to the blackboard and kept it up there for six weeks. Then she launched a contest to see if any of the students could write a better poem to replace it. Nobody could, so she eventually shut down the contest and gave me an award for having the best poem in the class.

That feeling of praise and approval opened up something inside me. I sat down at the piano and figured out a little melody to go with "A Song." Then I started writing poems and lyrics all the time. Whenever I finished one, I'd run to Ms. Burke for some more of that affirmation and positive feedback. She encouraged me to keep writing and sometimes made suggestions about how I could improve. That was the start of me really analyzing how to write and how to create something that could touch people. I give Edith Burke a lot of credit for igniting that spark inside me.

It wasn't until later that I looked back and realized how appropriate it was that my love for lyrics and poetry was awakened at Edgar Allan Poe Elementary School. I didn't even know who Poe was when I first started going there, but when I later discovered he was a writer, I felt like I'd connected with a bit of his spirit by going to that school.

Right next to the school was the house on West Forest where Charles Lindbergh was born. There was a plaque outside that I used to stop and read over and over. I had that fascination with fame and accomplishment, and I remember reading about him making the first transatlantic flight. I thought, *Wow, I wonder how that guy felt being the one to fly all the way across that ocean.* I'd get carried away trying to pick up on the energy of Edgar Allan Poe or Lucky Lindbergh. I would walk around talking to myself and thinking out loud about what made those people special. It was like I was talking to the spirits, trying to figure out how to connect, how to transcend.

My interest in history was always rooted in a fascination with how people achieved what they did. Trying to figure out that puzzle played perfectly into my tendencies as a people watcher. For example, I was always trying to eavesdrop on conversations when I was in a restaurant. I had an antenna up for interesting topics or a different way of saying something. Studying historical figures and modern-day people was my attempt to crack the code of human experience. What makes people tick? What makes some achieve greatness when others don't? I'd always been observant, but once I started writing, I was on full alert.

That's a core principle that I carry with me as a songwriter to this day. *Ideas are all around us if we keep an ear out for them.* **There are so many stories yet to be told, and the answers to a lot of our problems are lingering in places you wouldn't think they'd be. You just have to keep the antenna up. That's what I did then, and that's still what I do. If you want to be a great songwriter, you've got to absorb conversations, books, movies, TV shows, and art. You've got to experience the world with open ears and eyes to pick up on those universal truths that others might miss if they're not paying close attention. Be a people watcher. Listen to what others are saying. Heck, I've even found melodies by keeping my ears open to my surroundings. There's a rhythm to life. There's a sound to the everyday hustle and bustle of cars, planes, and people going about their business. I've even been known to open up my windows and listen to the melodies of the birds. Sometimes they come up with some really intricate stuff! What I was learning from that young age is that being a songwriter is a way of life. And that way is all about observation.**

As I was learning to express myself with words, I also began learning how to express myself in the kitchen. We never had a whole lot in terms of food, but there was usually some day-old bread, rice, beans, collard greens, and macaroni mixed with cheeses that was provided by the government. My mom was still working cooking and cleaning for other families in the suburbs, so she taught me how to cook so that I could get dinner ready for her and my siblings. When she came home from doing all that stuff for other people, she didn't have to do it for us, too. My siblings and I learned to keep the house clean for ourselves, and I learned how to prepare a few simple meals to take care of my brothers and sisters. I discovered that I really enjoyed making food for other people. I found out that a cook can try new things and put their own personal spin on different dishes. Over time, cooking food developed into a creative outlet for me that was a little bit like songwriting. In both areas the creator is working within the constraints of a particular template, but also has the freedom to push the boundaries, add some spice, remove or replace a few ingredients, and create something new that's a reflection of their personality. Food became a way for me to communicate and let others know I care about them.

After my mom left my father, he continued living in the same rundown house. Several times when I was around nine or ten I'd walk over there and sneak in the window when he wasn't home. The place was always filthy, so I'd clean up the kitchen, wash the dishes, and fix him a pot of beans and a hunk of cornbread. I had mixed feelings about my father, but I felt like somebody should cook him something to eat. It was a small gesture on my part. I'd always leave a little note that said, *I left you some food. Love, Lamont.* I never heard from him, and he never said anything about it, but I hope he appreciated it. I wanted to let him know how I felt about him, despite his flaws.

In later years I had the opportunity to really develop my skills in the kitchen. In fact, when I was on a promotional world tour as a Warner Bros. artist in the late 1970s, my then-manager, George Greif, introduced me to several Michelin Star chefs. I was thrilled to meet Roger Vergé in the South of France. I stayed at the Le Moulin de Mougins, which was an old sixteenth-century mill that was converted into an elegant restaurant and a small inn with only two guest rooms. Roger was renowned for his light cuisine de soleil and really taught me some amazing things when I was there.

As time went on, I became well known among my friends and family for my cooking. In fact, in the 1980s my wife Barbara and I became friends with Terry Semel and his wife Jane. Terry was the chairman and co-chief executive officer of Warner Bros. He loved my cooking, and at one point asked if I'd be interested in having Warners invest in a restaurant with me. He said I'd have to put music on the back burner for a while, so I said no. Thinking back on it now, I probably shouldn't have been so impulsive in making my decision. I wouldn't have had to give up music completely, and cooking is one of my great loves. I suppose it was just hard for me to think about switching gears at that point, but I often think that, had I not pursued a life of music, I would have loved to become a chef.

After I became the de facto family cook, I would go to the grocery store to buy the necessary staples. When I was there I'd see all sorts of exciting things that we couldn't afford. I always wondered what it would be like to walk in a store and get whatever you wanted without having to worry about how to pay for it. On a couple of occasions I even went into the store and walked up and down every single aisle filling up my cart with everything I wished I could buy. I'd push the cart up close to the cash register, but then I'd abandon it because I didn't have any money to pay for all that stuff. I just wanted to feel the feeling of being a person who could walk down each aisle and have anything they wanted. It was a way of hyping myself up. I made myself believe the scenario until the very last moment when the dream had to end. That kind of role-playing was all part of my longing for something greater, to reach for something more.

I heard about a study one time that applies to what I was doing without realizing it. In the study, one group of basketball players practiced shooting free throws for twenty minutes every day. Another group of players visualized shooting free throws but didn't actually practice. At the end of the study, the ones who had only visualized it had dramatically improved in their ability to hit their shots and were nearly as good as those who'd actually practiced it. Observing the behaviors and conversations of others, going to the movies, reading about historical figures, and filling up my grocery carts were all my way of mentally practicing what I wanted for myself in real life. I was effectively visualizing the future I wanted for myself. I don't know that I would have been able to put words to it back then, but I was almost doing this stuff by instinct.

By the time I graduated from elementary school, I had the heart of a poet, the head of a dreamer, and the desires of a hopeless romantic. I started at Hutchins Junior High School, where word got around that I could write. Other guys started coming up to me to ask them to write love poems they could give to their girlfriends. If they made their girl mad, I could write them a heartfelt letter to help woo her back. When I was in seventh grade, an eighth grade boy that I didn't even know came up to me at my locker. "Hey man," he said, "I heard you can help me out. I'm having trouble with my girl. She quit me, man. What can I say to her to get her back?" That's the moment I became a professional writer. "I'll tell you what," I replied. "I'll write you a letter to give her that's guaranteed to get her back. It'll cost you fifty cents." He didn't hesitate. "Alright, man. It's a deal."

Before long I had a steady stream of customers. The other guys all started calling me Candy Man because I was selling my sweet words. I had stored up all the things I'd heard in my grandmother's beauty shop, and I knew what women wanted to hear. It was like I'd cracked a code that the other boys hadn't figured out. I even had a catchphrase: Get a woman's mind and the body will follow.

My job as the junior high love doctor developed to the point where some guys would hire me to call their girlfriends and pretend to be them. If they thought the voice on the other end of the line didn't sound like their guy, I'd say I had a bad cold. I'd tell these girls what they wanted to hear, and that would save my customer from his love troubles. Even though letters were just fifty cents, phone calls were riskier. I charged a dollar for that service. Depending on how many customers I had, I'd usually do alright each week and start the weekend with some spending money in my pocket. Amazingly, I never got caught. All the guys kept it quiet because they knew they might need my services one day!

My way with words got me out of a jam on a few occasions. There was this one girl in school that I used to tease. I was always calling her names and fooling with her like kids do. We'd go back and forth, and she could give it as good as she got. I was giving her all kinds of grief one day when she finally snapped, "You better shut your damn mouth or I'm gonna tell my brother." I shot back, "Oh, to hell with your brother." Well, it turned out her brother was in a gang. The next day a friend came up to me in the hallway after our last class. "Lamont, you better get your ass out of here," he said. "That girl told her brother you've been messing with her. He and his boys are sittin' out there, and they look like they're about ready to do you in."

I appreciated the warning, but I didn't have any way to escape because these gangbangers were on both corners outside the entrance to the school. I took a deep breath and stepped outside. This big guy came charging up to me almost immediately. "You're Lamont," he barked. I couldn't tell if it was a question or a declaration. "Uh, yeah," I said. "That's me." He took another step forward so that his face was only inches from mine. "I hear you've been messin' with my sister," he hissed. "What have you been saying to her?" I suddenly became aware that his buddies had formed a circle around us. I could feel a bead of sweat trickle down my back. I had to think fast if I was going to talk my way out of this situation.

I cleared my throat. "I'm sorry," I said. I surprised myself with how steady my voice sounded. "It's just that …." He drummed his fingers on his chest impatiently. My heart was pounding in my ears. "It's just that what?" I looked down sheepishly. "It's just that I like your sister so much. I was just trying to get a date with her, man. I'm sorry." Suddenly the girl pushed through the tight circle that had formed around us in anticipation of watching me get my ass kicked. "He's lying," she shouted. "He don't want no date! All he does is make fun of me and call me names. Cut him! You need to cut this bitch!"

Her brother looked at her and seemed to study her face for a moment. Then he turned back to me. We locked eyes. I slid my hands in my pocket so he wouldn't see them trembling. "No, it ain't like that, man," I replied. "I love your sister. I don't know why she's gotta do me this way. I just want to take her to the movies. There's nothin' wrong with wanting to take a girl to the show, is there?"

He stared at me silently. It felt like a full minute went by, but I'm sure it was probably only a few seconds. My temples were wet with sweat, but I tried to hold myself steady. Finally, the guy turned back to his sister. "If you don't like him, then don't like him," he said, "but don't try to get him in trouble." With that, he turned and walked away with his boys in tow. She called after him, "Lamont don't like me. That's some bullshit right there. He's full of shit. Come back here and take care of this fool." Those gangbangers never even looked back. Of course I didn't really like that girl, but I wouldn't be the Candy Man if I couldn't talk myself out of that situation.

I might have been a smooth talker, but talking to girls was easier when I was doing it for someone else. In some ways I was living vicariously through the guys who paid me to communicate with their girlfriends. There were a few girls I'd see every now and then, but I was kind of afraid to find a serious girlfriend of my own. My mother was always telling me and my brother, "Don't you be bringing no babies back here. My hands are full enough as it is dealing with you all." She used to say, "If you're going to be out there foolin' around, you better make sure you've got your raincoat on." That's what she called rubbers. We'd kind of roll our eyes at her, but she did actually scare us pretty good. I was afraid of getting a girl pregnant.

Whether it was fear or respect, my siblings and I didn't get in trouble when we were young. My mom had a hard enough time just trying to survive. I'd pick up these little odd jobs to try to help her put food on the table instead of getting into stuff I shouldn't be into or spending time around people who might drag me down. We were all clean-cut kids and well behaved because we were all trying to spare my mother any more grief. I felt blessed to have a mom who really cared and looked out for us. I wasn't going to do anything to hurt her. To stay out of trouble I joined the track team, and I was a pretty good little runner in junior high. They were even talking to me about training to become an Olympic runner. That would have been an opportunity, but my heart was already somewhere else.

I wasn't the only student at Hutchins Junior High School who dreamed of a life in music. One of the older boys who went to Hutchins was Marv Johnson, who ended up getting together with Berry Gordy to release the first record on the pre-Motown Tamla label. He scored a couple of Top 10 pop hits and was an important part of the Hitsville community in the early days. Actress and singer Freda Payne also went to school there. Our paths would cross down the road when she had a hit with Holland-Dozier-Holland's "Band of Gold."

Another of my Hutchins buddies was Otis Williams, who would go on to great success with The Temptations. Otis and I were pretty tight when we were in school. We'd talk about our futures and how we were going to get record deals one day. We were always imagining how we were going to make it big and make a serious splash with our own music one day. While we were talking about it, another of our classmates was actually doing it.

I didn't know that Aretha Franklin could sing when I first met her in school, but I knew her dad was a famous preacher. The best-known congregation in our area was the New Bethel Baptist Church, which was led by the Reverend C. L. Franklin. When I was about nine years old, they moved into a great big new facility on Hastings Street, where hundreds and hundreds of people packed the pews on Sunday mornings. One Friday at school, one of my buddies came up to me and asked, "Are you gonna go down on Sunday to hear Aretha?" I was confused. "Hear Aretha? Hear Aretha do what?" He explained that a group of kids was going over to her father's church to hear Aretha sing that weekend. I was curious since it was the first I'd heard that she might have some musical talent.

I went along, and I couldn't believe my ears when Aretha sat down at that piano on Sunday morning and opened her mouth to sing. She was phenomenal! People were shouting and screaming and jumping in the aisles. It was electrifying. I'd never heard someone that age sound that good. I said to myself, *Damn! This girl has got it.* That lit a fire under me to take some steps to get my own music heard by the world.

Chapter Four

I CAN'T HELP MYSELF

By the time I started at Northwestern High School, I was regularly writing songs. I'd start plunking out piano chords and finding notes to go with my words. I'd just fool around until I got a decent pattern of movements and chord changes that fit the feeling of the lyrics. It was just a process of finding the right notes to hit the melody I heard in my head. I didn't have any extra money, so I would take some scissors and cut paper grocery bags down to the size of a regular sheet of paper. I had this little stack that I'd use to write lyrics on. Even using those paper bags, I didn't have any extras to waste. Before I put anything down on paper, I had to really think about it and go over it in my mind to make sure it was right. I was fine-tuning my lyrics before I committed them to the page, which was making me a stronger writer. Since most people today write lyrics on computers, tablets, or even their phones, that's not the kind of concern budding songwriters would have anymore. I do think it was a good practice, though, and one that today's writers can still adapt.

The principle I'm talking about here is the principle of taking your time. *Think about what you're trying to communicate before you throw down the first line or idea that comes to your mind.* **Let the song reveal itself to you. Marinate in the idea so that it can properly emerge. There's no set amount of time that will take. Some songs come in a rush like a freight train, but others want to be chased for a while. Whether you've got a speedy one on your hands or a slow-mover, you've got to be mentally prepared to spend the time it takes to get that particular song to where it needs to land.**

I was starting to understand that concept as a teenager, but I had no idea how people got into the music business. In my attempt to figure it out, I was always looking for music companies in the yellow pages. I'd get these addresses, put all my cut-down grocery bags into another grocery bag, then go walking all over town, knocking on doors. "Is this a record label? Are you guys looking for singers? Is there somebody here who might be interested in hearing some new songs?"

I found this guy named Harry Nivens, who was a songwriter, producer, manager, and all-around music industry hustler. He was working with local acts like The Royal Holidays and would go on to manage The Royaltones. Harry also had a little local label called Penthouse Records for a while that he pretty much ran out of his house. Basically, he had his hands in all kinds of stuff and had some connections with some larger companies in New York.

I didn't know any of this when I appeared on Harry's doorstep as a fourteen year old desperate to make a connection with someone in the "actual" music industry. I had just seen a listing for his company somewhere and was taking another shot in the dark. I took a deep breath and knocked on the door. Harry opened it up to find this skinny kid standing there with a grocery bag full of more cut-up grocery bags. He wrinkled up his nose. "What do you want, son?" I shuffled my feet. "I'm a songwriter," I told him. "At least I think I am. And I sing, too." He opened the door wider. "Well, come on in and sing!"

I noticed right away that Harry was a jittery, nervous kind of guy. He had me come into his little makeshift studio and sing a couple of things for him. "You've got a nice sound to your voice," he told me as he lit a fresh cigarette. "I'd like to work with you a bit to see if we can't get something going. Can you come back again about the same time tomorrow?" I don't know what made him want to spend his time working with a kid. Maybe he could sense my hunger and determination, but I walked out of there feeling like Harry Nivens was going to be my ticket to the big time.

I started going over to Harry's place pretty regularly, and he taught me a lot about singing. We'd record demos in his little studio. Some were songs he wrote, and some were my earliest songwriting efforts. I don't remember what they were, but I can't imagine they were all that good. But that didn't matter because I had the fire! If he asked me to do something vocally that I wasn't able to do, I'd go home and work on it until I could. He taught me a lot about harmony, too. We'd do multitrack recording where I'd sing several harmonies over my own lead vocal. Harry would work the hell out of me stacking those harmony vocals. He would push me and push me, not letting me give in or settle for anything less than perfection. "You're going flat, Lamont! Don't you hear it? C'mon, now. You can do better!" Even though I felt like he was putting me through the ringer, I see now that it was all really valuable training. All that hard work gave me a good ear for harmony and how to construct vocal parts.

One day Harry and I were in his studio, and he was just drilling me on those harmony parts. I finally burst out in tears. I was embarrassed and tried to turn away so he wouldn't see, but I'm an emotional person, and there was no hiding my feelings from him. He put his hand on my shoulder and pretended to ignore my tears. "You know what, Lamont? I think it's time I met your mother. You've got what it takes, and I'd like to take you to New York to introduce you to some folks and make a proper record. But your mother will have to give her permission, of course." I wiped my cheek with the back of my sweater sleeve. "Really, Harry? You think so? New York? Man, that would be something!"

A couple of days later, I took my mom over to Harry's. She was skeptical before we even got there. *Who was this man who wanted to take her teenage son to New York?* She didn't like the sound of it, and she definitely didn't like the looks of Harry Nivens when we sat down and started talking. She took one look at this guy twitching and shaking and shit, and I could immediately see in her eyes that the answer was going to be a big fat "no." She was cordial during the meeting, but as soon as we got outside, it was a different story. "Lamont, have you lost your damn mind? Do you think for one second I'm going to send my boy off to New York City with this unstable guy that's acting all erratic and obviously popping Benzedrine pills? I don't trust him, and there's no way you're making that trip!"

Boy, was I upset that my mother was going to stand in the way of my dream. "This is my chance, Mama," I pleaded. "Why would you do this to me? Why would you stop me when I finally have an opportunity to make something of myself? You're just trying to hold me back because you're jealous!" I went on and on saying all kinds of terrible things that I'm sure must have really hurt her feelings. But she didn't budge. I refused to speak to her the rest of the way home. When we arrived, I went straight to bed.

My silent treatment went on for several days. Any time I saw my mother, I just scowled at her and maybe grumbled a few rude comments under my breath. She finally called Bishop Martin Tompkin, the minister over at The Spiritual Israel Church and Its Army and told him about the situation with this guy who wanted to take me off to New York. The minister invited her to bring me down to the church so we could talk it over.

Bishop Tompkin was kind of a strange guy, and I remember wanting to bolt for the door as the three of us sat there in his study. "Your mother told me what's going on," he said as he leaned forward in his chair and placed his hands on the desk. We locked eyes. "Lamont, I sense that it's not your time. You wouldn't have made it with this guy anyway. Nothing would have come of it." I could feel my eyes starting to get water. "What are you talking about?" I shot back. My mother put her hand on my knee in a way that said, "Boy, you better watch your tongue!" The minster straightened his back and cleared his throat. "Like I said, it's just not your time. There's gonna come a day when you're gonna be successful beyond your wildest dreams, but this isn't that day. You have to take your time, learn your craft, learn what you need to learn, and—most importantly—don't disrespect your mother. She's not trying to stop you. She's trying to protect you, do you understand? She's got her hands full trying to raise you, and she doesn't need any more problems. I know you're frustrated now, but you're going to win in the end. Believe that."

So that was the end of Harry Nivens. My mother went back over there and told him it wasn't going to happen. I'm sure he must have been disappointed after putting all that time into recording our demos, but there wasn't a damn thing in the world I could do about it. It just wasn't meant to be. I never heard from

Harry again, and I have no idea whatever happened to him, those songs, or our demo recordings. Maybe out there in some attic somewhere is a box of tapes of my earliest songs, but I'd probably cringe if I heard them now!

Not long after my great disappointment with Harry, I reconnected with my friend Tyrone Hunter. I'd known Ty since we went to school together at Barstow Elementary in Black Bottom. We both ended up living in the Jeffries Projects, and he was trying to figure out how to become a singer too. In those days it seemed like everyone in the neighborhood was trying to sing. If you didn't have any education, the dream was to become an entertainer. Vocal groups like Billy Ward and His Dominoes, The Mello-Moods, The Five Keys, The Cardinals, The Chords, The Moonglows, and The Platters were big at the time, so different guys around the projects were joining up and putting together ensembles of their own. Ty and I decided to align our efforts.

We were hanging out at a record shop one day when we met up with a group called The Counts, which was made up of Eugene Dwyer, Kenny Johnson, Bobby Alexander, and Don Davenport, who was a white bass singer. Ty and I started singing with those guys a little bit. Interracial groups weren't totally unheard of in the 1950s—you'd see some mixed groups from New York or Philadelphia back in those days—but it was still somewhat unique for us to have Don in the lineup. When Bobby split, we recruited Leon Ware into the group and started calling ourselves The Romeos.

Don Davenport lived out in the suburbs somewhere. He'd come in, and we'd all sit out in the middle of the projects in this big open area where people would come together to sing and hang out. We were out there harmonizing one day when Little Willie John walked up and started listening to us. He'd grown up in Detroit, and everyone knew he was making a big splash on

King Records with hits like "All Around the World," "Need Your Love So Bad," and the original version of "Fever." When I saw who it was, I just kept cool and really leaned into my vocal part. I'm sure we were singing whatever the doo-wop hit of the day was. When we finished, Willie flashed a smile. "What are you guys doing out here?" I shrugged. "Just singin' a few songs, I guess." He nodded. "Well, you guys sound pretty good, but can I give you a few pointers?" He really got down into the nitty-gritty, making suggestions and sharing helpful hints. He showed us how to sing vocal riffs while keeping it precise and professional. Willie was a great singer, and all of us were eager to soak up his expertise.

It turned out that Willie's sister, Mabel John, was living in the Jeffries Homes at the time. He'd come around to visit with her pretty regularly, and he kind of took me under his wing. I was really impressed with Willie, and I always appreciated his pointers and his encouragement. He was very generous to share his tricks of the trade, and I think I became a much better singer thanks to his help. I was pretty taken with him, not only because of his talent, but because of his rising fame. He'd found a way to make it as an entertainer, and I was determined to do the same. I just enjoyed being around him and hoped to soak up some of that positive energy.

The Romeos didn't get a lot of gigs at first, but I remember hearing about an "up-and-coming" contest at the Graystone Ballroom over on Woodward Avenue. I went down there to find out how we could sign up. The man gave me a big stack of pamphlets. "What you need to do," he told me, "is write your group name on the back of this flyer. Anyone who shows up at the door with one of these gets fifty cents off the admission price." Man, I went crazy with those pamphlets. I was giving one to anybody I saw. I had my aunts and my cousins and everybody passing those things out. We blanketed the city with those damn things! Don Davenport's mother scraped together a little extra money to buy us group uniforms. Actually they were just matching brown suits off the rack from J.C. Penney, but we thought we looked sharp.

When the big night came, all these local doo-wop groups were taking their turn, one after the other. We all listened to the same stuff, so every group was practically doing the same damn song! The Romeos put in a decent showing. We weren't terrible, but we definitely weren't the best, either. At the end of the night, the emcee came out and announced the third place winner. They came up to collect their twenty-five dollars or whatever it was they won. Then the second place winners were called up for whatever prize they got. "And finally," he said, "tonight's winners of the Graystone Ballroom's up-and-coming contest are … The Romeos!" We couldn't believe it. We won $100 for taking the top spot, but we knew we didn't win because we were the tightest or most polished group. We won because we passed out the most pamphlets!

Still riding high off our big win at the Graystone, The Romeos became honest-to-goodness recording artists in mid-1957. Don knew this guy named George Braxton, who was enamored with the idea of getting into the music business. He was a real estate broker, but he also published a little magazine called *Teen Life*, so he knew that teenagers were spending money on records like never before. He launched a label called Fox Record Company and set up a recording date for us at United Sound, which was already well known at the time for recording Charlie Parker, John Lee Hooker, Little Willie John, and other important national acts.

At our first session, we recorded "Gone Gone Get Away" and "Let's Be Partners." I wrote the songs and sang lead on both sides. When the record was released that summer, the label credited "The Romeos with the band of George Braxton." We were actually backed up by Hal Gordon's group, which was best known for appearing with Soupy Sales on his nightly show called *Soup's On* that aired on Detroit's WXYZ-TV. I guess since George was paying for the record he could put whatever he wanted on there. Not that it mattered. The record was a total flop, and I don't know if anyone even saw the label anyway.

For whatever reason George decided to keep investing in Fox Records and The Romeos. We went back to United Sound not long after our first record was released to cut two more songs, "Fine Fine Baby" and "Moments to Remember." It was released in August with band credits going to Lucky Lee's group. If I remember right, that was actually a country trio that George Braxton had decided to record, so it made sense for him to use the musicians who were already there. They did a pretty good job, too.

Even through it wasn't the first thing The Romeos recorded, I think "Fine Fine Baby" was the first real song I wrote for the commercial market—at least the first one I'd want anyone to hear. Sure, Harry Nivens and I had been working on some different things prior to that, and I'd been coming up with different things since elementary school, but all of that was just preparation to really figure out what I was doing. "Fine Fine Baby" was a simple little R&B song. It was just a diddy with a slight cha-cha beat, but it had a catchy melody. I had figured out how to properly structure songs at that point, and I was pretty serious about making music my profession. I had just turned sixteen, but I thought The Romeos might be my ticket to success.

Fortunately we had pretty good luck with that record. Those were the days when an act could have a regional hit, which is what happened when Frantic Ernie Durham started spinning "Fine Fine Baby" on WJLB. It made it into the Top 5 of "Ernie's

Picks to be Clicks," and then other DJs started playing it too. We got invited to appear on the *Saturday Dance Party* TV show just across the river in Canada, and then we were asked to open a show for Della Reese.

Before long, Atlantic Records took notice of the attention our record was getting around Michigan. One of their promotion men called up George Braxton. "Looks like you've got a hit on your hands over there," he told George. "We'd like to buy it." That October our record was rereleased on Atlantic's Atco imprint with "Fine Fine Baby" on the A-side and "Moments to Remember You By" (a slight variation on the original title) on the B-side.

The busier I got with The Romeos, the more high school began to take a back seat. I would be out late at these record hops, and I found myself falling asleep at my desk. I came in late to my homeroom class one morning, and the teacher, Mr. O'Neal, quipped, "Oh, here comes our superstar" as I slid into my spot in the back row. "I ain't no superstar," I shot back, "and there ain't no reason for you to try to embarrass me." He crossed his arms. "Mr. Dozier," he said as he raised his voice, "This is my classroom, and I'll say what I please." I can see now why he wanted me to take school seriously, but at the time I just felt like he was standing in the way of my musical dreams. I was pissed off. I stood up. "Man, go to hell," I said on my way out the door. I walked down the hallway and right out the front door of the school building. I never went back. I became a sixteen-year-old high school dropout. I didn't care at the time. All I wanted to do was make music. Looking back with the wisdom of a few years, however, I really regret that I never finished school.

When my mother found out that I walked out of Northwestern High School, she was furious. "What do I need to go to school for?" I asked her. I'm gonna make music for a living.

I think I could be a star." She thought I was crazy when I talked like that. "You're just dreaming, Lamont," she sighed. "You need to get your head screwed on straight and figure out what you're gonna do with your life." My Aunt Jennie recognized that I had talent, and she would frequently speak up for me. The rest of the family pretty much thought I was nuts for trying to build a music career. My mother gave me an ultimatum. "I'm not gonna have you laying around my house playin' around at tryin' to be some kind of singer," she said. "If you don't want to go to school, then you can go to the army."

I definitely didn't see myself as a military type. I was a lover, not a fighter. I was too young to enlist in the service on my own, but my mother was ready to sign for me. She put me in the car to drive over to Fort Wayne on the Detroit River, which was the main military recruiting center in the area. It was winter time, and the roads were icy. On the way there, another driver lost control on the slick surface and rear-ended us at a traffic light. It didn't do too much damage to the cars, but I hit my face on the dashboard and broke my nose. When we finally showed up at Fort Wayne, I had blood running down my shirt, and it looked like I'd been punched in the face by Joe Louis himself. The recruiters took one look at me and refused to take me. And there was nothing my mother could say about it, so I dodged that bullet. The broken nose was a small price to pay.

In the meantime, The Romeos might have landed on Atlantic Records, but it's not like we were living the glamorous life. Having left school, I had no choice but to work. Before long I was balancing three jobs. I was a stock boy at the grocery store and also worked the night shift making bagels at Epstein's, a Jewish bakery on Dexter Avenue. On Saturdays I shined shoes at Andy Pellicano's hat blocking and shoe shine place in Highland Park. There were about ten of us lined up at a row of shoeshine seats in there. I didn't mind hard work, but I wanted my efforts to be going toward music. Needless to say, I was ready to advance my station on the music scene, so I hatched a plan to move The Romeos ahead and catapult us to music industry success.

Even though I was still just a teenager, I'd been studying the music business closely, and I thought I had a better handle on what I was doing than I actually did. Atco sent me a letter after the release of "Fine Fine Baby" to let us know they wanted to get The Romeos into the studio to record another single. The legendary Jerry Wexler was the A&R man then. Thinking I had some kind of negotiating power, I wrote him back telling him that we weren't interested in only doing a single and were ready to make a full album instead. In so many words I said that if Atlantic wasn't going to get on the stick and let us record an LP, then we would take our talents elsewhere.

Talk about overplaying your hand! I didn't even have a hand to play. Here I was, a sixteen-year-old kid, giving Jerry Wexler an ultimatum. It was probably only a week or so before I got another letter back that said something like, "Dear sirs, we understand your position. While we are not prepared to record an album of material on The Romeos it sounds like you have someone lined up to work with your group in that capacity. We certainly don't want to stand in your way. In order to facilitate your other opportunities we hereby release you from all contractual obligations. Goodbye and good luck."

I was stunned. I thought, "Oh man, the other guys are gonna kick my ass. I got us tossed off the label!" I couldn't bear to tell them what really happened, so I made up a lie and said I'd gotten a letter from the label informing us that our deal was just a one-off and that they didn't want to do anything else with us. I never told any of the other guys about the actual letter from Jerry Wexler or how I'd stepped in it trying to be a businessman.

Some lessons I've learned along the way have been hard-learned. That's definitely one of them. One of the most important things I tell songwriters and others looking to make a living from music is that *you must educate yourself about the business. Then, once you've educated yourself, you've got to be realistic.* I thought I knew something about the music industry when I sent that letter, but I actually only revealed how inexperienced I really was. A little humility and a lot more understanding of how things work would have served me much better. If you want to live the life of a songwriter, read some reputable books about how the music business works. Or consider taking a class or two. Then, ask good questions and draw from the wisdom of those who have gone before. That can help you get your songs to the artists you want to hear them or get your own material to the right person in the appropriate way without thwarting your own efforts or putting your foot in your mouth.

I don't know why we didn't return to working with George Braxton after the Atlantic thing fell apart. Though he'd launched Fox Records specifically to record The Romeos, he was getting pretty serious about his recording efforts and actually spun off several additional imprints, including Brax and Chant Records. He even hit the national charts at the start of 1959 with Danny Zella's recording of "Wicked Ruby," but for some reason we didn't go back to Fox. We went to see some different record people around Detroit but weren't really able to get anything going. Ultimately, The Romeos just kind of petered out on its own.

Despite my screwup with Atlantic, not everyone in the group had the same ambition I had. The other guys were having a ball with the girls screaming and carrying on, but that wasn't why I was doing it. I didn't mind a little female attention, but to me music was about much more than impressing girls. I viewed music as a long-term career more than some of the other Romeos did, so I have a feeling it would have eventually fizzled out whether we'd gone on to make another record or not. The Romeos had its time, but it just wasn't meant to be.

After we disbanded, I kept thinking about this guy we'd met toward the very end while we were still looking for a new recording deal. Eugene Dwyer had run into him somewhere, and he invited us to come over to this little makeshift studio he'd set up in his sister's basement. He told us, "You guys sound good. I think we could probably get some things going if you're willing to hang in here with me for a while until I can get things off the ground." He was real positive and full of energy. I liked him, but The Romeos were done before he really got his situation together. Little did I know that our paths would cross again before long. The guy's name was Berry Gordy, Jr.

Chapter Five

SOMEDAY, SOMEWAY

One of Detroit's legendary music venues was the Flame Show Bar. The biggest black touring acts in the country would play there, including Billie Holiday, Dinah Washington, Dizzy Gillespie, Ella Fitzgerald, Count Basie, Joe Turner, Etta James, and many more. There was a successful photo concession business in the club run by a pair of beautiful sisters named Gwen and Anna Gordy. The very popular Gordy girls would wind their way through the crowd offering to take pictures, which were developed in the back by a couple of their brothers and then sold to the customers. The patrons loved Gwen and Anna for their glamor and charm, and the club loved them because they got a percentage of their sales. Needless to say, they were great saleswomen!

The venue's manager and talent booker was a guy named Al Green—no relation to the famous soul singer of the same name. Because he was a powerful figure on the local music scene, Al was able to launch a music publishing company and management firm of his own. He began working with some local artists, including LaVern Baker, Johnny Ray, and Jackie Wilson. When Jackie left Billy Ward and the Dominoes in 1957, he became one of the most popular singers in Detroit thanks to his legendary performances at the Flame Show Bar. It was no surprise when Al secured him a record deal on Decca's Brunswick imprint.

With Jackie preparing to record for a national label, Al was looking for songs—preferably ones that could be signed to his own publishing company. About that time, he met Gwen and Anna Gordy's younger brother, Berry, an aspiring songwriter who was hanging around the club in hopes of making inroads on the local scene. Given the popularity of his sisters, Berry was quickly embraced as part of the Detroit music community. When Al found out he had songs, he suggested that Berry come by his office. That's where Berry met Billy "Roquel" Davis, a fellow aspiring songwriter, who was writing for Al's company. Billy and Berry began working together, often as a trio with Gwen Gordy.

Billy Davis, Berry, and Gwen ended up writing Jackie Wilson's first hit, "Reet Petite." Then they wrote his next one, "To Be Loved." In fact they wrote Jackie's first six or seven hit singles, including the classic "Lonely Teardrops." By the start of 1959, they were bona fide hit songwriters, and Billy Davis and Gwen Gordy were in a romantic relationship. Everything was going great until Berry butted heads with Jackie's second manager, Nat Tarnopol, and the songwriting trio lost access to their hit-making artist.

Gwen came up with the idea of launching their own label so they could keep writing songs and release them by their own stable of artists. I think she was pretty surprised when Berry told her and Billy that he would rather do his own thing than work with partners. He would continue to work with them, but wanted to try his hand at launching a separate label of his own. Moving forward as a duo, Gwen and Billy established Anna Records, named for Gwen's sister. Berry, recently separated from his first wife, had already set up shop in his sister Lucy's basement. There he worked to develop a handful of artists, including a vocal group called The Matadors that was fronted by a teenager who called himself Smokey Robinson. Little Willie John's sister Mabel, whom he used to visit in the Jeffries Homes, got with Berry around the same time and ended up being the first female artist signed to his Tamla label. Even though she didn't have any hits with Berry, she would later go on to back up Ray Charles as a Raelette and have a hit on Stax Records called "Your Good Thing (Is About to End)." All of these seeds were being sown in that little basement studio, which is the same place were Berry was working when I first met him with The Romeos.

Thanks to their connections and songwriting success, Gwen and Billy were able to make a distribution deal with Chess Records in Chicago, which would give their Anna Records releases a wider reach. They opened their doors early in 1959, launching their efforts with a couple of singles by a group called The Voice Masters that was co-managed by Berry Gordy and Billy Davis. At some point in 1960, a couple of The Voice Masters left the group. The label aired radio ads to announce auditions for new singers, so I went down to their little storefront studio at the corner of Farnsworth and St. Antoine Street and tried out. I guess they liked what they heard, because I was invited to join the group on the spot. They asked me if I knew any other good singers, so I suggested my friend Ty Hunter from The Romeos.

When Ty and I signed with Anna Records as part of The Voice Masters, we also made a deal where we could record as individual artists as well. By the end of 1960 they'd released two singles credited to Ty Hunter. The first, "Everything About You," made it to the Top 20 on the national R&B chart, while the follow up, "Free," was also pretty big locally. Meanwhile, I was waiting my turn to record as a solo artist. To help make ends meet, Gwen Gordy hired me to work at the label. In addition to singing with The Voice Masters, I took on the glamorous tasks of mopping the floor, packing records in the back for shipment, cleaning up the place, and that kind of thing—just doing whatever needed to be done. I was basically a glorified janitor itching to get into the studio to make my splash.

Of course being there meant I had a front row seat to everything that was going on. Anna Records released singles by Johnny & Jackey (Johnny Bristol and Jackey Beavers), who later ended up as writers and producers at Motown, and are best known for going on to write "Someday We'll Be Together." The Anna label also recorded some of Joe Tex's early sessions just before he broke through with the big hit "Hold What You've Got." Future Temptations singer David Ruffin was part of the Anna family, too. Like me, he sang with The Voice Masters and also helped pack records for shipment while waiting to cut a solo record.

I first met Harvey Fuqua and Marvin Gaye during my days at Anna Records. Of course I already knew about Harvey and his group, The Moonglows, from their songs like "Sincerely," "See Saw," and "Ten Commandments of Love." At some point, the original lineup had split up, and Harvey hooked up with a group called The Marquees that included Marvin. The Marquees effectively became the New Moonglows, backing up Harvey on tour and on his Chess Records releases. There was a strong relationship between Anna Records and the Chess label. When the New Moonglows began to splinter, Leonard Chess suggested that Harvey move to Detroit and hook up with the folks at Anna. Marvin came with him, and we became buddies. Marvin and I just hit it off. He wasn't really writing a lot of songs in those days, but he had a great voice, was a really solid drummer, and played piano well, too. It wasn't uncommon to see Marvin in the studio playing on various sessions for the label.

I remember going over to Billy Davis's house one time when I was working for Anna Records. He stepped into the other room to pour us drinks, and I spotted all these plaques on the wall. I got up from the couch and started examining them closely. Each one had the name of one of the hits he and Berry and Gwen had written for Jackie Wilson: "To Be Loved," "Lonely Teardrops," "That's Why (I Love You So)." Suddenly Billy was standing next to me. He handed me my drink, and I took a sip, trying to seem casual. "What are all these?" I asked him. "Those are BMI awards," he told me. "Every time a radio station plays a song, they have to report it to BMI so the songwriters get paid. If a song gets a lot of airplay and you have a big hit record, BMI awards a plaque to the writer." I took another sip and nodded slowly. "Wow," I finally responded. "You know, one day I think I'd really like to have something like that." Billy squeezed my shoulder, which startled me. I turned, and we locked eyes. "Lamont," he said, "listen to me. If you want it bad enough and you work for it hard enough, then one day you will have some of these on your wall, too." Billy went on to co-write "I'd Like to Teach the World to Sing (In Perfect Harmony)," so I guess Billy Davis knew what he was talking about when it came to finding songwriting success!

Finally, after months of waiting, I got the chance to make my record for the Anna label. Released at the tail end of 1960, "Let's Talk It Over" was a mid-tempo ballad written by Harvey Fuqua and Gwen Gordy. I was more excited about the B-side, an original song of mine called "Popeye." Marvin Gaye played drums, Harvey Fuqua was on the piano, and future Motown musicians James Jamerson and Robert White played bass and guitar, respectively. Those guys were cookin', and it was a really cool funky record. I think it was Billy Davis who suggested that I choose a stage name. They felt like "Dozier" wasn't particularly memorable, so I picked Lamont Anthony. That's not my middle name or anything; I just thought it had a ring to it. It sounded like someone who could be a star.

The deejays weren't too interested in "Let's Talk it Over," but when Frantic Ernie Durham flipped it over and started playing "Popeye" over the WJLB airwaves, other local stations followed, and the record took off. Almost immediately I had a serious local hit on my hands. Then it became a regional hit. "Popeye" was spreading like wildfire, and I was going to all these record hops to promote it. Things were finally starting to click for me, and I figured I could set aside that mop once and for all.

I came in the office one day to find Billy Davis shuffling some papers on his desk. "I've got something here you need to see," he told me as I stood in the doorway. "It's not good news. We got this letter from King Features that says they are the sole owners of the Popeye cartoon character and we are infringing on their copyright with our references to Popeye in your song. It says we must cease and desist from production and distribution immediately or face a lawsuit. They sound serious."

I felt like someone had just punched me in the stomach. How could this be happening? It was like every time I took a step forward with my music career, I kept getting shoved five steps back. "Man, Billy," I muttered with my head hanging low, "what are we gonna do?" He thumped his pencil on a desk a few times as if he was thinking. "We've got a hot-sounding record," he said.

"Let's go back in the studio and use that same track. We'll just change the words."

I wasn't convinced, but soon "Popeye the sailor man" became "Benny the Skinny Man." Anna Records re-pressed the single and sent it out to the radio stations, but by then the buzz had already died down. There just wasn't a way to recapture the momentum we had going on the original release. To this day, that's one of the great disappointments of my career. I really thought "Popeye" was going to be the start of something big for me, but it wasn't meant to be.

As a songwriter, I picked up a tip from that experience that has served me well over the years. *You have to recognize what's beyond your control.* **You can write a song, record it, release it, find success with it, and sometimes something can still go awry. There are certain things that are just out of our hands. It's important to be diligent to control what you can control. Beyond that, you have to release the songs into the wild and trust that the right thing is going to happen. I believe it's the Master Muse who gives us our songs in the first place, so if there's a master plan for it that's different than what we might have envisioned, we have to be willing to accept it. The life of songwriting is full of joys as well as disappointments. The key is to stay on top of what we can control and trust that the rest will unfold as it's meant to.**

The "Popeye" disappointment was discouraging, but it turned out Anna Records was winding down anyway. Having decided not to join Gwen and Billy Davis, Berry Gordy had started his own independent operation called Tamla Records. He'd set up shop in a house at 2648 West Grand Boulevard, converting a garage and an old photography dark room into a little studio. Unlike his sister, Berry didn't have distribution, but the first Tamla release, "Come to Me" by Marv Johnson, was picked up by United Artists and hit the Top 10 on the national R&B chart. It even snuck into the pop Top 40. Berry released another half dozen Tamla singles in its wake, but none of them broke through to the national market.

In the summer of 1959, not long after I started working at Anna Records, I was mopping the floor one day when Berry came bursting through the front door with an acetate record under his arm. "Hey, man," he yelled as he headed my direction. "Can I get your opinion about something?" I leaned the mop handle against the wall. "Sure, man." I shrugged. "I could use a little break." He motioned for me to follow him into the little studio. "We just cut this thing," he said breathlessly as he pulled the acetate from its paper sleeve and set it on the turntable. "This is the first session we cut over at my own studio, and I want to know what you think." He lowered the needle onto the disc. I heard a bar of solo piano that was joined by a lone tambourine before erupting into a very danceable groove with a full band. Suddenly the lead singer's soulful shout took over: "The best things in life are free …"

That was the first time I ever heard Barrett Strong's "Money (That's What I Want)." Of course it would go on to become a classic, but at the time, the rest of the world hadn't heard it yet. Berry was pacing back and forth across the floor the whole time it played. As soon as it faded out, he snapped his head in my direction. His eyes widened. "Well?" He shoved his hand in his pocket and started fiddling with his change. "What do you think, man?" I smiled. "Sounds like a hit to me, Berry!" He nodded as if he was both agreeing with me and trying to convince himself at the same time. "Do you really think so?" Before I could answer, he wrinkled up his nose and dropped the needle back on the record. "*Really* listen to this part again." We listened to almost the entire back half of the song again. "Yeah, man," I said. It's really good. That's a hit!" He smiled. "What about that instrumental section? Do you feel like it works?" I couldn't help but chuckle a little. "What do you want me to say, Berry? To my ears, that sounds like a hit!"

Berry had really invested serious funds and sweat equity in "Money" and was looking for validation from everyone around him that it was, in fact, a hit. He was probably also thinking about the bigger picture. Was this new studio of his the kind of facility he could use to churn out successful singles? He shouldn't have worried. Berry always had great ears and an uncanny ability to identify a hit song. And, of course, he was right. The Tamla release of "Money" caught fire on Detroit radio. Then it spread to Chicago, St. Louis, Atlanta, and other cities. Since Berry didn't have national distribution, he leased the master recording to Gwen and it was reissued on Anna Records, which was able to distribute it through their deal with Chess. It hit the national charts in January of 1960 and climbed all the way up to the number-two position on *Billboard*'s R&B rankings in about a month. The record crossed over to the pop charts and became a Top 20 hit, as well.

In the meantime, Berry had released a record called "Bad Girl" by The Miracles on a sister imprint to Tamla that he named Motown Records. That one was leased to Chess for distribution and landed on the national pop charts. Berry was finding success, but he soon grew tired of sharing the proceeds with United Artists, Anna, Chess, and other third parties. In 1960 he finally secured distribution of his own, and everything just seemed to snowball from there. He signed a teenager named Mary Wells that year, and her debut single, "Bye Bye Baby," became the first Top 10 R&B hit released and distributed by Motown. The Miracles' "Shop Around" became the company's first million seller soon after, with The Marvelettes' recording of "Please Mr.

Postman" becoming its first number-one single on the national pop chart just before the end of 1961.

The Gordy clan was probably the most tightly knit family I've ever seen. Several of Berry's siblings were involved in Motown early on, and, with the tidal wave of success dwarfing Gwen's efforts at Anna Records, the family decided that Motown would become the focus. At some point, Billy Davis and Gwen Gordy's romantic relationship had fizzled out, so he left Detroit and moved to Chicago to take a job heading the creative department at Chess Records. Gwen Gordy and Harvey Fuqua got married and sold Anna Records to Berry. They launched a couple of new imprints, Tri-Phi and Harvey Records, but eventually they went to work for Motown, too. Marvin Gaye ended up marrying Anna Gordy and, of course, became part of the Motown family. Ultimately Anna Records (and many members of its cast of characters) was simply absorbed into Motown.

I didn't go over to Motown right away. Keep in mind that my goal at that point was to be a singer, and Berry had plenty of singers. Several of us from the Anna Records crew, including me, Ty Hunter, and David Ruffin, continued to record for Billy Davis even though he moved over to Chess. They launched an imprint called Check-Mate in the summer of 1961. The first release was a record of mine credited to La Mont Anthony called "Just to Be Loved."

I remember going to Chicago to record in the Chess studio. I was still pretty much a teenager, and that was the first time I'd ever traveled outside Detroit for work. We had some relatives in Chicago, so I'd visited the city before, but I'd never traveled in a professional capacity. I took the train over and, since I didn't have any musicians with me, we used the guys at Chess. I was already a fan of a lot of the stuff they were doing. Little Walter performing "My Babe"? Damn, he could play his ass off on that harmonica, and that record sounded like magic. I met Chuck Berry when I was there, and I also got to meet Howlin' Wolf. I was mesmerized by that guy. That voice! I used to love the energy that he had. His voice sounded like he was chewing gravel or some shit, and he was a giant in my mind. It was thrilling to go be a part of the Chess Records scene for a couple of days, but unfortunately that record didn't do anything. I was starting to get discouraged.

By that point, I was twenty years old, and the pressure was on to make the music thing work. I had a wife and daughter but wasn't very well equipped for the responsibilities of family life. I met my wife, Elizabeth Ann Brown, in the Jeffries Housing Projects when we were still teenagers. She stayed down the street from me, and we became friends. One thing led to another, and we started dating. When Ann discovered she was pregnant, I thought the right thing to do was to get married. I was just seventeen, and my mother thought I was too young to be striking out and starting my own family. Ann's mother didn't leave much room for debate, though. "Y'all are just gonna have to get married, and that's that," she told us. She was adamant. Since my mother wouldn't sign for me, we had to wait until I turned eighteen so we could go down to the Justice of the Peace and make it official.

I didn't feel pressured to get married, but I felt like it was my obligation. I thought it was the right and responsible thing to do, but we were so young and inexperienced that we were probably doomed from the start. I don't know if I loved Ann, but I cared for her. I certainly didn't mind being with her, but I was just a kid. I might have been writing songs about it, but I didn't really know anything about "forever" or what love truly meant. It would take me years to understand what love was really about.

Ann and I got married because there was a baby on the way. Ironically, we experienced a miscarriage soon after we got settled into our new life together. That was tough on both of us. Even though the baby was a surprise, we had just gotten adjusted to the idea when that rug was pulled out from under us. Strangely, going through that sad time together drew us closer. Within a year, Ann was pregnant again, and our daughter, Michelle, was born in 1960.

Ann, Michelle, and I lived in a tiny one-room studio apartment with a little kitchen and a Murphy bed that came out of the wall. We both had to work to make ends meet, so when Anna Records folded, I needed a job. I began working for Hires Root Beer as a "helper," which was basically their word for delivery guy. I made five dollars a day, which they paid in cash. Ann was a pretty good typist and bookkeeper, so she got a job in the secretarial pool over at Motown.

Then Berry Gordy called me up one afternoon out of the blue. "Hey, Lamont," he said, "why don't you come over here and jump on board, man? I need you!" It was obvious that, after years of struggle, Berry had hit on something big, and I was ready to be a part of it. Plus, Ann was already over there, so it made sense. "Yeah, man," I replied. "I think that sounds like a pretty good idea." Berry said he could pay me twenty-five dollars a week as an advance against future royalties. That meant I would make just about enough money to pay for my bus rides to and from work, but it was the same I was getting from the root beer job, and at least I would be focused on music again. I'm sure that my mother and Ann's parents thought I was a fool for continuing to chase a music career when I had a family to support, but I couldn't get music out of my system. I had to give it one more go.

Of all my family members, my Aunt Jenny and Uncle James were the most supportive of my musical pursuits and my most consistent cheering squad. James drove me over to Motown's headquarters on my first day on the job there. As we pulled up to the now-iconic house on West Grand Boulevard, I was a little nervous, but I was also excited. Something felt right about the place. It was as if I was exactly where I was supposed to be at that time. James slipped the car into park and turned his body toward me. He pushed his hat back off his forehead with his index finger as a big grin broke out across his face. "Well," he said slowly, "how do you feel?" I looked out the passenger side window at the big sign that read "Hitsville U.S.A." above the large front window. "You know," I said, "I've got a funny feeling that through this little house I'm gonna do some really big things." Uncle James slapped his palm on the dashboard so hard it startled me. "Yeah, man," he practically howled. "That's what I'm talkin' about! If you feel it, then I *know* that's what's gonna happen. You go in there, Lamont, and you kill 'em, baby! They never heard nothin' like you! Get yourself in there and you go kick some ass!"

After James's pep talk, I felt like a boxer about to go in the ring. He was pumping me up. As I headed up that walkway to the front doors, I thought about Joe Louis and how my folks always emphasized what a champion he was back when they'd tell stories about him training on the playground at Barstow Elementary. I felt like maybe this was my chance to become a different kind of champion. Whatever was on the other side of that door, I was ready!

Chapter Six

FOREVER CAME TODAY

When I walked into the reception area at Hitsville U.S.A., I was greeted by one of the women who worked in the front office. I introduced myself, and she walked me over to the punch clock, which was located in the hallway beyond the front room that led back to the recording studio. It's kind of funny to think about now, but everybody who worked at Motown punched a clock when they arrived each morning. Berry just adopted that from what they were doing at the Lincoln-Mercury plant where he once worked. He didn't know any better. None of us did. The assumption was just, "Well, sure, when you come to work you punch a clock." We'd clock in at nine in the morning and clock out at six in the evening. If we had a late recording session or something that stretched until two in the morning, we'd just punch in later the next day.

On that first day, Berry had me come in a little later for some reason, maybe because he wanted to introduce me to everybody at once. As they were showing me the punch clock, there seemed to be a lot of activity in the hallways. People were coming out of the studio and heading upstairs. Just then Berry came walking down the hallway. "Lamont," he smiled, extending his hand. "Welcome aboard. Let's get upstairs and get something to eat." That's when I found out that Motown provided lunch every day for the whole staff. I got myself a bowl of stew, and Berry introduced me around to some of the people I didn't already know.

After lunch we headed into Berry's office to make everything official. He put all kinds of contracts and paperwork in front of me. One was for my publishing as a songwriter, one was an artist agreement, and another was a producer contract. I didn't know any better, so I just signed whatever was put in front of me. In those days, Motown was famous for not letting you take the contracts out of their offices to get reviewed by a lawyer. Not that I would have known where to find a lawyer or where to get the money to pay one. I was eager to get on with it, so I signed on the dotted line. And the other dotted line. And the next dotted line. And so on.

When I started at Motown, Brian Holland was Berry's fair-haired boy because he'd produced "Please Mr. Postman" with his songwriting and production partner Robert Bateman. The pair had been with Berry since virtually the start. They provided the backing vocals on his early production efforts along with Sonny Sanders and Raynoma Liles, who would later become Berry's second wife. Dubbed The Rayber Voices (a combination of the names Raynoma and Berry), all four members involved themselves in various creative aspects of Berry's early business efforts, including songwriting and arranging.

Once things began to take off for Berry at West Grand Boulevard, Brian Holland and Robert Bateman started writing and producing together under the banner of Brianbert Productions, a combination of their first names. After their success with The Marvelettes and "Please Mr. Postman," they teamed up with Motown's A&R Director Mickey Stevenson to write the follow-up singles "Twistin' Postman" and "Playboy."

Robert was actually my next-door neighbor, and I happened to run into him on the sidewalk one evening in the spring of 1962 as I was getting off the bus on my way home from work. "Hey, Lamont," he said, as we walked toward our apartment building, "I don't know if you heard, but I'm moving to New York. Berry and I keep getting into scrapes, and I don't need him on my ass anymore. I've got an opportunity at a company over there, and I'm gonna split, man." I didn't know Robert well, but I liked him and was sorry to hear he was leaving. We chatted for a few more minutes until we arrived at our respective doors, and I went in to have dinner with Ann and the baby.

An hour or two later there was a knock on my door. It was Robert. "Hey, man, I don't mean to disturb you, but can you come over for a quick drink?" I shrugged. "Sure, why not?" I followed him into his apartment and saw that Brian Holland was sitting at the kitchen table. I sat down and the three of us shot the shit for a little while. Finally, Robert said, "Brian, I know how you work, and Lamont, I've heard what you do. If you guys were to link up, there would be some real chemistry there. Something tells me you two would fit together like a hand in a glove." That sounded like a great idea to me. "Yeah," I said, "we oughtta give it a try." Brian nodded his head. "I like it. Why don't we get together tomorrow?"

Since I didn't yet have an office at Motown in those days, I would write songs on one of the pianos in the hallway. My preference was to go in the studio when there wasn't a session going on so I could use the grand piano. It sounded better, and I had more privacy in there. The day after I'd chatted with Robert and Brian, I was in the studio picking out a melody of a song I'd been working on for a few days. When I paused, I heard Brian's voice behind me. "*Man,* I like that. What is it?" I spun around to face him. "I call it 'Forever,'" I said, "but something's missing." Brian nodded his head slowly. "Let me hear it again." I played what I had as he leaned on the piano with his eyes closed. "Yeah, man, that's great," he said as the last chord rang in the air. "I love it, but you need a bridge … May I?" He motioned toward the piano bench. I scooted to the left, and Brian sat next to me and started plunking out some chords. As soon as he'd try something, I'd know exactly where it needed to go. Then I'd start something else, and he'd come up with the perfect answer. It was like Brian and I could complete one another's musical ideas the way certain people can finish one another's sentences. I realized right away that we shared a secret language of creativity. We finished up the music for "Forever" within an hour, and I felt like there was electricity surging through the room.

"I'm producing a session on The Marvelettes soon," Brian said as we headed up to the kitchen to refill our coffee cups. "Would you mind if I brought Freddie in to finish the lyrics so we can go ahead and get started on some more musical ideas?" Freddie Gorman and Brian had been in a group together called the Qualitones at one point, but then Freddie got a job as a mail carrier after they broke up. He got to know Berry Gordy on his mail route and eventually co-wrote "I Want a Guy," the first Supremes single, with Berry and Brian Holland. It didn't chart, but Freddie was later brought in on "Please Mr. Postman," likely because of his practical experience on the subject. After that, he was signed to Motown as an artist and writer.

After the great feeling I'd just experienced writing music with Brian, I was happy for Freddie to complete the lyrics so we could keep cranking. The Marvelettes were still the hottest act at Motown at the time, and the more chances I had to get them to record my songs, the better! Within the course of a few days, Brian, Freddie, and I had come up with a batch of songs for the group, including "Someday, Someway," "Too Strong to be Strung Along," and "Strange I Know."

As a songwriter, *it's crucial to be open to new situations.* Though it didn't ultimately end up being the long-term writing partnership that led to my biggest success, it was exciting to start working with Brian and Freddie. When you're starting out as a writer, there will be opportunities to collaborate with different people, and I always encourage newer writers to get in the habit of saying "yes." Some of those encounters will lead to nothing, but you never know who you'll click with or where a particular collaboration will lead you down the road. Don't get too locked in to one way of doing things. Be open to experiment and try new things. By staying open and positioning yourself for new encounters, you'll be more likely to find the partners and situations that will bring out the best of your talents.

In July The Marvelettes released their fourth single, "Beechwood 4–5789," which was produced by Mickey Stevenson. He wrote the song with my buddy Marvin Gaye and Berry's brother, George. It was a big national hit, and our song, "Someday, Someway" was on the B-side. Every time a record was sold, the songwriters got paid, which meant that if you'd written the flip side of a big hit you got paid the same on every record as the folks who'd written the hit side. Not only that, but we also got paid any time a song was played on the radio. Fortunately for us, enough disc jockeys turned over "Beechwood 4–5789" and played "Someday, Someway" that it wound up hitting the Top 10 on the national R&B charts. That was the first time I ever appeared on the *Billboard* charts as a songwriter, and I was thrilled.

By that point, Ann had quit her job at Motown to take a better-paying opportunity working at a department store. That meant I had to step up my role as a father with Michelle just as things were starting to get more active at Motown. It wasn't uncommon for me to bring her in to the office. Michelle was really well behaved, so she would just sit over in the corner and listen while Brian and I worked away on new melodies. There were other people in the building with kids, too, so it wasn't frowned upon. Brian didn't seem to mind at all, so we just did what we needed to do. Sometimes Michelle would start dancing, and that's how we knew we were on to something good. It was instant research.

In the wake of the success of The Marvelettes' double-sided single, the label put together an album called *Playboy*. Not only did it include "Someday, Someway," but it also had "Forever" and a song Brian and I wrote called "Goddess of Love." On top of that, both sides of the next Marvelettes single were Holland-Dozier-Gorman songs, "Strange I Know," another Top 10 R&B hit that also became the first song I wrote to hit the pop charts, backed with "Too Strong to be Strung Along."

When we went in the studio with The Marvelettes, my job was to make sure the background vocals were covered. To be honest, sometimes the girls' harmonies and voicings were a little suspect. They'd sing their parts, but they didn't always hit the standard I was looking for. Man, they could drive me crazy sometimes. I

might say, "No, that's the wrong note. You're going flat right there."
But many times they just weren't having it. They'd shoot back,
"Well it don't sound flat to me." There were a few occasions I'd
get to the end of my rope and tell them, "OK, don't worry about
it. You go on to lunch now and we'll fix it in the mix." But I had
my secret weapon. Jackie Hicks, Marlene Barrow, and Louvain
Demps, known as The Andantes, sang background vocals on a
whole lot of Motown hits. When The Marvelettes would go out
the front door, I'd open the back door to the studio and let The
Andantes in to fix the background vocals. They'd knock it out in a
hurry, so it was nice and smooth, and then they'd be out of there.
I don't think The Marvelettes ever knew. They'd come back in
and listen to the playback. They'd look at each other, saying, "Ooh,
listen to that. We sound good, don't we, girl?" Brian and I would
just look at each other and roll our eyes.

After that early success with The Marvelettes, I got my first
royalty check, which was for $1300. I took that thing to the bank
and asked them to cash it with only one and five dollar bills. The
teller looked at me kind of funny for that, but I didn't care. I went
straight home and dumped all that money out on the bed, which
looked like a lot with all those small bills. Hey, to us it *was* a lot!
Ann and I were celebrating and dancing around that tiny little
apartment like we'd just won the lottery. It was a brief moment of
happiness in a relationship that would soon become strained. As I
began to get my footing in the music industry, I was increasingly
away from home. Motown was a competitive environment, and
achieving success today meant you had to work twice as hard to
keep that success tomorrow.

Not only did my family life go on the back burner, but my
dreams of having a singing career were sidelined, too. In June of
1962, I recorded my one and only Motown single as an artist.
"Dearest One" backed with "Fortune Teller (Tell Me)" was issued

on Berry's brand-new Mel-o-dy label, but they didn't push it. Why would Berry want me to get distracted with an artist career when I was showing promise as a songwriter and producer? I was disappointed, but I had no time to dwell on it.

Brian, Freddie, and I kept writing and producing songs for the Motown roster, including "Mr. Misery (Let Me Be)" for The Miracles and "Pa (I Need a Car)" for The Contours. Sometimes we'd work with Janie Bradford instead of Freddie. She was the first secretary hired at Motown but was also a songwriter who'd found early success collaborating with Berry on Barrett Strong's "Money." Brian, Janie, and I wrote "Contract on Love," which was one of Stevie Wonder's early singles, as well as a few others.

Stevie was a trip, man. For a blind kid, he was always into some shit. He'd be running around all over Hitsville, playing tag with Berry's children, and getting into everything. He had a sixth sense or something where he could play games with other boys and girls and be good at it! He could do all kinds of things you wouldn't imagine a blind person doing. Once he came into his own as a songwriter, it was unbelievable. He was doing what everyone else was doing, but he worked around the clock. I'd hear him in one of the rooms at the piano pounding away for hours, finding chords and melodies and everything. His dedication was unparalleled.

If I'm honest, some of those early songs just didn't really resonate with me. I don't particularly like "Someday, Someway." I don't remember anything about writing it, and it just never spoke to me. It was OK, but it's lacking something I've never really put my finger on. "Strange I Know" was just a song. I don't have any kind of emotional connection to it. Brian and I were finding success with Freddie and Janie, but something was missing. We even had some conversations with Freddie and Janie about trying to form an exclusive partnership as a collaborative team, but that was short-lived. Something was "off," but I didn't quite know what it was. I'm a person who operates by feeling, or gut instinct. My gut was telling me that Brian and I could do great things, but our puzzle was still missing a piece.

Then the strangest thing happened to me in the fall of 1963. I was visiting someone in the neighborhood near Central High School on Tuxedo Street one night when I decided to cut through the school's athletic yard on the way back to my car at around 11:00 PM. It was a clear night, and I could see some stars, despite the lights of the city. For some reason I suddenly had the urge to stop and sit down. I dropped to the grass for a minute or two before leaning back to lie flat on my back. What happened next can only be described as a spiritual moment.

I started thinking about my music and what I hoped to accomplish at Motown. I closed my eyes and began to pray. I spoke to God, "I believe things are about to change, Father. I believe you have something great in store for me." My body suddenly felt light as a feather, and I started to levitate. When I tell people this, they think I'm nuts, but I know what I experienced. I wasn't asleep. I wasn't dreaming. I wasn't under the influence of any substances. But I was floating. It wasn't much, maybe ten inches off the ground, but it scared the shit out of me. It was a weird feeling. It lasted a few moments, and then I was gently returned to the grass as if a giant invisible hand was carefully lowering me back to earth.

Years later I told my friend Deepak Chopra about my experience. "I've done that," he assured me. "You tapped into something that very few people tap into." I'm not entirely sure what that experience meant, but I do know that things started changing in my life after that. I first noticed it a couple of months after the levitation when I bought a raffle ticket for two different Christmas raffles on opposite sides of town. I won first prize in both of them. It's not like these were life-changing winnings. One of them was a check for one hundred fifty dollars. The other was a large holiday turkey. But both raffles had a lot of entrants. It was just bizarre that I happened to win them both. When the new year started, everything began falling into place. That missing puzzle piece appeared, and an unprecedented season of success began that would dramatically impact my life. Hell, it would dramatically impact the future of pop music.

Chapter Seven

COME AND GET THESE MEMORIES

In the summer of 1962, Brian suggested that we work on a song for his older brother, Eddie, who was one of Berry's artists even before Brian came into the picture. Berry would use him to sing the demo recordings of the songs he, Gwen, and Billy Davis were writing for Jackie Wilson. Then Berry started producing Eddie as an artist in 1958 and leased several singles to the Mercury and United Artists labels, though they didn't land any national hits. Nevertheless, Eddie was pretty well known around Detroit as a good singer. When I was with Anna Records, he and I used to cross paths when we'd be doing these local appearances to promote our singles. On more than one occasion we ran into

each other on the bus on the way to a record hop, and we'd
become friendly with one another as a result. I didn't know Brian
when I first came to Hitsville, but I did know Eddie, so I was
certainly happy to work with him.

Eddie had finally landed a national hit in early 1962 with a
song called "Jamie" that Mickey Stevenson and Barrett Strong
wrote together. It was the first Motown record with strings on it,
which would become a defining characteristic of the "sound of
young America" that we would wholeheartedly embrace in the
next few years. Unfortunately, Eddie's next three singles didn't
connect, but Brian thought he and I might be able to come up
with something. We wrote a song with Eddie called "Darling, I
Hum Our Song." It didn't go anywhere, either, but that was the
first Holland-Dozier-Holland song ever released by Motown. It
might not have been a hit, but "Darling, I Hum Our Song" gave
Eddie Holland an idea.

Eddie had a good voice, but he suffered from stage fright.
He liked making records, but he didn't really want to go out
on the road because he didn't enjoy getting up in front of a
crowd and being an entertainer. He wanted to stay in the game,
but he wanted to stay home. Eddie could see that Brian and I
had our hands full with keeping up with the demand for new
material, so he proposed to Brian that he permanently join our
team to take up some of the slack. Not only that, but Eddie
had worked out a system for exactly how to structure our
partnership. Brian usually worked on music, while I worked
on both lyrics and music. Under Eddie's plan, I would be the
idea man. I'd bring in a lyrical concept and Brian and I would
develop a piece of music around it. Once we had a title or a
chorus lyric or a framework mapped out, we'd hand off the
song to Eddie to finish the lyrics. That way we could move on
to the next song while he completed and fine-tuned the words.

If Motown was a hit factory, we could be a factory within a factory. It would make the team of Holland-Dozier-Holland more efficient because we could churn out more work but keep quality high.

That idea was the birth of Holland-Dozier-Holland. Eddie taught himself to be a great lyricist, so I didn't have to worry about that side of the equation. He learned the craft and worked on writing and rewriting until Brian and I were satisfied. The three of us were a songwriting team while Brian and I continued to work as a duo on the production side. We'd finalize the song and cut the master while Eddie was working on the lyrics. It was very rare that the three of us would sit down in a room together and create a song from beginning to end. Instead, Eddie would go away and do his thing, so Brian and I could go back in the studio to come up with more ideas. Then Eddie would come in and sing the vocal on the track as a guide for the artist who would later record it. Brian was all music, Eddie was all lyrics, and I was the idea man who bridged both. It was that division of labor that was the secret to our success, and it became the template by which we functioned for the rest of our years at Motown together.

We started working as a songwriting trio around September of 1962. In January of 1963 we took The Marvelettes in the studio and cut "Locking Up My Heart." That was one of a few songs that I'd brought with me when I came to Motown. It was pretty much all finished up, but Brian and Eddie put a little polish on it, and that became the first Holland-Dozier-Holland song to hit the *Billboard* charts. The label decided to put "Forever" on the B-side, since it had only appeared on a Marvelettes LP up to that point. Both sides wound up charting in the Top 25 on the R&B chart and both appeared on the lower end of the pop chart, too. It didn't take the world by storm, but it was a good start.

Where "Someday, Someway" and "Strange I Know" seemed to be lacking something for me personally, "Locking Up My Heart" had the flavor I was looking for. There's no big story behind that song or anything; it just had a feel that seemed to click for me. The Holland brothers and I grew up going to church, and we were trying to capture that church energy to accompany the story of unrequited love. One of the common characteristics of our songs that would develop with time was an upbeat, happy feel with lyrics about sadness and heartbreak. If you really pay attention to the lyrics of some of our classic songs that make you feel good when they come on the radio, you'll notice that the words are often pretty bleak. We felt like the beat was the optimism. The lyric was sad, but the beat and the feel was the injection of hope that things could get better. We were all about taking a dark poem and transforming it into a ray of light with our music and production approach. That was a very conscious thing on our part. "Locking Up My Heart" was a good early example of that pattern, and it gave me a good feeling about the future for Holland-Dozier-Holland.

Over time, The Marvelettes' records began to stumble in the charts. The group kind of took a back seat to Martha and the Vandellas, who rose up to become the top female act at Motown prior to the ascendancy of The Supremes. The Vandellas' first charting single was "Come and Get These Memories," which also became the first Top 10 R&B hit for Holland-Dozier-Holland.

Some people are surprised when I tell them I originally wrote the song with Loretta Lynn in mind. As a lyricist and a storyteller, I've always been a fan of country music. There's nothing like country music when it comes to learning about strong lyrics or how to translate real-life situations into compelling stories. I was listening to country radio and buying country records, and I thought it was just magnificent. I knew that a lot of people looked at country as white music, but I didn't care about that. I was learning from a great art form. Hank Williams was one of my favorite songwriters. He could take very simple lyrics and ideas and deliver them in ways that were really profound. To me, the song was king. If a song is good, it can be sung by anyone in any style.

I think I liked Loretta Lynn so much because she told great stories, and I felt like she was speaking the truth. She was authentic. For some reason, I just heard Loretta's voice in my head when I wrote "Come and Get These Memories." I wrote it pretty quickly, and it's still one of the easiest songs I've ever written. It was a country song with a country lyric, but I was a black kid in Detroit, so how in the hell was I going to get my song to Loretta Lynn or get someone to open that door for me? And even if I did have a way to get a song to Loretta, by 1963 I was under exclusive contract to Motown. I couldn't have given her a song even if I had the opportunity! When I realized that my country songwriting debut was not to be, Brian and I went to work and did a little surgery on "Come and Get These Memories." We reworked the groove, the chord progression, and added all these eleventh and ninth chords to make it more complex and turn it into an R&B-influenced pop song. It turned out to be a good fit for Martha Reeves's voice.

Mickey Stevenson knew Martha could sing, but he had originally hired her as his secretary. She was answering phones, typing, handling paperwork, and that kind of thing. She was great at it, too, so Mickey was probably a little hesitant to record her for fear of losing a good worker. But Martha wanted to be a singer, and there was no denying her talent. Mickey's the one who took her in the studio first, but they weren't able to get any traction with her debut single. Everyone around Motown quickly realized that Martha was a great artist with a great voice. She just needed the right break to get started. Once she and the Vandellas established themselves with "Come and Get These Memories," they were set up for future success.

There's a lesson there that has proven very helpful in my career: *Be flexible enough to change your ideas when it's appropriate to do so.* **I had written a song with a particular artist in mind, but if I hadn't allowed myself to be flexible enough to reshape it, then it's very likely that nothing would have ever come of it. Our songs are like our babies, and it's easy to get precious about them sometimes. I'm not saying that writers should compromise their vision or change things on a whim, but I am saying there are situations where we must avoid being rigid in order for the song to emerge as what it was meant to be in the first place. Have confidence in songs to create them the way you think they should be, but never become so rigid that you're not willing to at least consider changes that will tip the scale to help the song earn the attention it deserves.**

When I showed up for work every morning, I would go through a little ritual to get the creative juices flowing. It usually involved sitting down at the piano and playing through a piece of music that I was working on, or maybe something I'd already completed that just hyped me up and made me feel inspired. I remember coming in one morning in the early summer of 1963 and sitting down at the piano to pump myself up with a piece of music I'd been playing around with. It was a pulsing shuffle, and the more energy I put into it, the better it sounded. I'd been messing with it for a few days, but didn't have any words coming to mind, so I was digging in harder and harder. It was an unusually hot day out, and I could feel my undershirt begin to get damp with sweat as I really got into the groove. The music business has changed a lot over the years, but back then we actually wore suits and ties to work. All of the men at Motown would wear those little narrow ties and those stovepipe pants with form-fitting jackets. All that stuff's back in style again now, but it's not the most comfortable thing a guy could wear on a sweltering day. After a few minutes, I stood up from the piano bench, removed my jacket, and rolled up my shirtsleeves. "Man, I'm hot," I said to no one in particular. "If we're having this kind of heat wave already, this summer will be unbearable." I sat back down, but what I'd just said played back to me in my mind like a recording. A heat wave! Suddenly, the song began to fall into place.

Things moved quickly at Hitsville back then. We finished recording "Heat Wave" with Martha and the Vandellas in late June, and it was out by early July. That became our first number-one on the *Billboard* R&B chart and our first Top 5 single on the pop chart. It even earned a Grammy nomination for Best R&B Recording, which I believe was the first time a Motown-associated act got a nod from the Recording Academy. We followed that up with "Quicksand," a Top 10 pop hit with a similar feel to "Heat Wave." We wanted to follow that pattern of a two-syllable hook that would just grab you, and "quicksand" was a good word to sing. It's evocative. What is quicksand? It's something that sucks you in. Once you get in it, you can't get out of it, and the more you fight it, the deeper you go. It was one of those words that just started the ideas flowing, and then the lyric could practically write itself.

At first Brian and I would meet in the studio to work out our songs, but if someone was in there, we could always grab one of the pianos in the hallway. When we started coming into our own, they gave us an office. It was more like a little cubby room with a small desk, a spinet piano, a little Webcor reel-to-reel tape machine, a pencil, and some paper. It was bare bones, but that's where you could find me and Brian if we weren't in the studio cutting records. We practically lived in that little room, and once we had our own space, everything started moving faster and faster. We were more productive than ever, and royalty checks started coming in for over one hundred thousand dollars.

Unfortunately, our next couple of singles for Martha and the Vandellas didn't do as well as our first ones. "Live Wire" probably pushed the "Heat Wave" and "Quicksand" formula a little too far. We cut that song twice for some reason but ended up going with the first version after all. I probably should have listened to my gut that we needed to do something different, but there was a lot of pressure on us to keep cranking out hits. It did OK, but it didn't make the Top 10 on the R&B chart or the Top 40 on the pop chart.

I was much more disappointed when the follow-up, "In My Lonely Room," didn't fare much better. We did get an R&B Top 10 on it, but it did a little worse on the pop chart than "Live Wire." That one has always been one of my favorite Holland-Dozier-Holland songs. I really like the melody and the feeling of the chords. I mentioned that we often wrote happy-sounding upbeat music to go along with sad lyrics, but the way it actually worked was that I would come in with a sad idea, and Brian and I would write the melody as a ballad. Then, once we were finished, we'd speed it up to give it that pop feel. If you slow down some of those feel-good Holland-Dozier-Holland hits, you realize a lot of them are hurtin' songs. "In My Lonely Room" is a prime example.

In January of 1964, I traveled to New York for BMI's annual awards dinner. Berry's Jobete Music Publishing was the second most honored publisher that night with a total of seven awards. Three of those were for Holland-Dozier-Holland songs, including "Heat Wave" and "Quicksand." Just a few short years earlier, Billy Davis had shown me his BMI awards and told me

I could achieve the same thing if I put in the work. I never imagined that I'd be collecting awards for three different songs the very first time I went! The other writers who received three awards that night were Ben Raleigh, Phil Spector, and the team of Jeff Barry & Ellie Greenwich. Still others took home four awards each: Brian Wilson of The Beach Boys, the team of Jerry Leiber & Mike Stoller, and the team of Barry Mann & Cynthia Weil. Only one team took home five awards, and that was Gerry Goffin & Carole King.

That's some great company, but the songwriter everyone was talking about that night is a name that isn't as well known today.

Ronnie Mack was a young writer who had a big hit with a song he wrote for The Chiffons called "He's So Fine." It spent about a month at number one in the spring of 1963, earning Ronnie his first BMI award. Tragically, he was already sick with Hodgkin's lymphoma when he scored his big hit. Ronnie died a few months later at the age of twenty-three. At the BMI awards dinner, his mother, Louise, came to accept the plaque on her son's behalf. She talked about her boy and was holding up his award saying, "My baby will never be able to get another award." It was such a traumatic thing and there wasn't a dry eye in the place. To see that woman crying like that over her child really stuck with me.

When I got back to Detroit, I came up with a new melody, but didn't have any ideas for the lyrics. I started thinking about Louise Mack and her tribute to her son. She said he'd never get another award, so I decided to write a song called "Ronnie Mack." I thought if it was a hit, then it would be another way to honor his name and maybe bring some more attention to him. As we worked on it, however, we had to admit that "Ronnie Mack" just didn't sing as well as we wanted it to. We ultimately decided to call the song "Jimmy Mack" instead, but in my heart it was still a nod to that poor woman's son and a recognition of her loss. We cut "Jimmy Mack" with Martha and the Vandellas. I knew it could be a hit for them, but little did I know how long we'd have to wait.

Every Friday there was a "quality control" meeting in Berry's office with about a half dozen staffers, producers, and even some administrative people who weren't necessarily musical. Berry wanted them there because their opinions represented the average music buyer. The point of the meeting was to play recordings that had been turned in that week by the various staff writers and producers. These weren't demo recordings. These were all full-blown master recordings featuring Hitsville artists. The point was for everyone to give feedback about what they did and didn't like about each recording. Then we'd take a vote on which ones to release. The rules were that you had to be honest (it could get pretty brutal in there sometimes) and that you couldn't vote for your own production. If we recorded something with an artist that didn't get released, the cost of that session was charged back to us as writers and producers. Needless to say, the meetings could get intense. The bottom line, though, was that whoever had the best song got the release.

Just because you'd recorded something, however, didn't mean it would automatically get played in the meeting. Billie Jean Brown oversaw the tape room and kept all the recordings organized. Berry eventually put her in charge of the first stage of quality control. She would prescreen everything and then bring what she thought was the cream of the crop to the full Friday gathering. We finished the "Jimmy Mack" master in June of 1964 but, for some reason, Billie Jean didn't think much of the song, and she wouldn't ever bring it out for the meeting. Since the quality control team never got to vote on it, the tape just sat on the shelves, and we missed out on getting the next Martha and the Vandellas single. That opportunity went to Mickey Stevenson, who brought in "Dancing in the Street," a song he'd written with Marvin Gaye and Ivy Jo Hunter that he'd produced with Martha and the girls just a few days after we cut "Jimmy Mack." It was a great record. Hell, I voted for it in the meeting, but I thought it was too bad "Jimmy Mack" didn't get its chance. I figured maybe we'd try a different artist on the track another time.

We didn't have any time to lose sleep over "Jimmy Mack." We were still producing The Marvelettes and Martha and the Vandellas, but by 1964 the lineup of artists we were working with also included Marvin Gaye, Mary Wells, The Supremes, The Four Tops, and others. At the time, we usually recorded our sessions during the day. Motown was a thriving enterprise with a lot of people packed into a fairly small space. There were plenty of producers vying to get into the studio, but we'd usually try to get in at ten in the morning for a three-hour session. Once a recording session was over, we'd just go right back to the office and start banging away on the piano to see what we could come up with. As the company got hotter and hotter, it just became a nonstop treadmill. Since we had to work with the artists' touring schedules, when we got them in, we'd work our asses off to bank as many recordings for the tape library as possible. These acts might be out on the road for three or four months at a time, so we'd need a surplus of releases to issue while they were gone. Everything was accelerating, and it was easy to feel overwhelmed. But the job was the job, and our mandate was to try to meet the demand. That meant looking for song ideas wherever we could find them. Sometimes the turbulent cultural changes of the 1960s stirred our spirits to write.

In 1964 the US accelerated the number of troops it was sending off to Vietnam. I had met this kid who was about nineteen years old and had been drafted. They were about to ship him out, and his friends asked if I'd host a party for him at my place. A bunch of us got together, but this guy was kind of off in the corner with his girlfriend. He was looking really solemn because he had a feeling that he wouldn't be returning home. I tried to encourage him a little bit and help him look on the positive side, but he wasn't having it. I can't say I blame him. As a person who is in tune with his own feelings, I know what it's like to have a premonition. I felt bad for this young man. That night I was in bed thinking about his dilemma. I was thinking about how he felt trapped. There was no escape. There was nowhere to run.

I took that feeling of "Nowhere to Run" and started building a song around it. Berry was always committed to making music for everyone and was not interested in releasing records with overt political statements. I was able to take that idea of feeling trapped by the draft, however, and channel it into a song about running from heartbreak. I think the spark that inspired it, however, gave the song a certain urgency that came across to listeners. Everyone in the quality control meeting agreed. When we brought it in one Friday in the fall of 1964, everyone agreed it should be Martha and the Vandellas' next single. The song wound up going to the Top 10 on both the pop and R&B charts. When it was used in a prominent scene in the film *Good Morning, Vietnam* some years later, I felt like it was validation that the heart of the idea for the song was evident to those who were really in tune with those changing times.

We didn't have synthesizers in those days, so if you wanted a certain sound in the studio, you had to come up with it yourself. We would get pretty creative with percussion and weren't above banging on pots and pans if needed. Winters could get pretty cold and icy in Detroit, so everybody had snow chains in the trunk of their car. When we cut "Nowhere to Run," we actually grabbed a set of chains from somebody and used them as a percussion instrument. Creative percussion was a big part of a lot of Motown hits. Those distinctive sounds you hear on some of those hit records were made by slamming a tire iron on a concrete floor or stomping on a piece of wood. Pretty sophisticated stuff!

After "Nowhere to Run," Martha and the Vandellas released a handful of singles that didn't do much. None of them were Holland-Dozier-Holland songs. About a year and a half later, they issued another one of ours called "I'm Ready for Love." It was a positive song about seizing a new day and rejoining the game. By December of 1966, Martha and the girls were back in the Top 10 and they were ready to lock into a more consistent run of hits like some of the other artists on the label. Martha came up to our office one day in January of 1967 and shut the door behind her. She was really pissed off. "Look," she said, "we're getting the short end of the stick here. Why are we fooling around releasing all these different things when we all know damn well there's really good stuff in the can that isn't being considered? We need to follow up 'I'm Ready for Love' with another surefire hit. I'm gonna talk to Berry because this ain't right!"

She must have gotten through to Berry because at the next quality control meeting he said, "I want to bring out all the unreleased Martha and the Vandellas stuff from the library. Let's see what we've got. Billie Jean finally brought in "Jimmy Mack" and everyone loved it. Everybody in the room gave it a thumbs up. Berry scrunched up his brow and pounded his fist on the desk. "How long," he demanded, "has this been on the goddamn shelf? This is a hit!" When he found out it had been sitting there for two and a half years, he got really angry. "I want this record out," he barked. "And I want it out next week!" I was just sitting there with a little grin on my face. I never complained about "Jimmy Mack" getting shelved because I knew it was a good song, and I knew it would find its time. Though it might have been delayed, "Jimmy Mack" became Martha and the Vandellas' sixth and final Top 10 pop hit. With the exception of "Dancing in the Street," we wrote and produced all of them.

That's yet another example of the principle I mentioned I had to learn when "Popeye" didn't pan out as I'd hoped. There's only so much about a song's fate that we can control. Sometimes you write a song, and the circumstances are right for it to find an audience immediately. Sometimes that song sits on a shelf and never gets heard at all. Other times, it might get rediscovered years later and finally get its due. We do our very best to create something that's just right, but then we have to trust that the right thing will happen in the right time. That doesn't mean that we don't put in the work to try to make sure our songs gain exposure, but it does mean we have to recognize our limits and understand that we can't force it. In the case of "Popeye," not much happened. With "Jimmy Mack," however, we ended up with a very happy ending.

Chapter Eight

DEEPER & DEEPER

Even though we worked really hard to churn out great songs, there was admittedly an element to our success that seemed a bit mystical. It was as if we were playing the lottery and winning every time. There was a period of a few years where I felt like I had a particular blessing on me. For example, I was never much of a gambler, but Berry, Smokey Robinson, Eddie Holland, Mickey Stevenson, and some of the guys used to love to play cards in the rare moments of downtime in the office. They recruited me for a game one time, and I barely had any clue what I was doing. But that didn't matter since I just kept getting all the right cards. I was winning hand after hand, and these guys were all protesting and everything, "Lamont! We thought you couldn't play!" I just shrugged my shoulders. "I can't," I was telling them. "It's beginner's luck." I ended up winning about a thousand dollars but decided to retire as a gambler while I was ahead.

I ended up having much better luck thanks to a card game I decided to sit out in the summer of 1963. Eddie, Mickey, Berry, and some of the other guys wound up getting into a game in our office one day. I figured they wouldn't take very kindly to me banging on the piano in the corner while they were concentrating on their bets, so I went out to one of the pianos in the hallway and started messing around with a melody that I'd had in my head all day. I started plucking out a Bo Diddley beat on the keyboard. I didn't have any words for my melody yet, so I sang some sounds that I thought would fit nicely. "Lum-dee-lum-dee-lie, lum-dee-dum-dee-lie." I was so lost in my own little world that I didn't hear Smokey coming up the back stairs.

"Hey, Lamont!" I was jolted back to reality. "Oh, hey Smoke. What's goin' on, man?" He pointed to the keyboard. "I like what you were doin' there. Who's that for?" Smokey and the Miracles were the biggest act on Motown at the time, and I was no dummy. "I don't know, man," I replied, "but I thought it might be a good one for you guys." He gave me a wink. "Go ahead and record the track. Let's do it!" The next morning, Brian and I finished up the music and handed the lyric over to Eddie to complete. Within a few days, we were in the studio. We wanted to create a real party kind of atmosphere on the record with a sing-along sort of vibe. We just went through the halls grabbing anyone in the building who could sing. Mary Wilson, Martha Reeves, the Vandellas, members of The Temptations, member of The Marvelettes, and even a local dee jay named Jay Gibson came into the studio with us and helped create the feel we were looking for. It was a lot of fun, and the record captures the spirit of the day.

"Mickey's Monkey" hit the streets a couple of weeks later and hit the *Billboard* pop chart just a week after Martha and the Vandellas' "Heat Wave." It rocketed to the Top 10 and became The Miracles' third million-seller after "Shop Around" and "You've Really Got a Hold On Me." I mentioned before that I received three BMI awards for hit songs in 1963. In addition to "Heat Wave" and "Quicksand," "Mickey's Monkey" was the third.

When I was at Motown, I made a rule for myself that I should *never count out a possible opportunity*. Everybody knows that Smokey wrote most of the Miracles hits—not to mention a whole bunch of hits for other artists—but when he asked me about the song, I took the opportunity to pitch it to him. I could have said, Oh, there's no point in trying to give Smokey a song since he writes his own stuff. Instead, I went the optimistic route. It's funny how sometimes our minds want to jump right to the reasons something might not work instead of considering how we can make something possible. I try to live my life and pursue my writing career in such a way that I hope for the best outcome rather than restrain myself with negative "what-ifs." Don't decide that someone will probably give you a "no" and miss out on an opportunity for them to give you a "yes!"

In the wake of the success of "Mickey's Monkey," we wrote the Miracles' follow-up single, "I Gotta Dance to Keep From Crying." It was a Top 40 pop hit and a Top 20 R&B hit, but it wasn't as big as "Mickey's Monkey." Smokey and his bandmates wrote most of their own material, so we didn't do a lot with The Miracles. We had another hit with them in 1966 when "(Come 'Round Here) I'm the One You Need" hit the pop Top 20 and the R&B Top 5, but those three songs were pretty much the extent of our work with Smokey.

The bottom line was that Smokey certainly didn't need outside songs, but he also had that team spirit, and he would happily cut someone else's tune if it was the best song on the table. The same was true when it came to other artists for whom Smokey wrote and produced. He had written all of Mary Wells's big hits, including the Top 10 pop singles "The One Who Really Loves You," "You Beat Me to the Punch," and "Two Lovers." After a couple of releases that didn't perform quite as well, Holland-Dozier-Holland was given a shot with "You Lost the Sweetest Boy." Smokey knew that the best song wins the day, so he was supportive. When someone has the songwriting talent that Smokey Robinson has, they don't need to hide behind ego. And it probably didn't hurt that Mary Wells' next single after ours was Smokey's "My Guy," which reached the top of both the pop and R&B charts.

After that, at the height of her popularity, Mary left the label for what she thought would be greener pastures. She had a little success, but never recaptured the commercial triumphs she'd experienced at Motown. She was actually one of the very first acts to record a Holland-Dozier-Holland song when the three of us began working together. We finished up a session for a song called "Guarantee (For a Lifetime)" with Mary Wells on the same day in 1962 that we finished another one with the Supremes called "I'm Giving You Your Freedom." Along with Eddie's "Darling, I Hum Our Song," I believe those were the first three HDH songs ever recorded. The one with Mary stayed in the vaults, and she ultimately left the label, Eddie eventually gave up his artist career, and our session with The Supremes hit the tape library with a thud. We assumed it was dead in the water, having no clue it would be issued as a B-side about a year and a half later. With the Marvelettes action drying up, we focused on our work with Martha and the Vandellas.

Though it seemed we were living in a remarkably productive and successful time, sometimes success results in unwanted attention. There was an entertainer who stayed downstairs from me and Ann in our apartment building. He was in a local group, though I don't recall the name of it anymore. They were pretty popular and had a few local hits. One morning I was getting dressed to go to work at Motown when there was a knock on the door. I opened it and saw this singer standing there in a sheet with a butcher knife. "Come with me," he said. I swallowed hard. "You want me to come with you?" I'm thinking to myself, *This dude's wrapped up in a sheet with a butcher knife. This only ends with me dying.* I didn't know what to do, so I stepped into the hallway and tried to put some distance between the two of us. "You're the one been stealing my songs," he shouted. "You need to come with me!" As soon as he turned around, I shot down the hallway and out on to the sidewalk.

When I got to Motown I was telling Berry what happened. "Oh, I know who you're talking about," he said. "He had a breakdown." I said, "Somebody needs to lock him up! He just came after me with a butcher knife and shit!" I guess Berry called somebody, and this guy's wife brought him over to Motown later in the day to apologize. Berry called me into his office, and the guy's sitting there kind of looking down at the ground. He'd changed out of his sheet and left his butcher knife at home. Apparently his mother had just died, and he had some sort of psychotic episode. He was kind of muttering, "I'm so sorry." He didn't say much, but his wife was very apologetic. I never heard from him again, but a couple weeks later they arrested him walking down the street naked and screaming. I kind of felt sorry for the guy, but he scared the hell out of me that day.

Marvin Gaye and I came to Motown about the same time, but he wasn't interested in being an R&B singer. Marvin wanted to be the black Frank Sinatra. He was a smooth crooner in the style of Nat King Cole, and that's the kind of stuff he was recording at first. He was also playing drums on sessions for other artists and—like most people around Hitsville in those days—jumping in the studio to help out whenever voices were needed for backgrounds or feet were needed for stomping. It wasn't until Mickey Stevenson practically tricked him into recording some R&B material that he started finding success with hits like "Stubborn Kind of Fellow," "Hitch Hike," and "Pride and Joy."

In the summer of 1963, we recorded Marvin singing "Can I Get a Witness." That idea came from the saying that people would holler in those old Pentecostal churches. There's no big story to that song except that it's another example of the church influencing our musical instincts. Brian and Eddie and I sang background vocals along with The Supremes, who weren't yet having hits of their own. The record did well. It was a Top 5 R&B hit, though it didn't quite make the Top 20 on the pop chart.

A few months later, Berry released "You're a Wonderful One," which did better for us. The record was another Top 5 R&B hit, but also made it to number 15 on the pop chart. It was Marvin's second highest single up to that point, after "Pride and Joy."

In the summer of 1964, Berry showed up in our office. "Hey guys," he said, "Marvin is getting ready to go out on the road for a while, and we need to stockpile as much stuff for him as we possibly can. I need you to come up with some stuff right away." Several days later, I was coming out of the office when I ran into Berry in the hallway. "Hey, Lamont, what have you got for me for Marvin?" I smiled as casually as I could. "We're working on it, Berry." He let out a long breath. "I told you a week ago I needed something right away. That means yesterday. We're racing the clock here, man!"

With my back against the wall, I had to do something I didn't want to do. I had to give up a song that I'd secretly been holding on to for myself. When I came to Motown, I signed contracts as a songwriter, producer, and artist, but the artist part of the deal had fallen to the wayside. After my one-off single for their Mel-o-dy imprint, they released another one credited to Holland & Dozier. "What Goes Up Must Come Down" was a recitation set to a swelling chorus courtesy of The Four Tops and The Andantes. Neither it nor the instrumental flip side, "Come on Home," did a damn thing. Berry had plenty of artists, so he wanted me to write and produce. He needed good songs and good productions more than he needed another singer, but I'd been working on this thing that I thought would really blow him away and maybe get me another shot as an artist. It was called "How Sweet It Is (To Be Loved by You)." When the heat was on to get something recorded by Marvin, though, I panicked and gave it up.

With no time to spare, we cut the track, and Eddie put a vocal on it for Marvin to learn. Marvin was notoriously late for everything. When we booked the studio to put his vocal on the song, he was nowhere to be found. We waited and waited, but no Marvin. Finally somebody called him, and he eventually appeared in the control room with his golf clubs. I was sitting at the mixing console when he walked in. Without turning around I said, "Man, you're late. We need to get going on this thing. You ready?" He set his clubs down. "Sure, man. What are we doing?" My eyes widened as I spun around in my chair. "What are we *doing?* We're doing 'How Sweet It Is.'" Marvin kind of shrugged. "We gave you the tape," I continued. "You did learn it, right?" He flashed an easy grin, which instantly pissed me off. "Nah, I didn't get a chance to listen to it," he said slowly. "Shit, Marvin. We've been sitting around here waitin' for your ass to show up, and you're not even ready!" He took a few steps toward me. I stood up and took a couple of steps toward him. Suddenly, our faces were inches apart and nobody dared blink. You could have heard a pin drop. "Relax, man," Marvin hissed through clenched teeth. "Just play me the goddamn song so we can get out of here."

"OK, guys," Eddie spoke up. "We're all on the same team here. Let's just hear the song." Brian started the machine as Marvin stepped back and took a seat. He closed his eyes, but after a few seconds, he started waving his arms. "Stop! Stop! Stop!" Brian switched the tape off. "The key is too goddamn high," Marvin barked. "What the fuck is wrong with you guys? You're always cutting this shit too high for me to sing." I shook my head. "Marvin," I shot back, "it *feels* better in this key. You can hit those notes." He dropped his head down for a moment before swinging it up and locking eyes with me. "You listen to me, motherfucker," he started. I cut him off. "No, motherfucker, *you* listen to *me*. We know what we're doing. This is the key for the song and we don't have time to be fucking around here, so get it together!" Marvin smirked. "Brian," he called out, "play the goddamn tape, man."

Brian hit play where we'd left off and Marvin listened through to the end of the song without saying a word. Brian rewound it to the start and Marvin listened from beginning to end—the first time he'd heard the song in its entirety without interruption. He was silent when it ended. Brian rewound the tape and started it again. After a few bars, Marvin stood up. Brian stopped the tape. "What's wrong?" Eddie asked Marvin. He straightened his shirt. "Nothing's wrong," Marvin replied.

"I'm ready. I've got it." He sauntered into the vocal booth and put on his headphones. Brian hit record, and Marvin sang the hell out of "How Sweet It Is" in one take. He nailed it. And he knew he nailed it.

Marvin walked out of the vocal booth and came back into the control room. He picked up his bag of golf clubs and swung it over his shoulder. "I'll see you guys later," he said over his shoulder as he headed for the door. Brian shot back, "Hey, wait a minute, man. We haven't even listened to it yet." Marvin just laughed. "You got what you need," he shouted as he disappeared out into the parking lot. We listened back to the take, and our jaws were on the floor. It was perfect. The performance you hear on the record is Marvin's one take after barely hearing the song twice. Since the key was high, he slid into his falsetto, which sounded beautiful. Marvin could do things with his voice that we hadn't even thought of when we were writing the songs.

Since Berry was pushing for us to stockpile Marvin recordings, we managed to get him back again a few days later. We pulled an old unreleased session we'd done with The Supremes, took their vocals off, and put Marvin on instead. The song was "Baby Don't You Do It," which was released in September of 1964. Motown issued "How Sweet It Is (To Be Loved By You)" the following month, and it climbed to number six on the pop chart—Marvin's most successful single up to that point.

I knew that "How Sweet It Is" was a hit song. I wish I could have recorded it, but once Marvin had his hit with it, I accepted that an artist career just wasn't in the cards for me at Motown. I still wanted it, but I was constantly being bombarded with the demand for more songs and more productions for the growing roster of artists. Berry always saw me as a studio man whose job it was to churn out hits. There was no way I was ever going to get a fair shake as a Motown artist, so I buried that dream deep in my heart to save for another time. I knew it would come when the time was right. For then, my purpose was to be a songwriter and producer.

We didn't do a ton of stuff with Marvin Gaye at Motown, but we did have another Top 10 R&B hit with him when Berry released "Little Darling (I Need You)" as a single. That's a song I wrote for my grandmother when she was dying. I remember taking it over to her before it hit the streets. "I brought you this new song, Grandma," I told her. "It's a special one that I wrote just for you, and Marvin Gaye recorded it." She listened for a couple of minutes, but she was kind of drifting in and out. She died soon after at the age of fifty-seven. It was at her home that I fell in love with the piano and got some real insights into the minds of women thanks to eavesdropping on her beauty shop conversations. She was a very important force in my life, and it wasn't easy to say goodbye to her at such a young age. The Doobie Brothers ended up rerecording that song in the late 1970s, so it had a second life. Whenever I hear it, I think back to my grandmother, Melvalean, and remember what a great woman she was.

There was an extraordinarily important element to the hits we were making at Motown that I haven't mentioned yet: the musicians. The Funk Brothers were the legendary house band at Hitsville, and those guys had a lot to do with helping us translate our ideas onto tape. Those guys were on salary, so they showed up to the studio every day without knowing whether they'd be working with Smokey, Norman Whitfield, HDH, or someone else. Their salaries were actually bigger than ours, but they deserved it. There were various musicians who comprised the Funk Brothers, but we had our favorites. We always liked to get Joe Hunter or Earl Van Dyke on piano; we always used three guitar players for every session, usually Joe Messina, Robert

White, and Eddie Willis; Clarence Isabell was great on vibes; and our rhythm guys were James Jamerson on bass and Benny Benjamin on drums. That was our nucleus, and if we didn't have those guys, we'd cancel the session until they were available. That core group worked with us so much that they knew exactly what we wanted. We could get so much done in a relatively short amount of time because they understood what we were looking for. You didn't have to tell Benny Benjamin or James Jamerson twice. You explained what you wanted and they'd take it home for you. They knew how the song should feel, and it was all about that *feel*. There's playing the notes, and then there's selling the notes with the right feeling. When it comes to musicians, these guys were some of the best there's ever been.

When we made records, we would cut the tracks with the Funk Brothers first, and then bring the vocalists in later to replace the guide vocal Eddie had recorded for them. Then we'd put the horns and strings on last as sweeteners. The studio was small. We could get about eight string players in the room. Then another room had the horns, which we tried to record at the same time as the strings. We were all crammed into that little cinderblock studio, but we were making magic.

The studio was only four tracks when Brian and I first started making records at Hitsville. Michael McClain ordered all the equipment from Germany and built that studio into what it was. He was the designer and engineer and was really a genius at putting that stuff together. He was actually a little weird. He was always telling jokes that weren't funny, but he was a master at tuning a room and putting together an amazing recording environment despite serious space limitations. At first we'd put all the musicians on two tracks. The rhythm would go on one and the guitars on the other. We'd put the lead vocal on the third track and the backgrounds on the fourth. If we were adding strings or horns, we'd have to bounce everything down to make more room. Later on we knocked out the walls, got better equipment, and moved up to eight tracks, then sixteen, and then twenty-four. But it's amazing how many classic records were made when we were up against the greatest limitations in terms of space and technology.

Bob Dylan came over to Motown one time. We were standing around talking in the lobby, and he said, "Where does that sound come from, man? I wanna see the room where you're making these records." I took him back and opened the door to the studio. He looked around and said, "No, I mean the real room, man, where you guys cut all those hit songs." I said, "This is the room, man. This is it. This is where the Motown sound comes from." He almost looked disappointed. It might not have looked like much, but it worked.

That's another great lesson: *If you want to find success, surround yourself with the right people.* **Motown was never about the facility. It was about the people working inside the facility. I can play piano, but I'll never be as good a musician as one of the Funk Brothers. I know my way around a recording studio, but I don't have the technological talents of Michael McClain. This business is about knowing what you do best and then surrounding yourself with the right people who know how to complement your talents. Iron sharpens iron, so if you're a great songwriter, find a great recording engineer you can work with. You'll inspire one another, and you'll walk away a better writer while that person will walk away a better engineer. If you play guitar really well, then play guitar. But find someone else who plays bass better than you and use that person's skills instead of doing a merely passable job of it on your own. Nobody is an island, and the right combination of people will not only serve your skills but will also give you a sense of artistic community**

and encouragement to make you better at the important piece that you bring to the puzzle.

Because I practically lived in that little studio, however, my marriage suffered. I was an absentee husband and father, and Ann and I fought about it all time. "You're never here," she'd say, and she was right. I would shoot back, "I'm doing this because this is what I do and it's who I am. You just have to accept that." The bickering only added to my exhaustion and anxiety over the grueling pace of cranking out hits. The truth was that I was working around the clock, and even when I wasn't working, I was preoccupied with work. The harder I worked, the more Ann resented me. We'd gotten married far too young, and I think we both probably wanted different things for our lives. We both wanted a way out, but I didn't believe that was the right thing to do. Even if Ann and I couldn't get along, we had a daughter to think about, and I was resolved to stick it out no matter how miserable our relationship became.

One day, however, we got into another huge blowout, and I guess it was just one fight too many for Ann. "I want you out, Lamont," she screamed. "You need to get out of this house. I don't want you here anymore!" I didn't fight it. I grabbed a few things and left. Soon we were legally separated, and the divorce was eventually finalized. Ultimately Ann and I just couldn't resolve our differences. I was young and didn't know much about balancing my work life with my home life, but the harsh reality is that if we didn't keep up the pace at Motown, we were in danger of losing what we'd worked so hard to build. I had never wanted a divorce, primarily because of Michelle. I was the product of a broken home, and I didn't want my daughter to become a "statistic" as well. It was heart-wrenching to have to leave my little girl. Brian and I held on to our position at Hitsville but at the cost of our families. That was the price we paid for success. Neither of us was proud of it, but the reality—at that time in my life—was that Motown came first. By the end of 1964, I'd had over two dozen hits at the cost of one failed marriage.

Despite the personal problems, however, I was flooded with ideas. HDH was already exploding all over the place, but it was about to get even crazier. Eddie, Brian, and I were about to take over the world.

Chapter Nine

YOU KEEP ME HANGIN' ON

The no-hit Supremes. That's what everybody called Florence Ballard, Mary Wilson, and Diana Ross around the Hitsville offices back in 1963. They'd been around Motown longer than I had. Diana—or Diane as she was known in those days—was acquainted with Smokey Robinson, who helped them get an audition with Berry in the early days of the label. He liked their voices but wasn't ready to sign a group of high school girls to a recording contract. They eventually began hanging around the studio almost every day until Berry finally gave in and officially brought them into the fold in early 1961.

The Supremes' first single was "I Want a Guy," written by Brian, Berry, and Freddie Gorman. It was released in the spring of 1961, but went nowhere. Then the next one went nowhere. And the next one. Finally they released a Berry Gordy tune called "Let Me Go the Right Way" that barely crawled into the R&B Top 30. The flip side, "Time Changes Things," was a song Brian and I had written with Janie Bradford before we formed our partnership with Eddie. It didn't exactly open the floodgates.

After a couple more failed releases, Berry was determined to get a Supremes hit. He asked us to take a crack at working with "the girls," as everyone called them around Hitsville. We took them in the studio in the fall of 1963 to record "When the Lovelight Starts Shining Through His Eyes." Girl groups were very popular at that time. Not only was Motown finding success with The Marvelettes and Martha and the Vandellas, but The Crystals and The Ronettes had just had recent hits with "Then He Kissed Me" and "Be My Baby" on Phil Spector's Philles label. I always had my ears open to what was going on in pop music and was keeping track of guys like Phil and Brian Wilson. "Lovelight" was our answer to Phil Spector. We kept our own flavor but set out to mimic his "wall of sound" that was taking the charts by storm at the time.

The Supremes finally got their first Top 20 pop hit with the release of "When the Lovelight Starts Shining Through His Eyes" in October of 1963. It was the first Holland-Dozier-Holland song the girls released, and it finally made a little bit of noise for them. It even went to number two on the R&B chart, but it *still* didn't open the floodgates. It did do well enough that we got the first crack at a follow-up single called "Run, Run, Run." It charted, but not very high. By that point I think Berry might have been the only one who still believed in The Supremes. We liked the girls on a personal level, but they just couldn't catch a break for some reason. The Holland brothers and I were doing just fine with other artists on the label, so I just figured we'd put our main efforts into the hitmaking artists and continue to work with The Supremes until Berry decided to throw in the towel.

In the meantime, I'd come up with "Where Did Our Love Go," and we cut a track of it for The Marvelettes to sing to. Of course we put it in Gladys Horton's key since I couldn't imagine any reason why The Marvelettes might not want to record it. We just assumed they'd do it, but they were pretty hot at the time, so I guess they could afford to be contrarian. We played the song for Gladys. "Uh, uh, baby," she said after she heard it. "We don't do shit like that. Why would you write something like that?" Apparently Gladys thought it was too simple, too pop, and too cutesy. I could tell she was adamant, and we weren't going to get any traction with her. I knew that if we didn't get a record on the track we'd recorded, then we'd have to pay for the session ourselves. I was determined to find somebody else to do it. I couldn't think of any act who I thought could pull it off, so I went and got a list of the entire artist roster. All the way down at the bottom was the no-hit Supremes. I didn't have a lot of hope of them getting a hit at that point, but I wasn't looking to get charged for that session, either. The Supremes didn't have the clout to reject it, so I figured we could cut it on them, not be out any money, and make Berry happy that we were still giving it a go with his girls.

I saw Mary Wilson coming in the front door one day, and I pulled her aside. "Mary, I wrote this song just for you and Diane and Flo. It came to me in a dream, and I knew it was a special song just for The Supremes. It's called 'Where Did Our Love Go.'" Mary cocked her head to the side. "Is this that song that Gladys turned down? She said it was a piece of shit." I thought, *Uh oh. I'm sittin' here tellin' all these lies about how I came up with this thing just for them. What am I gonna do now?* It was time to channel the Candy Man. I smiled and looked deep in Mary's eyes. I spoke softly, as if I'd been hurt by her words. "What are you talking about? Sure, I played the song for Gladys just to get a second opinion, but 'Where Did Our Love Go' has always been for The Supremes." She looked skeptical. I don't know where the hell this came from, but I said, "Listen, Mary. You never know if the apple's ripe until you bite it. Let me give you a tape so you can take it to the other girls."

When it came time to bring them in to do their vocals, none of the Supremes were excited about the song. I thought Mary should have sung the lead vocal because it was better suited to her key, but Berry had recently decreed that Diana was going to be the permanent lead singer of the group. I suggested cutting it with Mary out front anyway, but Brian and Diana were beginning to get romantically involved at that point, and he pushed for letting her sing it. She didn't want to record the song in the first place, so by the time we rolled the tape, Brian and I were pissed off at each other, Diana was pissed that she had to sing the song, and Mary and Flo were pissed about being reminded that they were in the process of being relegated to backup singers. There was a very negative vibe in the room.

Diana went in the vocal booth and started singing, but it sounded all wrong. Her voice was high and clear and it didn't fit the track. Brian suggested that she sing it in her lower register. We tried again, and I could see her crossing her arms in the vocal booth. "It's just not working," she said. "It's not right for my voice!" Brian had her try again. And again. And again. By that point Diana was practically fuming. Then something clicked. She started channeling her anger into the vocal performance. It took on an attitude. It wasn't anything like the way we heard the song in our heads, but it worked. Her annoyance had turned into an edginess that had a sexy growl. Brian and Eddie and I were looking at one another like, *I think we might really have something special here!*

After a few takes, Diana stormed out of the vocal booth. "We always get the leftovers that nobody else wants," she hissed as she walked straight out of the studio. We figured she just needed a moment to herself, so we had Flo and Mary head on into the booth to record their backup vocals. I had worked out these intricate harmonies for the background parts, but they weren't in the mood. Flo said, "There's only two of us. How are we gonna do all these parts?" I got frustrated after going back and forth with them for a few minutes. Finally, I reached the end of my rope. "OK," I said, "let's just make this simple. When I point to you, you just say 'baby, baby,' OK? Can you handle that?" I just scrapped all the background parts I had designed for the song. They rolled their eyes, but they did it. Things had already gotten heated enough, and I knew nobody was feeling inspired. I wasn't going to push it.

A few minutes later, Berry came into the studio with Diana trailing behind him. "What's going on here?" Berry's brow was furrowed, and I could tell that Diana had run crying to him. "Let me hear this song," he said. Brian rewound the tape and hit play. The music came blasting from the speakers as Berry walked back and forth across the control room with his hands in his pocket. He started chewing his tongue, which he used to do whenever he was deep in thought. When the track ended, Berry stopped pacing. Everyone was quiet. Finally he clapped his hands together. "This thing is a hit, baby," he said to nobody in particular. He turned toward Diana, who was leaning against the door frame sulking. "Diane, this is a hit. What are you talking about?" She stared at her shoes. "I don't like it," she mumbled. Berry studied her for a moment before speaking. "Brian," he finally said. "Mix this thing and get it ready to go out. I want a test pressing as soon as possible. We don't need to bring this to the quality control meeting. This is The Supremes' next single." With that, he spun on his heel and walked out, patting Diana on the shoulder as he departed. "Cheer up, girls," he called behind him. "You're about to be the big-hit Supremes!"

Berry Gordy had the greatest ears in the business. He knew his shit like nobody else. He could tell what would sell and what wouldn't. He had an almost magical instinct for spotting a hit a mile away and could usually tell you in the first eight bars if a song would be successful. Berry believed in The Supremes when everyone else had given up, and he believed in "Where Did Our Love Go." From Diana's unexpected performance to the change in background vocals, the record became something much different than what we originally wanted it to be. What I once imagined might sound grandiose was a thin track with very basic background parts. Sure, I had all kinds of plans for it, but the song wanted to be something else.

There's a mystical dimension to being a songwriter that's hard to describe. Sometimes you think a song should be one way, but that song will tell you if it's meant to be something else entirely. Don't fight it! As I said before, that doesn't mean songwriters should compromise their vision, but it does mean that one of the most important things in songwriting success is to set aside your ego. If I had insisted that "Where Did Our Love Go" be recorded exactly as we'd envisioned it originally, then things might have turned out very differently. It's a delicate balance to pursue your vision while having the humility to be willing to let the Master Muse guide you along the right route. That's one songwriting principle that can only be perfected with practice: *Always put the song ahead of your ego.*

Berry put a lot of money behind "Where Did Our Love Go." It was released in mid-June of 1964 and by the second week of July, it was sitting at the top of the pop charts. It was The Supremes' first number one, and it was also the first Holland-Dozier-Holland song to hit number one on the pop chart. Motown promoted the hell out of that record, and suddenly, The Supremes were the biggest act on the label. Everybody in America was clapping along with our record. Well, actually, there weren't claps on the record at all. What everyone thought were handclaps was actually just a teenager named Michael Valvano stomping on a piece of plywood. Meanwhile, Motown and The Supremes were about to stomp down the door of American pop music dominance. Finally, the floodgates *had* opened.

The girls were out on tour with Dick Clark's *Caravan of Stars* when "Where Did Our Love Go" hit number one in August of 1964. Fortunately we'd finished some new recording with them just before they left, so when Motown released the *Where Did Our Love Go* album, we had a couple of new songs to add to the previously released singles. One of them, "Baby Love," became the follow-up single. Brian came up with the idea for that one. The word "baby" appeared sixty-eight times in "Where Did Our Love Go" and that seemed to work, so we decided to double down on the repetition of the word "baby" as a little trademark for The Supremes. "Baby Love" was released in September, and it, too, reached the top of the chart, making The Supremes the first Motown act to earn more than one number-one hit on the pop rankings. Not only that, but "Baby Love" remained in the top slot for four weeks and went on to receive a Grammy nomination for Best R&B Recording.

Berry called us to his office one morning as The Supremes' career was exploding, "Listen guys," he told us. "Drop everything else you're doing and don't worry about nobody else. We need to give our attention to The Supremes right now while they're hot. I want you to pull out all the stops on these girls, OK?" Berry was the boss. That's what he wanted, and that's what we gave him! We went guns blazing to take advantage of the moment.

To be honest, it was nerve-wracking. Brian and I would spend hours sitting side by side at the piano. When one of us got tired, the other would take over and keep banging away. As a songwriter and producer, I'd reached the top of my game, but I was feeling more anxious than I ever had. It felt like there weren't enough hours in the day to crank out the hits we needed to provide. I would have trouble falling asleep at night worrying about how we would get everything done, and I'd wake up in the morning worried about getting back to Hitsville to keep cranking out ideas.

In the meantime, "Come See About Me" from the *Where Did Our Love Go* album was issued as the next single in late October. It hit number one the week before Christmas, and the girls made their debut appearance on Ed Sullivan's show several days later. It was their third consecutive single to hit number one in 1964, but there was no time to stop and enjoy the success. We had Beatles crawling up our back!

It's impossible to think about the music of 1964 without thinking about The Beatles. "I Want to Hold Your Hand" hit the charts in January and was sitting at number one within two weeks. After they made their debut performance on Ed Sullivan in February, Beatlemania gripped the country. "I Want to Hold Your Hand" remained at the top of the charts for nearly two months until The Beatles knocked themselves out of the top spot with "She Loves You," which then got knocked out of the top spot by another Beatles song, "Can't Buy Me Love." That one camped out at the top for six weeks. By the time The Supremes' "Where Did Our Love Go" started climbing up the charts, the Beatles were a constant presence in the Top 10 with songs like "Do You Want to Know a Secret," "Love Me Do," and "A Hard Day's Night."

In the wake of The Beatles, the British Invasion was on. Acts like Peter and Gordon, The Animals, and Manfred Mann were topping the US charts when The Beatles weren't. In fact, other than Bobby Vinton, The Supremes were the only act other than The Beatles that hit number one multiple times in 1964.

The Holland brothers and I always had our ears open to what was happening in pop music, so we were paying very close attention to what was going on with John, Paul, George, and Ringo. I really liked what they were doing and thought they were coming up with some really inventive stuff. As much as I admired their music, however, I knew they'd bury us if we didn't keep bringing our best material to the market.

As 1965 dawned, The Beatles had knocked The Supremes' "Come See About Me" out of the number-one position with "I Feel Fine." Then, in mid-January, "Come See About Me" bumped The Beatles out and reclaimed the Top position once again. It was a real fight for chart position. Not only did we have the pressure of battling The Beatles, but Berry was on us about churning out new material for The Supremes, who were America's best defense against the lads from Liverpool.

In January we were already hard at work on the album that would be called *More Hits By The Supremes*. Every track was written by Holland-Dozier-Holland and produced by me and Brian. It included "Stop! In the Name of Love," which was issued as a single and knocked The Beatles' "Eight Days a Week" out of the number-one position. The girls' follow-up single was "Back in My Arms Again," which was yet another chart topper. For those who are keeping score, that's five consecutive chart-topping hits we wrote and produced for The Supremes in 1964 and 1965.

At one point virtually all the songs in the Top 10 on the pop chart were written by either Lennon and McCartney or Holland-Dozier-Holland. Man, I just loved Paul's writing. He's a year younger than me, but we're both Geminis. I was born on June 16 and Paul was born on June 18. Would you believe that I've still never met him? We were both in London one time for the Ivor Novello awards, which are the top songwriting awards in the UK. We were both doing the red carpet thing, with Paul talking to an interviewer on one side and me talking to an interviewer on the other. We were practically touching one another back-to-back, but we didn't have a chance to say hello. I used to go up to Ringo's house in LA to hang out and was out at George's place in England a few times. I even met John one time at a New York club called Regine's. Somebody took a picture of us reaching across a table shaking hands. I've always wondered who took that shot, but I've never found it. For years I asked if anyone knew where that picture might be, but I never did find out. And I still don't know Paul McCartney!

That era when we were racing The Beatles was an unbelievable run of success, but the curse of creativity is that you're always looking at the next horizon or searching for a new milestone. It's hard to feel satisfied. I don't recall which one it was, but I remember looking at one of those number-one songs and wishing it could have done something better. But what? You can't get higher than number one! There was still a nagging sense of restlessness that made it hard for me to really enjoy our success. "You're black," my grandmother used to tell me. "Society sees that as a strike against you, so have to be better than everybody else. You can't give 100 percent if you want to succeed. You've got to give 120 percent." Her words helped push me, but they always haunted me. It left me with some self-doubt about whether my achievements were good enough or if they could be pushed farther.

It took me a long time as a songwriter to realize that you have to recognize when things are good and just let go. I listen back to some of my old songs today—even some of the classics—and think, *I probably could have said that better.* **But I don't stress out about it. If you don't let go of your songs and let them be done when they're done, then self-doubt can eat at you and ultimately destroy your creative impulses. In other words,** *do your best work, enjoy your successes, and don't get stuck in the paralysis of overanalysis.*

In June of 1965, The Supremes and Holland-Dozier-Holland were knocked from the top of the charts yet again. This time it wasn't a British act like The Animals, The Beatles, Petula Clark, or Freddie and the Dreamers. This time, we were knocked out of the number-one spot by ourselves. "Back in My Arms Again" was toppled when another of our songs, "I Can't Help Myself (Sugar Pie Honey Bunch)," became the first chart-topping pop hit for The Four Tops.

Chapter Ten

RUN, RUN, RUN

Levi Stubbs, Duke Fakir, Obie Benson, and Lawrence Payton got together when they were still in high school and formed a doo-wop group called The Four Aims. Lawrence's cousin was Billy Davis, who I'd worked with at Anna Records. Thanks to his connection with Chess Records, Billy was able to get them a deal with the Chicago-based label, where they changed their name to The Four Tops. Unfortunately they didn't land any hits. They bounced around to a few other labels, including Columbia Records, but nothing really clicked for the guys for several years.

Berry eventually signed The Four Tops to Motown, where they started out singing standards and vocal jazz that stayed in the vaults for years. They did some background vocals on other artists' records in their early days at Motown. We even used them on The Supremes' "Run, Run, Run."

Many months before things began to pop with The Supremes, Brian and I wrote a complete piece of music without any lyrical ideas. Sometimes, when we had extra time at the end of a three-hour recording session, we'd lay down a musical track with the idea of coming up with a story or lyrical concept later on. That's what we'd done at some point in 1963 with a particular piece of music. It must have been a year later that I came into the office one day and got handed a two-line gift from the Master Muse: *Baby, I need your lovin.' Got to have all your lovin.'* I sketched out some additional lines and handed the song off to Eddie to complete. Everything fell together quickly from there. It's yet another reminder that sometimes a song just isn't ready until it's ready.

We knew The Four Tops had been waiting around for a hit song for a while, so we offered "Baby I Need Your Loving" to them. Our plan was for Levi Stubbs to sing the lead vocals, but—just like Diana Ross with "Where Did Our Love Go" and Marvin Gaye with "How Sweet It Is"—he thought the key was wrong for his voice. "I don't know, guys," he said when we played them the track. "I think this is really suited for Lawrence to sing lead more than me. His voice is lighter and smoother and really fits the key best." But we didn't want light and smooth. There was something about Levi stretching to the top of his range that had a certain sense of pleading and urgency that was particularly effective. The others agreed that it worked well, and that's how Levi became the lead singer of the Tops.

Released in the summer of 1964, "Baby I Need Your Loving" was the first Four Tops single issued by Motown and the group's first national hit. It didn't make it into the Top 10 on the pop chart, but it went to number eleven, so that was a pretty great start. When it came time to write and produce a follow-up song, we came up with "Without the One You Love (Life's Not Worth

While)." We were caught up in The Supremes whirlwind at the time, and it shows. We tried to simply duplicate "Baby I Need Your Loving," but the song didn't have the same magic. It didn't crack the Top 40.

Given that we hadn't really hit on a winning formula for the Tops, we didn't write their next single, "Ask the Lonely." That was Mickey Stevenson's baby, and it did pretty well. It hit the R&B Top 10. From there, The Four Tops could have moved on to work with other Motown producers, and Holland-Dozier-Holland could easily have become a mere footnote in their story. But then I came up with the song that gave them their first number-one hit and provided me that unique experience I mentioned of having one of our songs bump another of our songs out of the number-one position on the pop chart.

I was sitting at the piano one day messing around with some chords. When I'm writing, I often let my mind wander back to events from my formative years. I let myself get nostalgic to try to tap into the purity of some of those youthful feelings and emotions. That's one of the reasons I would often drift back to Bernadette. It allowed me to access the feelings of puppy love and translate those universal emotions into a song. On this particular day, I started thinking about my grandmother's beauty salon. I often thought back to the conversations I heard among the women there, but this time I pictured myself as a kid sitting on the front porch of my grandparents' home from which she ran her shop. I thought about my grandfather, who was often out front piddling around in his garden. I smiled to myself thinking about how he'd flirt with all the women as they came up the sidewalk to visit my grandmother's salon. "Good morning, sweetie," he might call out as a customer passed by. He'd come up with endless flirtatious greetings, which I found really entertaining at the time. I started thinking back to some of his pet names: "How're you doing, baby doll? Hey, sugar pie! Hi there, honey bunch!" Sugar pie. Honey bunch. Suddenly I got the rush of excitement that every songwriter gets when they know they've hit on something. "Sugar pie, honey bunch" sang perfectly with the chords I'd been playing. Once I had those first four words, we were off to the races and "I Can't Help Myself" was soon on its way to number one.

I mentioned that The Four Tops had been signed to Columbia Records before coming to Motown. With "I Can't Help Myself" topping the pop and R&B charts, somebody at Columbia got the idea to cash in on our success. They rereleased an old Four Tops single called "Ain't That Love" in hopes that the public would think it was the group's new record. As soon as Berry got wind of it, he came to our office on a hot July day. "We've gotta come up with something for the Tops right away," he said. "Like right now. We can't let these guys over at Columbia get a free ride on our coattails."

We had a partially completed track in the can that fit the bill perfectly, but no lyrics. I had already been thinking about the concept of songwriters coming up with something that's reminiscent of a previous hit and had been playing around with the title "It's the Same Old Song" in the back of my mind. With no time to spare, we ran with it. The lyrics were written on Tuesday, we finished up the track and got the Tops in the studio on Wednesday, it was released to radio stations all over the country on Friday, and was available for the public to purchase in their local record store the following Tuesday. The whole thing happened within a week!

Columbia's single did enter the *Billboard* chart at the end of July, the same week that "It's the Same Old Song" appeared. Theirs lasted only a week and topped out somewhere in the nineties. Ours kept going for a month until it reached the

RUN, RUN, RUN | 135

Top 5 on both the pop and R&B charts. Thanks to our ability to move quickly, we were able to bury the competing record. Nowadays there's so much politics and bullshit, you could never get something out that quickly. It just doesn't work that way anymore.

That episode reminds me of another songwriting lesson: *You can have the success you dream about, but you've got to have a relentless work ethic.* **To truly "make it," you have to want it bad enough and be willing to put in the sweat equity. The reason we were able to get that song written and out to the market so quickly is because we were already in that mindset of putting in the long hours and the difficult work. We wouldn't have been able to do it if we weren't already in that rhythm. We were determined, and that meant we always gave it our all. If you want to succeed, you can't play around at your career because there are other people out there dedicating their lives to it, and they'll beat you out every time. I was guilty at times of neglecting the right balance between work and regular life, but there's no getting around the reality that it does take a ton of commitment and focus.**

Even though "It's the Same Old Song" happened in such a pressurized way, it didn't really seem that unusual at the time. I lived in a constant state of pressure anyway, so it just came with the job. Success breeds the demand for more, more, more, and all my waking hours were devoted to writing songs, making demos of songs, cutting records, and trying to keep up with the demand.

Even though my marriage and my mental health took a hit as a result of our achievements, there were definitely benefits to our success that I look back on very fondly. When I first started out in the music business, I told my mother, "If I ever come driving up to your place in a Cadillac, you'll know I bought you a house." In 1965 I got my first Coupe de Ville. It was red with a black fabric top. I drove over to see my mom in the projects one Sunday afternoon and found her outside working on her little flower garden. I pulled up and honked the horn. "Wow," she said as I stepped out of my new Cadillac, "is this your car? It's beautiful!" I said, "Yeah, Mama. I just wanted to come by to see if you'd like to take a little ride." She grabbed a sweater, jumped into the passenger seat, and we sped off down the street with the windows down. It was a gorgeous sunny day, and I remember feeling a rare moment of peace and calm.

We drove up Hamilton Avenue for several miles until we reached the Detroit Golf Club, "Hey, Mom," I said, "I told a friend of mine that I'd check on his place while he's out of town. Do you mind if we take a little detour?" She shook her head no, so I turned left on to 6 Mile Road and over to Birwood Avenue, a few blocks beyond Marygrove College. We pulled up into the driveway of a house. "I can just wait in the car while you make sure everything is alright," she said. "I think you ought to come in," I replied. "It might take me a few minutes." She got out, and we went up to the front door. We walked in, and she started looking around. "Oh, Lamont, your friend has a very nice house. Everything looks so new. Look at this furniture! Who did you say lives here?" Her back was turned so I held out the keys. "You live here," I said. My mother spun around and saw what I had in my hands. She broke down crying, ran over, and threw her arms around my neck. After she had sacrificed so much for our family, it felt good to give her something that showed her how much I appreciated what she'd done. I'm an emotional person, so my mother's tears brought on the waterworks for me, too. "I told you," I said as my voice broke, "that if I ever showed up in a Cadillac, that meant I'd bought you a house. I paid cash for it, too, so nobody can ever take this home away from you." She squeezed me tight, and I felt like that might have been the first time my mother really believed that music was a respectable occupation.

That was the first house I ever bought. I wanted to give a home to my mother before I bought a place for myself. Then I bought another home for cash and quitclaimed it to Ann. Even though we'd already split up, I wanted to make sure my daughter grew up in a good neighborhood. I wouldn't buy a house for myself until the following year when I got a place in the exclusive Palmer Woods neighborhood. It was very upper class, whatever that means, and I was the first black person to move to that area. I didn't get any pushback because the neighborhood association preapproved me as a result of my "status" or whatever bullshit. I loved my new house, but providing homes for my mother and daughter were a great joy for me in the midst of all the pressure.

The pressure intensified in September of 1965 when our latest Supremes single, "Nothing But Heartaches" stalled out at number eleven on the pop chart, failing to make the Top 10. Normally a single that charted that high on the national pop chart would be considered a success, but coming off five consecutive number ones, Berry saw it as a warning signal that The Supremes' reign could be in question. He sent a memo to the Motown creative staff that stated that the company would release nothing less that Top 10 product on any artist. He added that, since The Supremes were the biggest act on the label, they would only release number-one records. Obviously such a decree was largely out of our control, but that didn't mean we could ignore it. Holland-Dozier-Holland was under the microscope, and anything less than perfection would not be acceptable to the company.

While "Nothing But Heartaches" largely followed the formula of The Supremes' previous hits, we decided it was time to try something new. The original plan had been to release the song "Mother Dear" from the *More Hits by The Supremes* album as the follow-up single after "Nothing But Heartaches," but Berry had thrown down the gauntlet. It was time to try something musically fresh and sophisticated. I had no idea what it was going to be, but after that memo went around, I sat down at the piano and took a deep breath.

I used to watch movies all the time growing up, and I started thinking about how the main characters would have their own theme song as they entered a scene. I thought about how funny it would be if someone was walking around with their own theme song behind them all the time in real life. That would be melodramatic, but young love is melodramatic, so I started thinking about my first muse, Bernadette. I took myself back to those feelings of love and longing that we have as kids when we get our first crush. Suddenly, a chord pattern began to emerge, and I got a title: "I Hear a Symphony."

Eddie finished the lyrics, and we went in the studio right away. We recorded the song, pulled "Mother Dear," and issued "I Hear a Symphony" within a week of recording it. Within three weeks, it had entered the national charts and, by Thanksgiving, it reached number one.

Since "I Hear a Symphony" was more musically adventurous and commercially successful, we felt we had a license to keep pushing ahead into new territory. We cut "My World Is Empty Without You," which explored a moodier vibe with its minor key chorus. We finished it up in early December, and it was released just a few days before the end of the year.

In 1965 we were on the charts all the time. Our major triumphs in that year alone were "How Sweet It Is," "Stop! in the Name of Love," "Nowhere to Run," "Back in My Arms Again," "I Can't Help Myself," "It's the Same Old Song," "I Hear a Symphony," and a Top 5 R&B hit with Kim Weston's recording of "Take Me in Your Arms (Rock Me a Little While)." It was exhausting, but it was good to be on top of our game. I never took it for granted. I knew that getting to the top didn't mean staying at the top, and I tried to remember that as I interacted with those around me. I was never interested in trying to posture or act like a big shot. That's a lesson I learned early on when my Aunt Jenny took me to see a doo-wop group back in the fifties.

I loved this group called The Spaniels, fronted by Pookie Hudson. They were a pretty big doo-wop group, and they were appearing at the Arcadia, a skating rink in Detroit that occasionally hosted concerts. Aunt Jenny took me to see them when I was around twelve years old, and we had a great time hearing "Baby It's You," "Goodnight Sweetheart, Goodnight," and the other Spaniels hits. After the show, I wanted to get Pookie's autograph. Jenny said, "You go up there by the stage to meet him, and I'll catch up with you over there by the door."

I made my way through the crowd and up to Pookie. "Mr. Hudson," I said, "I enjoyed the show. I would really love to have your autograph if I could." He spun around and waved his hand. "Get the fuck away from me, boy." With that, he simply walked off. I was shattered, of course. I went back to Jenny, and she could see that I was troubled. "What's wrong?" she asked. I tried to force a smile. "Nothing," I replied. "He was just busy." Jenny knew me better than that. "Come on, Lamont," she said. "Something's wrong." I hesitated. "Well," I finally confessed, "He was pretty rude to me, but maybe he was having a bad day or they didn't get paid or something." I was making excuses for him, which I have a tendency to do. I usually try to look for the best in people, but it was hurtful that he'd been so abrasive toward me when I was just a kid.

Years passed, and The Spaniels' popularity faded. I had told Berry, Eddie, and Brian about my encounter with Pookie Hudson at some point, so Berry thought it was kind of amusing when Pookie came over to meet with him in hopes of getting a deal and reviving his career. I was in the office one day when the phone rang. It was Berry. "Hey, Lamont," he said, "guess who I've got waiting for me here outside my office? Pookie Hudson." I didn't see any point in bringing up that old childhood wound, so I just said, "Oh, yeah. He has a great voice." The Hollands could hear what Berry was saying on the phone, and they started falling out laughing. "I think he wants us to sign him to Motown," Berry continued, "but I think I should leave that up to you. Should I say 'yes' or should I say, 'Get the fuck away from me, boy?'" I just kind of laughed it off. "You're the boss, Berry," I said. "Your call."

A few minutes later Berry was giving Pookie a tour of Hitsville. He brought him into our office. "This is the team of Holland-Dozier-Holland," he said. Pookie's eyes got wide. "Wow," he said. "Holland-Dozier-Holland? Man, you guys are great writers! This is the hit machine right here!" He seemed genuinely excited to meet us. Berry introduced Pookie to Eddie and Brian first, saving me for last. "And *this* is Lamont Dozier," he said. I reached out my hand to shake his. Berry and the Hollands were all shooting me side glances and trying to stifle their laughter. I decided not to go for a cheap shot. "It's great to meet you, Pookie," I said. "I've loved your voice for years."

Those two encounters with Pookie have always reminded me of a cliché, but just because it's a cliché doesn't mean it isn't true. *You meet the same folks on the way up that you meet on the way down, so always treat others the way you want to be treated.* **I can tell you that I've met a lot of people in the music industry, and I know firsthand that you never know where life's circumstances will take you or who you might need help from in the future. You might be struggling today, but you could be on top tomorrow. Then you could go back to struggling once again and then crawl back to the top all over. I've always tried to steer clear of the drama and the**

backbiting and the politics that come along with the dirty business of music. It's easy to get sucked into it, but if you want to do it right, don't forget about the Golden Rule that you learned back in kindergarten or Sunday school.

Hitsville was a fiercely competitive environment, but it was mostly friendly competition. We were all in a battle to get our records released, but we weren't cutthroat about it. There was an underlying sense of camaraderie and an understanding that we were ultimately playing for the same team. If one of us won, we all won. If someone else got their record released over mine, then they were just helping to keep the operation going so I could continue doing my thing. I think most people there understood that, but sometimes jealousy and complaining got the better of some of our colleagues.

One time I was hanging out with Bobby Rogers from The Miracles. He said we needed to drop by the studio to meet with some of the other Motown producers. I remember that we'd just recorded "This Old Heart of Mine" with The Isley Brothers, so this would have been late 1965. When Bobby and I walked in, everyone suddenly stopped talking. They all turned and looked at me. It was an incredibly awkward moment, and I could feel the tension in the room. I didn't know what was going on, but I got a bad vibe, so I left. It came to light that some of the producers were plotting to discredit Holland-Dozier-Holland because they were envious that we were getting so many releases. These guys' songs weren't getting chosen in the quality control meetings, so they were looking for a way to get rid of us.

In reality, everybody had a shot to record with any of the Motown artists, but whoever had the best songs at the quality control meeting on Friday would win the day. They would assess all the material that had been recorded on that particular artist for that week, and whoever had the best song won. In theory, if somebody else had come to the meeting with an undeniably better song during our huge run with the Supremes, they'd get the next single. It doesn't matter what happened before. You had to keep up your winning ways, and you were starting over every single week. No matter who won the day, the cumulative work fueled the environment in which all of us got to continue to create. The people at Motown who understand that—people like Smokey Robinson, Norman Whitfield, and Mickey Stevenson— were the ones who had the greatest success. Those who let themselves be overcome by pettiness and jealousy were pouring their energy into the wrong thing.

When Berry found out about the plot to unseat us, he hit the ceiling. "Listen," he told them, "HDH are keeping the doors open around here. They're the reason you have a job, so cut out the bullshit and get your head screwed on straight before you shoot yourself in the foot. We vote on what to release, and as soon as you guys start coming up with better material than HDH, you'll get the vote. For now, they're the reason you have a job. If they go, you won't have a job, so I don't want to hear another goddamn word about anybody talking shit about Holland-Dozier-Holland." Fortunately those moments were rare at Motown. Because of the quality control meetings it truly came down to who had the best songs. It just so happened that we hit a streak where we had a whole lot of really damn good ones.

As I mentioned before, we thought of HDH as a factory within a factory. I think one of the reasons we did so well at the quality control meetings is because we were our own quality control group within the official quality control system. Our rule was that the music *had* to be infectious. If we felt like it was infectious to us, then we believed it would sell. We would toss around ideas among ourselves, and if it didn't feel right, we could just look at each other without even speaking and, no, it didn't meet the standard. So we'd just keep on working. If we hit it, we could look at each other, and tell there was a gut-level unanimous thing happening. The great thing about our collaboration was that we had similar sensibilities, and we got to where we knew one another by instinct.

It certainly didn't hurt that Berry gave us the freedom to do what we wanted to do. He wouldn't sign someone if he didn't think they were good, so he'd made a deal with the talent and then let you do what you do. He didn't really question anything we did because he had come from a songwriter background. He understood what we were doing, and as long as we came up with the goods, we had freedom.

As 1965 drew to a close, however, I wasn't looking backward. I was thinking about how we were going to use our freedom to keep up the pace in 1966.

Chapter Eleven

I CREATED A MONSTER

At the start of 1966, Eddie, Brian, and I were the kings of Motown. It's easy now for me to look back and marvel at the success we had in that era, but at the time, we were only as good as our next hit. I felt anxious most all the time, and I'd started drinking to calm my nerves. I'd seen what alcohol had done to my father, but I felt like I could handle it. Besides, it was the quickest and easiest way to cope with the unrelenting pressure we had on us to continue cranking out hit songs. It was definitely something that I kept quiet about. There were drugs around Motown, but Holland-Dozier-Holland were known as choir boys. Brian wouldn't drink anything but milk. Eddie would drink a little white wine, but we were pretty much all clean-living guys. We didn't have time to mess around with drugs, and I was always frightened about being out of control. Besides, Berry was clean and more or less demanded that the drugs and stuff stay out of sight. You came to Motown to work, not to get into a whole lot of boozing and partying. We weren't there to fool around, so I did my best to keep it in check. As time went on, that would become more difficult.

The Supremes' "My World Is Empty Without You" hit the charts in mid-January. It climbed all the way to number five on the pop chart, which should have been great news. Instead, it felt like a setback. The Supremes' next release, "Love Is Like an Itching in My Heart," barely made the Top 10. On top of that, our previous two Four Tops singles, "Something About You" and "Shake Me, Wake Me (When It's Over)" just squeaked into the Top 20. By any other measure, our accomplishments in the first part of 1966 were a success, but we had set the bar so high the previous year that nothing short of perfection would be acceptable.

Motown's Ivy Joe Hunter unseated us to produce a song he wrote with Stevie Wonder called "Loving You Is Sweeter Than Ever" that became The Four Tops' next single. I started to wonder if maybe we were losing our mojo. Little did I know that we were about to be caught up in another tsunami of success. About the time "Loving You Is Sweeter Than Ever" was stalling out at number forty-five on the pop chart, we were in the studio with The Supremes recording "You Can't Hurry Love." The song was rooted in the gospel music that Brian and I grew up with, but had a contemporary feel that continued the development of The Supremes' sound. It was out within three weeks and had climbed to number one by September.

The Supremes sang "You Can't Hurry Love" on Ed Sullivan's show that summer wearing matching sparkly sequined dresses. They exuded confidence and charisma, and it was clear that "the girls" were all grown up. One time Brian said, "Hey, Lamont, come on and let's go pick up the girls." They'd been out making TV appearances and touring Europe and were scheduled to land back in Detroit. I remember them coming down the ramp from the plane and they all had Chihuahuas. Brian and I looked at them with those little ugly dogs, and we started laughing about them struttin' their stuff and doing their star thing. At the same time, we had a real sense of pride. When they came off that plane, they were glamorous superstars. It was a far cry from a bunch of immature girls yelling at one another in the recording studio, and we felt gratified to have helped The Supremes become one of the biggest acts in the world.

We followed up "You Can't Hurry Love" with "You Keep Me Hangin' On." That provided a great opportunity to experiment in the recording studio. My dad used to listen to Walter Winchell's news bulletins on the radio, and I remembered that staccato alert sound that preceded the announcement of the news. I got the idea to try to replicate that with guitars. We usually used three guitars on our sessions, but we got four guitarists and had them all play that opening pattern in unison. I thought that would be a cool way for us to sonically say, "Hey, pay attention!" I guess it worked since it became a number-one hit for The Supremes. Then it became a Top 10 hit for Vanilla Fudge the following year. Then it became a number-one hit once again when Kim Wilde recorded it twenty years later. A few years after that, country artist Reba McEntire cut a version of it that shot up the *Billboard* Hot Dance Club Play chart. I think that's probably one of my favorite songs in our catalog because of the way it has continued to resonate with different people through different versions for different generations over all these years.

In the second half of 1966, we came back with The Four Tops in a big way. Around the same time we were recording "You Can't Hurry Love" and "You Keep Me Hangin' On" with The Supremes, we were in the studio with the Tops cutting "Reach Out I'll Be There." To me, that's a song that perfectly captures what Holland-Dozier-Holland was all about. Brian came up with the instrumental introduction, which draws heavily from classical influences. He was at the piano one day playing that phrase over and over when inspiration struck. I said, "Slide over, man." I sat down at the piano and took over, playing as I sang, "Now if you feel that you can't go on …" That was the gospel feel coming in to mix with the classical influence. Brian lit up, and we started trading musical phrases back and forth. For some reason I was thinking about the way Bob Dylan phrased the verses on his song "Like a Rolling Stone," which provided inspiration for the feel of "Reach Out I'll Be There." That was another song where we raised the key to get Levi Stubbs singing with that pleading gospel shout, and it's another of our records that I'm particularly proud of today. If Brian and I weren't both raised in the church and didn't both have a love for classical music, I don't know if we would have stumbled on so many of the things we did.

Being in the studio with the Tops was always a great experience. With most of the other artists we worked with, things were strictly professional. They'd come in and do their thing, and then we'd all go on with our lives. I was never one to hang out or socialize much because I was too busy working. The Four Tops managed to find a way to combine work with fun. The guys spent a lot of time in Europe, so if we were doing an album project with them, we'd get into these marathon recording sessions until three or four o'clock in the morning to make sure we had plenty of stuff in the can. We'd bring food in from Brothers Barbecue, which wasn't too far down the street from the studio. We'd get us a bunch of ribs, coleslaw, baked beans, and several bottles of Cold Duck wine. Once you got those guys eatin' barbecue ribs, drinkin' Cold Duck, and tellin' lies, you knew you'd get their best performance. It created a party atmosphere, and you could feel it in the music. I'm proud to say we wrote and produced some damn good songs for The Four Tops, but if you want to know the secret sauce that made those records really pop, it might just be the barbecue sauce!

By 1967 The Four Tops, like The Supremes before them, had become superstars. In January they scored another hit with our "Standing in the Shadows of Love," followed soon after by the Top 5 single "Bernadette." Even though I'd been drawing on my childhood feelings of puppy love for the real-life Bernadette for so long, I hadn't really ever mentioned her to Brian or Eddie. Besides, we all had an unspoken rule that we wouldn't write a song with a girl's name for the title. Yes, we were artists, but we also saw what we were doing as creating a commercial product in the hope of maximizing sales. We figured no girl was going to buy a record that had some other girl's name on it. That's why we never wrote a song about "Maggie" or "Mary" or any other woman's name.

We were all sitting around the office one day talking about how to get inspired. I said, "You know, guys, there was this little girl named Bernadette that I was in love with when I was ten or eleven years old, and she became my first muse. I still tap into that feeling when I want to get down to the basic feel of being in love." Eddie let out a little laugh. "That's crazy, man," he said. "I had me a girl named Bernadette at one time, too." He looked over at his brother. "Hey Brian, you used to go with a Bernadette, didn't you?" Brian nodded his head, and we all started laughing. "Hey guys," I said, "if every one of us had a girlfriend named Bernadette, then I think we need to write a song about it. We've just got to make it so good and get such a good performance on it that it transcends any one girl's name." Since Bernadette isn't the most common name in the world, I figured that it must be some kind of sign. We wrote it, cut the track, and brought in The Four Tops. Levi sang his ass off and made the song a classic. The Four Tops had a few more hits with our songs, including "7 Rooms of Gloom" and "You Keep Running Away," but there'll always be something special about "Bernadette."

Now here's a songwriting guideline that I always keep in my back pocket: *Know when to break your own rules.* **We were right to avoid writing songs with a girl's name for the title. From a commercial standpoint, it limits your audience. But sometimes circumstances dictate that it's time to throw the rules out the window and follow your gut. Where some young songwriters make a mistake is thinking they don't need to listen to any rules or guidelines in the first place. That's not true. The better you know the rules, the wiser you are about when and how to break them. Soak up all the songwriting wisdom you can as you dedicate yourself to the craft, but recognize that there's occasionally a time and place to set it all aside and pursue something outside the box. After "Bernadette" we didn't go write twenty more songs with girls' names as the titles, but that one well-timed rebellion against our own rule really paid off because we followed our instincts.**

Speaking of the real-life Bernadette, once we moved from my grandmother's house into the Jeffries Homes, I didn't see her anymore. I guess there was just no real reason that our paths would ever cross. Then, one day in the mid-1960s, I was driving down Woodward Avenue in my Coupe de Ville. I noticed a woman walking down the sidewalk. She was pushing a double stroller with two babies in it, had another baby on her hip, and was obviously pregnant with yet another. I happened to see her face pretty clearly as I passed and I recognized her. It was Bernadette! She was a beautiful girl, and she still had that beauty. I took the next right down a side street and circled back around the block to get a second look. Yep, it was Bernadette. I didn't stop and, as far as I know, she was never aware that she inspired me to write that song.

Since we were having so much success with the Tops and Supremes, it seemed that nearly every other act on Motown was asking us for songs and wanting us to record them. Otis Williams was a buddy of mine from our school days, and he was after me to do something with his group, The Temptations. But there were only so many hours in the day and only so much we could do. I would have loved to do it, but we just never got around to it. Otis made me feel a little guilty about it from time to time, but we just didn't have the capacity.

One of the rare occasions where we did give in was with a group called The Elgins. Those guys were friends of Brian's, and I think one of them was actually his barber. He kept pestering Brian about giving him a song, so we went through our stash and found one in the can called "Heaven Must Have Sent You." We cut it on them as a favor and, lo and behold, it became a Top 10 R&B hit. It was an even bigger hit when it was rereleased in the UK in the early 1970s. We didn't need another act to work with, but we went in and cut a whole album of material to capitalize on their hit. Ultimately, the group couldn't get the same kind of promotion out of Motown as some of the other artists, and they disbanded.

By the late 1960s, change was in the air in Detroit and at Motown. We had always recorded with The Funk Brothers in our home city, but Berry started spending more time in Los Angeles and wanted us to cut some stuff with The Supremes on the West Coast. Our first trip there was in the summer of 1966. The night we got to town it was late—about one in the morning—and we were searching for some place that would be open where we could get something to eat. We ended up in an IHOP in Hollywood.

When we walked in, we saw Burt Bacharach with his wife, Angie Dickenson, who was pregnant with their daughter. The place was packed, so we had to wait a few minutes for our table. I was looking around and spotted a strange-looking guy with sunglasses on sitting alone at a booth. I nudged Eddie. "Hey man, is that Phil Spector over there in the corner?" Eddie craned his neck to get a better look. About the time Brian joined our gawking session, Phil looked up and saw the three of us looking at him. Other than The Beatles, he was our greatest competition. We all just froze and stared at one another, but nobody made a move. None of us had ever met him before, and no words were exchanged. Phil was a genius, but he was a strange guy. We didn't know quite what to do. I guess it's a good thing a bomb wasn't dropped on the Hollywood IHOP on that late summer night in 1966. It would've wiped out Phil Spector, Burt Bacharach, Holland-Dozier-Holland, and a whole lot of hit songs!

I was worried about working with a new set of musicians in Los Angeles, but I shouldn't have been. Those guys were all pros, and they were familiar with our records. They knew our sound, and they already knew what we wanted before we arrived. Plus, they were excited to be working on something for The Supremes, so they showed us all the greatest respect. I think the first thing we cut in LA was "Love Is Here and Now You're Gone," which became yet another HDH-penned number-one hit for The Supremes.

We were back in Los Angeles in the winter of 1967 to record "The Happening," which was the theme song for a movie of the same name. That wasn't one of my favorite songs, but even though the movie was a flop, the song took The Supremes to number-one yet again. It was the fourth in their second run of consecutive singles, and the tenth number-one pop hit we'd written and produced for them.

Learning to make records in a new city wasn't the only change going on in 1967. In July, clashes with Detroit police erupted into looting before developing into one of the bloodiest American riots of the twentieth century. The National Guard and the Army were deployed to try to stop the chaos that ultimately resulted in nearly twelve hundred injuries, more than forty deaths, and over two thousand buildings destroyed by fire. I remember watching tanks roll down West Grand Boulevard like it was some kind of war zone. Motown was a black-owned company, but there were plenty of white employees. We were sneaking people out the back door of the studio to their cars to try to get everyone home safely. It was a really scary time no matter what color your skin happened to be! I was reminded of "Nowhere to Run," which took on a whole new dimension of meaning for me in the wake of the riots. It came to be the song that, for me, defined that whole period of upheaval and unrest that stretched from Vietnam to the streets of America's biggest cities.

One positive change that happened in 1967 was that I became a father for the second time. After Ann and I split up, she intentionally kept Michelle from me, which was a mean thing to do. I loved the times I got to take Michelle with me to the Motown offices when she was little, but those days of spending quality time together were over. Her mother was bitter and angry at me, even though she's the one who kicked me out of the house. I didn't know if I'd ever get another shot at fatherhood or not, but it happened in 1967 when my first son, Andre Lamont Dozier, was born. Andre's mother was Hattie Williams, whom I'd known back in junior high school. Hattie and I ran into each other somewhere and reconnected. I was dating around a little bit after my first marriage, and though Hattie and I had a real connection, we never lived together or anything. Andre grew up with Hattie, but I made a point to spend time with him when I could. Unfortunately that wasn't as often as I wish it had been. From a career standpoint it was a hectic time.

The late 1960s weren't only a time of civil unrest and personal change, but also a significant period of musical change. When The Beatles released their album *Revolver* in the summer of 1965, everyone in the music industry was paying attention. The production techniques were truly groundbreaking. We'd listen to some of the tracks, thinking, *How'd they do that?* We bumped *Revolver* from the number-one spot on the album charts with *The Supremes A' Go-Go* LP, but we knew that the musical times were changing. The sounds that would give rise to the psychedelic era were all around us, and we knew we'd better start experimenting, too. The slowed-down psychedelic that Vanilla Fudge used when they covered "You Keep Me Hanging On" was something that the Hollands and I thought was pretty cool. Instead of getting stuck in the past, we were eager to keep setting the pace.

We recorded "Reflections" in the spring of 1967. Inspired by The Beatles' manipulation of studio equipment, we created the unusual sounds on that recording by running a test oscillator through a bunch of effects. Normally it was just used to test the frequency response of the audio equipment in the room, but we decided we could do something more adventurous with it. People must have liked the sound, because "Reflections" moved straight up the charts in August of 1967. It was on track to become the girls' eleventh number-one hit, but it got trapped at number two—shut out of the top slot by Bobbie Gentry's "Ode to Billie Joe." But, hey, "Ode to Billie Joe" was a great song. We even recorded a cover of Diana singing it on The Supremes' *Reflections* album.

Times were changing, sounds were changing, and the Motown spirit was changing all around us. The all-for-one-and-one-for-all family atmosphere that characterized Hitsville in the early days was fading. In 1967 The Miracles became *Smokey Robinson* and the Miracles; Martha and the Vandellas became Martha *Reeves* and the Vandellas. Similarly, "Reflections" was the first single issued under the new name *Diana Ross* and the Supremes.

The Supremes had been straining under the weight of their own success for some time. Today Diana is regarded as one of the most notorious divas in pop music history. Despite the drama surrounding the recording session for "Where Did Our Love Go," she was actually pretty down to earth in the early days. I guess she couldn't be a diva before she had any hits. She hadn't gotten the credentials to be a diva yet! When we wrote all those hit songs, though, we gave her the platform to catapult to diva status. As The Supremes' success reached unimaginable heights, it was no secret that Berry wanted Diana to be the primary focus of the group. That was hard on Mary Wilson, and especially hard on Florence Ballard. Flo was pretty depressed and started drinking heavily as she and Mary were increasingly relegated to the shadows. Sometimes Flo wouldn't show up at the recording studio, or she'd show up drunk. To say that relations between her and Diana were strained would be a serious understatement.

I think the session for "In and Out of Love" was the last one Flo came to before Berry fired her from The Supremes. It became a Top 10 hit after she'd left the group and had been replaced by Cindy Birdsong. It was also the last real hit written and produced for The Supremes by Holland-Dozier-Holland. "Forever Came Today," which we'd first recorded around the same time as "In and Out of Love," was released not long afterward and became a Top 30 pop hit, but by the time it hit the charts, Holland-Dozier-Holland was effectively on strike. Things weren't going well for us with the Motown brass, and yet another change was in the air. Things were about to get messy.

Me as a toddler in Black Bottom, Detroit in the early 1940s.

My mother, Ethel Dozier, holding (from left) me, my sister Laretta, and my brother Reggie while her friend, Miss Bessie, looks on.

The Dozier siblings (clockwise from upper left): Me, Laretta, Reggie, Zel, and Norma.

At the piano at Motown with Eddie Holland (center) and Brian Holland (right).

At the piano with The Supremes (clockwise from upper left): Diana Ross, Mary Wilson, Eddie Holland, Brian Holland, and Florence Ballard.

With Eddie (seated) and Brian (standing, right) when
we first launched Invictus Records.

With my mother in the home I bought for her in Detroit.

Performing on *American Bandstand* during the ABC Dunhill years.

When Barbara had our children, it was a wake-up call to take care of my health and dedicate myself to being the kind of father I had always wanted to be.

On the boat where we shot the cover for my 1981 album *Lamont*.

If I'm not at a piano, my favorite place to be is in a recording studio.

(From left) Barry Mann, Cynthia Weil, Eddie Holland, Brian Holland, me, Carole King, and Gerry Goffin at a BMI Pop Awards party.

Phil Collins and I became friends and admirers of one another from the first time we met.

With Phil Collins in Acapulco, where he was filming the movie *Buster*.

At the 1990 BMI Pop Awards, Barbara and I stood side-by-side as business partners to accept our awards for "Two Hearts." I held the award for the songwriter, while Barbara represented our publishing company.

In the studio with Eric Clapton.

(from left) Diana Ross, Brian Holland, me, and Eddie Holland on stage
at the Rock & Roll Hall of Fame induction ceremony in 1990.

With Barbara at our tenth wedding anniversary at Le Dome Restaurant in 1990.

Me and Barbara with Atlantic Records' Ahmet Ertegun
and Debbie Gibson at a BMI party at Spago.

(left to right) Berry Gordy, Eddie Holland, Brian Holland,
Michael Jackson, and me at a BMI luncheon.

(from left) Jimmy Jam, Ne-Yo, me, and Sean Garrett at a Grammy Career Day event.

After receiving the Thornton Legacy award in 2007, I had the honor
of presenting it to the 2008 recipient, Brian Wilson. In the center
is Robert Cutietta, Dean of USC's Thornton School of Music.

Chatting about great songs with Bono.

Eddie (left), Brian (right), and I received our stars on the
Hollywood Walk of Fame in February of 2015.

In 2007 I had the opportunity to return to Motown in Detroit, which is now a museum. It was great to stand in that tiny control room once again, but the most meaningful part of the experience was getting to share it with my children (from left): Paris, Desiree, and Beau.

Chapter Twelve

WHERE DID OUR LOVE GO?

As Eddie, Brian, and I saw it, Holland-Dozier-Holland was one of
the key ingredients in the secret sauce that transformed Motown
from a scrappy independent R&B record label into a worldwide
force in pop music. By 1967 we'd written and produced well over
half the successful singles that had built Berry's company into an
unstoppable hit machine. But our accomplishments came at a
cost. The relentless work and around-the-clock hours were not
compatible with a healthy personal life. My first marriage fell apart,
which resulted in ripple effects that damaged my ability to have the
kind of relationship I wanted to have with my daughter Michelle.

Brian and his wife split up, too. We all internalized a
tremendous amount of stress, but it wasn't something we talked
about with one another. In those days men weren't supposed to

talk about their feelings, express their fears, or appear emotionally vulnerable. Publicly, I tried to keep a stiff upper lip, but inside I felt like I was going to implode. My drinking continued to increase, and I developed serious anxiety problems that would reach a breaking point in the years to come.

Other relationships suffered in ways I couldn't have imagined. I remember one day we wrapped up our studio work early, and I actually got away from the office at a decent hour. I was feeling a little melancholy and decided I'd drive down to the Jeffries Projects to visit some of my old buddies from high school. It sounds kind of funny because I was still living in the same city, but I felt homesick. I thought maybe I could find some of my friends, and we'd have a good time catching up and talking about the old days.

I parked my car and walked over to the courtyard outside the apartment where my mother used to stay. I spotted a guy named James that I'd gone to school with, and he waved me over. "Hey, Lamont," he said, smiling. "What brings you around, brother?" I shrugged. "Oh, man," I said, "you know, it's been too long. I thought I'd just come by and see if I could buy a round of drinks and catch up with some of the guys." James nodded. "Sounds like a plan, man. Let me get some people together, and we'll meet you at the bar across the street."

I headed over and found a large booth. In a few minutes James came through the door with a half dozen guys I hadn't seen in a good while. We exchanged hugs and settled in around the table. We had a couple of rounds of drinks and were laughing and swapping stories about stuff that happened in the neighborhood back in the day. At some point, during the third round of drinks, there was a lull in the conversation. "Well, fellas" one of the guys at the table said as he locked eyes with me, "I guess Mr. Big Shit has finally come down from his fancy house in Palmer Woods to see how the poor folks live."

The vibe around the table instantly shifted. It was as if the temperature in the room had dropped dramatically out of nowhere. "No, man," I laughed nervously. "It ain't like that. I just wanted to come down here and see you guys." Somebody else spoke up, loud enough that it startled me. "You're down here slummin' with your Cadillac and your expensive rings on your fingers, man. You don't know us. Tryin' to buy drinks and throw your money around. We don't need your shit."

Things were turning nasty quickly. Someone else said, "Maybe we oughtta take this fool out in the alley and remind him what life's like in the projects." I was baffled by the display of hostility from my old friends. James pulled me aside, "Lamont, you better leave," he said quietly. "Thanks for coming, man. It was good to see you, and I appreciate the drinks, but you don't know these guys anymore. This could get ugly, and you need to get out of here now." I excused myself from the table, left some money with the bartender, and headed for the car. It was already dark when I walked out into the cool night air, and I suddenly felt very alone.

As I drove back home I began to cry. All I'd wanted to do was hang out with the people I'd grown up with, but it was all taken the wrong way. I thought back to when I was a kid and I was ostracized for wearing the clothes that the Goodfellows gave away to low-income families at Christmas time. Now I actually *had* some material possessions, and I was being ostracized for supposedly flaunting it. Of course there was nothing pretentious about me going down there, but I barely escaped with my life. I guess I've experienced rejection for having too little and for having too much. It was a harsh wake-up call that my so-called friends were no longer my friends.

That experience hurt me, but it illustrates an important concept that has served me well in life and in songwriting. *You have to be true to yourself.* People will come and go from

your life. Seasons will change. Fashions and fads will ebb and flow. Different people will want different things from you at different times, but you have to have a strong sense of self in order to stay grounded and centered. I said earlier that a songwriter needs to have perspective and a voice, but equally important is being able to hold on to that perspective when others want you to be something you're not.

Staying true to myself helped me stay strong at a time when things weren't going so well at Hitsville. I have no complaints about the success and the opportunities that my affiliation with Motown brought, but then Eddie, Brian, and I felt like we'd given our lives to make Motown a success, and we wanted a fair share of the pie that we helped bake. Specifically, we thought Berry should give us our own subsidiary label under the Motown umbrella so we could sign and develop our own acts while continuing to do what we'd always done for the larger company. We believed we deserved that kind of recognition after all we'd accomplished, but Berry didn't see it that way.

Additionally, Jobete, the music publishing arm of Motown, owned one hundred percent of our copyrights. We thought we should be able to keep a fair share of the songs we were writing that were flooding Jobete with cash. Again, the company didn't agree.

My natural inclination is to avoid conflict. I was unhappy that we weren't being financially rewarded for our important contributions at Hitsville, but I wasn't ever the type to go storming into someone's office demanding my rights. Even though he was a bit of an introvert, Eddie was more business minded than I was, and he could be confrontational if he had to be. He became the spokesman for the three of us and probably had conversations on my behalf that I was never aware of. I was fine with that because I shared his conviction that we deserved to be compensated fairly. Even though Eddie made our desires clear to Berry, we didn't get any real traction.

Berry, of course, was in a difficult position. He knew that Holland-Dozier-Holland was a fundamental building block of his company's success, but there was no way he was going to give up control. He'd built the company by doing things his way, even if others considered his tactics unfair. He had to figure out a way to try to keep us happy without risking his empire.

Berry took some steps to try to buy himself some time. He started by installing Eddie as the company's new A&R Director, a position that Mickey Stevenson had held since the label began. In addition to writing and producing songs like "Dancing in the Street," "Beechwood 4–5789," and "It Takes Two," Mickey oversaw the whole staff of artists and producers. The A&R director got an override, meaning he was paid a royalty on all the records, not just the ones he wrote or produced. The new appointment meant a bit more money in Eddie's pocket and a stronger voice for the interests of Holland-Dozier-Holland. In addition, Brian was put in charge of the quality control meetings. By simply shuffling the responsibilities, Berry didn't have to give up anything. Mickey was initially moved into another position but realized what was really going on and ultimately left the company.

As the A&R Director, Eddie could bring in new talent at Motown. One time Brian and I were in New York, where we'd heard about this up-and-coming songwriting team named Nick Ashford and Valerie Simpson. We scheduled a meeting with Nick at our hotel, and we were both blown away by the demo tape he played for us. We arranged for them to meet with Eddie at Motown, and they were signed as staff writers and producers. I was always highly impressed with Smokey Robinson. I also thought Norman Whitfield was really great. Looking back, though, I think the Motown writers who impressed me the most were Ashford and Simpson. Songs like

"Ain't No Mountain High Enough," "Ain't Nothing Like the Real Thing," and "You're All I Need to Get By" were masterpieces. Unfortunately they really got going at a time when we were starting to look for the exit door.

The leadership changes Berry made for the Hollands were a stopgap measure to keep them happy for a little longer, but it didn't really do anything to address my concerns that we weren't being properly compensated for our contributions. Not only that, but now that we all had a little money, the Hollands had gotten into horse racing. They were as likely to be at the track as they were at Hitsville. I found myself increasingly isolated, hammering away alone at the piano for hours. Though Eddie had often worked separately while Brian and I worked together, the dynamic was shifting. Now I was the one toiling away in solitude, and I missed the dynamic of bouncing ideas off Brian every day like we did in the beginning.

I probably should have spoken up for myself, but my stress and anxiety had taken a toll on my self-confidence. Sometimes I felt like fighting, but other times I struggled with self-doubt. What if I was kidding myself? What if I was overestimating Holland-Dozier-Holland's contributions to the success of Motown? Maybe Berry really *was* the sole reason for Motown's success. He was, after all, a charismatic personality, and he could certainly cast a spell. I was drifting, constantly second-guessing myself, and feeling a creeping sense of depression that was stalking my every move. And, remember, I was all of twenty-five years old.

Then something happened early one evening in 1967 that provided the moment of clarity I needed. I'd received a royalty check earlier in the day for about $100,000. As I was leaving I ran into Berry, who was chatting with some of the other producers in the lobby. He spotted the envelope in my hand and nodded in my direction as I was walking past. "Whatchya gonna do with all that money, boy?" I looked up as he winked at me, and a switch suddenly flipped in my brain. There was something a little too gleeful about Berry's demeanor, and it made me suspicious. Actually, more than suspicious. I knew that something was "off."

I'll be the first to admit that $100,000 was a good chunk of money in 1967 that would equate to around $750,000 in today's terms. I soon discovered, however, that Motown was raking in many times that amount thanks to Holland-Dozier-Holland. We didn't believe we were getting an accurate accounting of our US sales, and we weren't getting *any* accounting for overseas sales. I'd always been lead to believe that there wasn't much going on for Motown in Europe until I had a frank conversation with Duke Fakir of The Four Tops. He told me they attracted huge audiences across the pond, and I learned that "Where Did Our Love Go," "Baby Love," "You Can't Hurry Love," "Reflections," "Reach Out I'll Be There," and "Heaven Must Have Sent You" were all Top 5 records on the UK pop charts. Berry's off-handed remark somehow confirmed what I knew in my spirit: we'd been taken advantage of.

Reinvigorated with a fresh sense of resolve, I was ready to pull the plug on Motown. Shortly after that, I took Eddie aside after a recording session. "Listen, man," I confided, "you know I'm not happy here and we all know what kind of toll this place has taken on us. I understand that you've made the case to Berry, but I just don't think we're getting anywhere with setting up our own imprint or getting a bigger piece of our song royalties. I've been asking around, and I'm convinced they're not even paying us what they *say* they should be, which is already less than they *actually* should be. You and Brian are my brothers, and I'll always value what we've done together, but I can't do it anymore. I'm out. I wanted you to hear it from me before you heard it from someone else."

Eddie motioned for me to follow him, and we ducked into an empty side room. He shut the door behind him and scanned the small room to make absolutely sure there was nobody who might overhear him. He lowered his voice to a near whisper. "Alright man," he said, "calm down for just a minute. Can you hang on a little longer? I've already been talking to some other companies about you and me and Brian forming our own situation with a production company and label."

I was quiet for a moment. "I'm not sure, Eddie," I finally told him. "I think I want to do my own thing. I just want a fresh start, you know what I'm sayin'?" He nodded. "I know, man, it's the same for me and Brian. We all want a fresh start, but look at what we've accomplished together. Just imagine if we were to keep doing what we're doing now, but in a situation where we get to hold on to all the money. We know we've got a winning formula, and I think we can make more by sticking together than we've ever dreamed of. If you can hang in there with me for a little longer, we can make this work." I promised I'd think about it.

In the meantime, we agreed we'd essentially go on strike. We couldn't make any deals with any other company at the moment because we were still under contract to Motown. There wasn't much we could do about that, so we decided we'd simply stop turning in songs or booking recording sessions. We thought perhaps the added pressure might move the needle with Berry.

It didn't take long for the rumors to start flying around the company. The Motown brass had to figure out some kind of solution, but they weren't willing to give us what we wanted. Mike Roshkind was a white music industry veteran whom Berry had hired as the vice president and CEO of the company. Mike could be aggressive and intimidating when he wanted to be, and I'd heard rumors that he was connected to the mob in some way. I didn't know what to expect when he called a meeting with me but didn't invite the Hollands.

"Listen, Lamont," he said matter-of-factly as I settled into a chair across from his large desk, "we all know there are problems, and we want to find solutions. It's clear that you and the Hollands are looking for a way out here. I understand that, but honestly we don't need them. As far as I'm concerned, Eddie and Brian can go off in search of greener pastures. You are the heart and soul of Holland-Dozier-Holland. We'd like to keep you, and we can put the full force of the Motown machine behind you to support you and make you more money than you ever thought possible. We're family, right?"

I don't even know what Mike said after that. I just knew that I was disenchanted and wanted to wash my hands of the whole thing at that point. By the end I nodded and said I'd think about it. For all I know, he might have had the exact same meeting with the other two guys. I saw right through the divide-and-conquer strategy, and I wanted no part of it. I realized there was no future for me there. I was going to keep working my ass off without getting what I thought I deserved. The whole picture was becoming uglier and uglier, and my mind was made up. Even if Eddie and Brian had made a deal to stay at Motown, I wouldn't have stayed. I was leaving Motown, with or without the Hollands.

In the meantime, we just couldn't be found. Thanks to our little strike, we essentially ghosted Motown. We didn't show up at the office. We didn't schedule recording sessions. We didn't turn in songs to the publishing company. We didn't submit recordings for the quality control meetings. We were just gone.

Finally, in the summer of 1968, Motown sued us for four million dollars. We were charged with breaching our contracts, and the suit asked the court to bar us from working with any other company. Our position was that, yes, we were breaking our contracts, but we believed we had been taken advantage of. We were never given the opportunity to have those contracts

reviewed by an attorney, and we were all basically just kids
when they put those agreements in our faces and told us not
to worry about all the legal mumbo jumbo. We could just sign,
we were told, because they had our best interest at heart. But
more importantly, we didn't believe they were giving us a proper
accounting of our earnings. We countersued for twenty-two
million dollars. The court battle went on for years. Then there
were other lawsuits between us and Berry, all of which were long,
complicated, and unpleasant.

Just as I'd been a man without a home when I tried to visit
the Jeffries Projects, it happened again one day when I was
driving past Motown II, a second studio they'd set up on the
other side of town. I spotted James Jamerson in the parking
lot, and pulled in to say hi. I'd had a few drinks and was feeling
pretty loose, so when James invited me inside, I went with him.
When I walked in from the bright outdoors it took my eyes
a moment to adjust to the darkened studio. I could see that
someone was standing in front of me, but I couldn't make out
who it was. Then I recognized Smokey Robinson. A big grin
broke out on his face and he embraced me with a warm hug.
As I began chatting with some of the other musicians who'd
gathered for the session, I spotted Smokey out of the corner
of my eye whispering to a security guard on the other side of
the room.

The guard made his way over to me. "I'm sorry, Mr. Dozier,"
he informed me, "but you don't belong here. Motown is
off limits to you and I'm going to have to ask you to leave."
Jamerson got hot. He jumped up in the guard's face. "Man, don't
you know who this is? This guy made Motown what it is!" He
was ready to get in a fistfight with the guard, but I didn't want
any more trouble. "It's OK, James," I said as I turned and walked
outside.

Jamerson followed me out to the parking lot. "That's just not right, man," he said as he shook his head. I shrugged. "It's complicated. I guess you can't go back home, man." He was still angry, but I didn't want to see him get fired from the session. I opened the passenger door to my car. "C'mon," I coaxed. "Get in." James climbed in the car, and we shared a bottle. Neither one of us said anything, but we both knew that we'd all lost something. And Motown had lost its innocence.

Chapter Thirteen

GIVE ME JUST A LITTLE MORE TIME

Out of the night that covers me,
Black as the pit from pole to pole,
I thank whatever gods may be
For my unconquerable soul.

In the fell clutch of circumstance
I have not winced nor cried aloud.
Under the bludgeonings of chance
My head is bloody, but unbowed.

Beyond this place of wrath and tears
Looms but the Horror of the shade,
And yet the menace of the years
Finds, and shall find me, unafraid.

It matters not how strait the gate,
How charged with punishments the scroll,
I am the master of my fate:
I am the captain of my soul.

"Invictus" William Ernest Henley, 1875

As the courts were sorting out the disputes between Motown and Holland-Dozier-Holland, Eddie was setting up several new companies for us. Though the three of us were still under contract to Motown as songwriters—and Brian and I were under contract as producers—there was nothing to prevent us from establishing companies that utilized *other* songwriters or producers.

Eddie had a vision that we would be well suited to run a company because we were creative people and we spoke the language of creative people. He theorized that most artists felt like they weren't speaking the same language as the heads of the companies they recorded for, but we could be a new kind of business. We were looking for people who were wanting to express themselves creatively. It wasn't meant to be a top-down kind of thing. We didn't construct a vision to impose on others. We wanted to find those with vision who could partner *with* us. It was a bold move and a risky move, but we found inspiration in a poem from the 1800s called "Invictus." I can't recall where we came across it, but it described how we felt. We were coming out of the dark and taking charge as the masters of our fate.

Eddie set up two label imprints, Invictus Records and Hot Wax Records, as well as two corresponding production companies: Holland Dozier Holland Productions, Inc., which was affiliated with Invictus, and Stagecoach Productions, which was affiliated with Hot Wax. He additionally set up Gold Forever Music with the performing rights society BMI, while Holland Dozier Holland Music, Inc. was our company with the other major society, ASCAP. Everything was set up under an umbrella company with Eddie as the president and sole shareholder. I had no interest in the inner-workings of setting up a business, so I signed over power of attorney during that era and a lot of decisions were made on my behalf.

We opened up our offices in the forty-story Cadillac Tower in downtown Detroit and went to work establishing our new venture. We had been a factory within a factory at Motown, but now we had to build and manage an entire team, which was a challenge. Fortunately we were able to mine a lot of great talent from Hitsville. Berry Gordy was increasingly focused on Hollywood, and I think most people saw the writing on the wall. Motown was well on its way to leaving Detroit for the West Coast. The pending relocation and the various personal frustrations that some staffers had with the company gave us an opportunity to recruit some fellow Motown defectors, including songwriter and producer Ronald Dunbar.

Ron was buddies with Brian and Eddie, and the three of them formed a tight bond going to the race track together. He was loyal to the Hollands, so when we left Motown, he did, too. We also got a couple of Motown's great recording engineers in Bob Dennis and Lawrence Horn, who played a big part in designing and building our recording studio at the former Town Theater on Grand River Avenue. While we waited for our facility to be completed, we recorded early sessions at Tera Shirma Sound Studio on the northwest side of town.

Of course offices and recording facilities alone won't bring you any success in the music business. You've got to have artists and, more specifically, you've got to have the *right* artists. Jeffrey Bowen, another Motown refugee who'd made a name for himself co-producing The Temptations' *In a Mellow Mood* album, came on as our head talent scout and A&R guy.

Holland-Dozier-Holland had honed a formula for success at Motown that served us well. The Supremes were our primary female group, and The Four Tops were our primary male group. We were able to develop a distinctive sound for each, and we saw no reason to mess with the template that had carried us to the top of the charts. We just needed a new Supremes and a new Four Tops. I don't mean that to sound crass. Both groups were amazing vehicles for the Holland-Dozier-Holland vision, but we couldn't have done it without their unique talents. We never thought we could simply apply a cookie-cutter approach to any random group of people and duplicate our success, but we were looking for a similar situation where we could bring together some really talented singers and discover how to use the strengths of each member to the best possible effect—just as we'd done with the previous acts we'd produced.

The group that would become something similar to what The Supremes had once been for us was The Honey Cone. We had met singer Edna Wright out in Los Angeles when we were still at Motown and were impressed with her voice. Edna's sister was Darlene Love, who sang lead on "He's a Rebel," "Christmas (Baby Please Come Home)," and a whole bunch of other great Phil Spector records. Like Darlene, Edna worked constantly as a background singer in Los Angeles and even spent some time as one of Ray Charles's Raelettes.

One evening Eddie saw Edna singing on *The Andy Williams Show* with Shelly Clark and Carolyn Willis. Though they didn't work exclusively with one another as a trio before coming to us, Eddie signed them, and I think he's the one who came up with the name The Honey Cone. The first record we released by any act was The Honey Cone's recording of "While You're Out Looking for Sugar," which was issued in May of 1969 on the Hot Wax label. It wasn't a big hit, but it landed on the *Billboard* charts, reaching number twenty-six on the R&B rankings. I actually don't remember doing anything on that song. I didn't produce it or anything, but once we set up our company, we agreed that Holland-Dozier-Holland would function in a similar way as Lennon-McCartney. No matter which of us—or which combination of us—wrote it, it would be a Holland-Dozier-Holland composition.

We released the second Honey Cone single, "Girls It Ain't Easy," around the same time we issued our first single on the Invictus label, which was "Crumbs Off the Table" by The Glass House. The mixed-gender group was actually assembled as a studio creation and had not been a pre-existing act before we auditioned them. For the two male voices we chose Larry Mitchell and Ty Hunter, my old friend from The Romeos and The Voice Masters. The female voices were Pearl Jones and Scherrie Payne, whose sister, Freda Payne, was also signed to our company early on.

"Crumbs Off the Table" was a Top 10 R&B hit. When it was released, the label copy listed Holland-Dozier-Holland as the production *company,* but the actual producer credit was listed as "staff." Remember, our hands were still tied as a result of our entanglements with Motown. Similarly, the writer credits showed R. Dunbar and E. Wayne, which were the same writer credits on the first two Honey Cone singles. Everybody knows who

Ronald Dunbar was, but there's been much speculation about the mysterious E. Wayne, who was frequently credited as a writer on our early Invictus and Hot Wax releases.

When we launched our labels, people in the industry knew exactly who was writing the songs and making the records, but we couldn't use our own names for two years until our exclusive songwriting contracts with Jobete and our production contracts with Motown ran out. The name Edythe Wayne (sometimes spelled Edith or Edyth) showed up on a lot of our label credits during that period. Fans have often wondered if Edythe Wayne was a real person, or if that was a pseudonym we invented to avoid legal problems. One guy even wrote a book speculating that we combined the name of Detroit's Wayne State University with my mother's first name of Edythe. That would have been a stronger theory if my mother was actually named Edythe, and not Ethel. In reality, Edythe Wayne *was* a real person. It was a pseudonym for Edythe Vernelle Craighead, who was Eddie's girlfriend at the time. Known to everyone as Vernelle, she and Eddie later married. Once we were free of our Motown entanglements, however, the name Edythe Wayne pretty much disappeared from our credits. It doesn't take a rocket scientist to figure out what we had to do there.

With The Honey Cone playing a similar role that The Supremes once played in our creative output, Jeffrey Bowen was assigned the job of finding a male group that would become our equivalent of The Four Tops. He's the one who assembled The Chairmen of the Board, which gave us our third Top 10 R&B hit, and our first Top 5 pop hit, as well. The song was "Give Me Just a Little More Time," another title we collaborated on under the banner of Ron Dunbar and Edythe Wayne. The group consisted of Harrison Kennedy, Eddie Custis, Danny Woods, and General Norman Johnson. General turned out to be an important part of our organization, but when he first arrived, I thought maybe Jeffrey Bowen had made a mistake.

Back in the early 1960s, General was in a New Orleans group called The Showmen that had a hit with the song "It Will Stand." He had this cool halting vocal style on that record that I really loved. I remember working on "Give Me Just a Little More Time" and hearing that voice in my head as I was writing it. Once we got The Chairmen of the Board in the studio for their first session, however, something odd happened. General started singing in the vocal booth, but his delivery sounded nothing like the guy on "It Will Stand." I turned to Jeffrey Bowen, who was in the control room with us. "Man, are you sure you got the right guy?" Jeffrey raised his eyebrows. "That's him, man," he replied. "That's General Johnson."

After a few takes, I asked General to come out of the vocal booth onto the studio floor. We sat down at the piano and I walked through the delivery of the song. But I wasn't singing like Lamont Dozier. I was mimicking the version of General Johnson that I was familiar with. It was like he didn't recognize his own style. "Lamont," he said, "What's happening? I don't get it." I said, "You know, man, like 'It Will Stand.' I'm trying to get you to sing this song with that same style. You *are* the guy who sang that, right?" He nodded his head slowly. "Yeah, I sang it," he answered. "I guess my voice has changed some over the last few years." I was completely puzzled by the experience, but I kept working with him at the piano and kept mimicking his own style back to him to demonstrate what I wanted. We worked at it for a long time that day, but I was finally able to coax it out of him and remind him of the way he once sang. In the end, General's vocal performance on "Give Me Just a Little More Time" came out exactly as I'd hoped.

Hot on the heels of our success with The Chairmen of the Board, we had another big hit with Freda Payne's recording of "Band of Gold," which was another one the Hollands and I wrote together. I'd known Freda since we were in the same class together at Hutchins Junior High School, so we went back a lot of years. Freda was a sweet but pretty quiet girl in school. She had a great singing voice, though, and I think Berry had wanted to sign her in the early days of Motown. Freda's mother stopped it for one reason or another, but I never knew why.

Freda was really more of a jazz vocalist than a pop or R&B singer. I remember Eddie and I teaching "Band of Gold" to her and going over it many times to make sure she got the right performance we were looking for. Eddie was drilling her over and over while I sat at the piano to demonstrate the feeling we wanted. Once she finally caught on, she really got into it. Her performance on that record is really strong, which explains why, in the summer of 1970, it because our company's second Top 5 pop hit.

"Band of Gold" raised a few eyebrows when it was released. Lyrically, we would always try to stay abreast of what was going on. At Motown we often set the trend, and people would gravitate toward what we were doing. When we started our own thing, we could be a little more controversial, and that song is a great example. The lyrics describe newlyweds who spend their honeymoon night in separate rooms while the woman hopes her new husband will come back in to love her like he "tried" before. We wanted to create a little mystique about what was going on, but the scene we envisioned was that this guy wasn't able to make love to his new wife because he was actually gay. This was back in the days when it wasn't as accepted to be as open about who you were if you were gay, and there were plenty of situations where some guys would try to fit themselves into the mold of the straight world by marrying a woman. I started thinking about what that experience might be like for the women in those situations, and that's where that idea came from. As writers we were getting bolder about addressing topics that had been viewed as taboo, so we decided to just go for it with "Band of Gold." Though Motown wouldn't have been the right setting for that song, we knew we could stretch a bit further at our own company.

That's another of my songwriting principles: *Know when to push the envelope.* **The flip side of that coin is knowing when not to push the envelope. It usually isn't a good idea to write about something that's going to make your audience uncomfortable simply for the sake of making them uncomfortable. But there's also something to be said for writing songs that might leave people a bit unsettled for the sake of making them think or moving them emotionally. You can't make a gimmick out of that kind of thing, but a few well-timed envelope pushes usually make for a more interesting songwriter.**

Thanks to those early hits like "Give Me Just a Little More Time" and "Band of Gold," our company was quickly picking up steam. Hot Wax was distributed by Buddah Records, while Invictus was distributed by Capitol. We put some artists on Invictus and some on Hot Wax, but I don't think there was any real rhyme or reason to why a particular act would get assigned to one label or the other. All these artists were R&B or pop acts, so it wasn't as if one label was meant to have a different identity or a different slant in terms of genre. Since only so many artists from a single label will get played on the radio, we just split them up between the imprints to help us get more exposure and more airplay. It's the same thing Berry did with Tamla and Motown. Having two labels just gave us more bang for our buck, but it was probably a little unusual that our two labels were distributed by two separate companies. Buddha and Capitol both knew we had deals with the other, but they just had to trust us that it would work out in everyone's favor. And, for a while, it did.

Having hits right off the bat didn't give us much time to get philosophical or to sit around and analyze how we were doing what we were doing. I felt more like I was caught up in a tornado. Now that there were a lot more people in the mix, I wasn't working with Brian and Eddie as close as I once had. We also had to adjust to a more fluid situation in terms of the musicians we were working with.

When we were working with the Funk Brothers at Motown, we could pretty much count on working with the same group of guys at all of the sessions. Once we made the move, we still used some of the Funk Brothers when they were available, but we couldn't count on having them whenever we wanted. Some of those guys would play Motown sessions during the day and then head over to our studio at night. Many of our sessions were a mix of familiar faces and new blood that Jeffrey Bowen recruited. Fortunately, Jeffrey was very good at finding new talent.

One of the key people working with us at Hot Wax and Invictus was McKinley Jackson. He was the leader of a group called The Peps that later changed its name to The Politicians. They became the house band at the Twenty Grand Club and eventually became the core of our evolving studio crew. McKinley became the default arranger for almost everything we recorded, filling a crucial role that Paul Riser had filled when we were at Motown.

One of the guys that McKinley brought in as a studio musician was Ray Parker, Jr. The young guitarist was just a teenager at the time, but I was blown away by his chops. Of course he would go on to a great career writing, producing, performing, and playing on a bunch of hit songs of his own. Most people remember him for the *Ghostbusters* theme song, but he did a whole of great stuff after those early days recording with us in Detroit.

To be honest, that period at our company is kind of a blur, but at least it's a blur of success. Freda Payne had another hit with "Deeper & Deeper," which landed in the R&B Top 10 while her Invictus labelmates The Chairmen of the Board scored a string of hits, including "(You've Got Me) Dangling on a String," "Everything's Tuesday," and "Chairman of the Board." Our Hot Wax releases were doing great, too. 100 Proof (Aged in Soul) scored an R&B hit with "Too Many Cooks (Spoil the Soup)," and blue-eyed soul group The Flaming Ember had pop and R&B hits with "Mind, Body and Soul" and "Westbound #9."

Those were just the songs where Holland-Dozier-Holland was involved in the songwriting process. What I really liked about the company was that we could nurture the talents of a team of songwriters and producers that, in addition to Ron Dunbar, included Greg Perry, Angelo Bond, Barney Perkins, and General Johnson, who quickly expanded his role as a member of The Chairmen of the Board to become a key figure in the company. General co-wrote the second Chairmen of the Board single with us, "(You've Got Me) Dangling on a String," which became a Top 20 R&B and Top 40 pop hit. He also teamed up with Greg Perry, Ron Dunbar, and Angelo Bond to write "Pay to the Piper," which reached number four on the R&B chart and number thirteen on the pop chart. But he wasn't only writing songs for The Chairmen. General teamed with Perry and Bond to write "Somebody's Been Sleeping," which became a Top 10 R&B and pop hit for 100 Proof (Aged in Soul) in 1970.

General and Ron Dunbar also co-wrote a now-classic song that was included on The Chairmen of the Board's debut album. Though it was never a hit for The Chairmen, when Atlantic soul singer Clarence Carter heard "Patches" on their album, he released his own version. Carter made it a Top 5 pop single, and Ron and General won the Grammy Award for Best Rhythm & Blues Song. That kind of success helped strengthen our publishing company, Gold Forever Music.

The best example of our team's ability to flourish was the continued success of Honey Cone, which dropped "The" from its name and had a string of hits in 1971 that resulted from the great songwriting and production of General Johnson and Greg Perry. The first was "Want Ads," a song that had originally been recorded by The Glass House but was ultimately released by Honey Cone instead. It hit number one on both the pop and R&B charts and was followed by the extremely successful singles "Stick-Up" and "One Monkey Don't Stop No Show."

After the success of "Want Ads," Eddie gave Honey Cone the full Motown treatment. He sent them to charm school and secured them choreography lessons, courtesy of Cholly Atkins, who had worked with everyone who was anyone at Motown. Honey Cone became a priority for the company and were certainly our biggest stars.

That same year, Ron Dunbar and Clyde Wilson wrote a gold-selling single called "She's Not Just Another Woman" for an Invictus group called 8th Day that was actually the same guys from 100 Proof (Aged in Soul). Ron then partnered with Greg Perry, General Johnson, and Angelo Bond for another Top 5 R&B single for 8th Day called "You've Got to Crawl (Before You Walk)." And if that wasn't enough success for one year, Greg, General, and Angelo also wrote "Bring The Boys Home," a Top 5 R&B hit for Freda Payne from her second LP, *Contact*.

Released in 1971, the *Contact* album represents an important shift in that era. Up to that point, we had focused mostly on singles, but the album was becoming king, and concept albums were just starting to become important. Brian Holland and I worked closely together on seven of the songs for what would be the first real concept LP I'd set out to help write. Built around the themes of sadness and heartbreak, the album earned Freda a Grammy nomination for Best Female R&B vocal performance. But I primarily remember it because it was the last real project that I have fond memories of working on before I decided it was time to part ways with the Hollands.

Chapter Fourteen

IN MY LONELY ROOM

Despite our commercial success with the Hot Wax and
Invictus labels, I look back at the first half of the 1970s as a
time of turmoil and transition. To an outsider, it might have
looked like the team of Holland-Dozier-Holland was on top
of the world, but I wasn't happy about how things were going.
At Motown we were a well-oiled machine, and each of the
three of us had a distinct role to play that contributed to the
success of the whole. We were hyper-focused, and we knew
how to deliver the goods. Running a label group with various
producers, songwriters, and support staff, however, meant that
most days were dedicated to putting out whatever fire needed
to be dealt with.

Launching our own company was exciting at first, but as time went on, Brian and Eddie and I weren't working together as closely as we once had. The three of us were the quality control team, but we didn't continue that formal meeting format like we'd done at Motown. We rarely got together to discuss songs or who would cut them, and we each began traveling different roads as we got into our own responsibilities at the company. I began to get annoyed when I realized I was spending more and more time in the office rather than the recording studio. Berry Gordy and Eddie Holland are the kind of guys who have a love for the music business, but I'm not wired the same way. I've always been passionately in love with the music, so I don't want to be behind a desk. I want to be behind a piano or a recording console!

As the strongest personality of the three of us, Eddie usually took charge when it came to business matters. It got to the point where I was running around dealing with one little crisis or another, but half the time I didn't even know what was going on with the bigger picture. Plus, even though Brian and I had always been close, when you're in a partnership with two brothers, you're always going to feel like the odd man out. Brothers stick together because blood is thicker than water. That's just how it is.

One of the early signs that we weren't on the same page with one another was an increasing difference in our response to some of the music that was presented to us. One example really sticks out in my mind. Laura Lee had been a successful singer on Chess Records with R&B hits like "Dirty Man" and "Up Tight Good Man" before she moved over to Hot Wax in 1971. She had some hits with our company, too, including "Women's Love Rights," "Rip Off," "If You Can Beat Me Rockin' (You Can Have My Chair)," and a cover of "Crumbs Off the Table." Laura was also known for her off-and-on relationship with soul singer Al Green, who credited her as the inspiration behind some of his songs, including "I Can't Get Next to You" and "Tired of Being Alone." Because of his relationship with Laura, Al brought us what would become his first big album to see if we'd be interested in distributing it. I thought it was fantastic, but the others didn't get it. I was dismayed when our company passed on Al Green.

That wasn't the only creative decision that concerned me. One of the acts on the roster that I didn't think we handled well was George Clinton's Parliament. George had been at Motown as a producer and songwriter for a while before his five-man vocal group, then known as The Parliaments, scored a hit with "(I Wanna) Testify" on Revilot Records in 1967. After the label went bankrupt, George shifted the spotlight from the singers to the backing band, redubbing the group Funkadelic. They signed with Detroit's Westbound Records and started finding local success with their blend of funk, soul, and psychedelic rock when their 1970 album debuted.

Jeffrey Bowen saw an opportunity. If Funkadelic was basically a showcase for The Parliaments' backing band with support from the vocalists, then why couldn't they also record under a different name showcasing the vocalists with support from the band? He signed George's group and suggested the name Parliament. Just as we had two distinct labels with two distinct distributors, George could have two distinct band names that recorded for two distinct companies. Funkadelic would remain a Westbound Records act, while Parliament would record for Invictus.

We released Parliament's *Osmium* album in 1970, but it didn't work out. For starters, this was around the time when Clarence Carter released his cover version of "Patches." Jeffrey Bowen was pissed off at one of the local radio stations for playing Carter's single instead of promoting the original Chairmen of the Board version, so he wouldn't give them promotional copies of the next single we released. That single happened to be Parliament's "I Call

My Baby Pussycat." As a result, we weren't able to build that local buzz that creates the spark needed to ignite a national hit. On top of that, our company eventually tried to stop George from recording as Funkadelic on the Westbound label, even though he was actually with Westbound first. Things got contentious, George got upset, and that was pretty much the end of the story in terms of Parliament's relationship with Invictus Records. George went on to release about a half dozen Gold and Platinum albums for the Casablanca label later in the decade. Things could have turned out very differently for Invictus had we not botched that first release.

One of the groups that George Clinton greatly influenced was The Ohio Players. That's another group that we passed on. When they weren't signed to Invictus or Hot Wax they went over to Funkadelic's home at the Westbound label, eventually moving to Mercury Records, where they released a string of Platinum-selling albums and hit the top of the singles chart with hits like "Fire" and "Love Rollercoaster." Again, I really liked them, but it wasn't Eddie's cup of tea. I've often wondered what would have happened if our company had embraced Al Green, Parliament, and The Ohio Players when we had the chance.

When I realized that the Hollands and I weren't going in the same direction, I became despondent, and I admittedly disengaged from the business. I felt like they were really shooting themselves in the foot by missing out on opportunities to find success with the kinds of acts that would redefine R&B music in the 1970s. I thought, *If we're turning down people like this, what does it say about our company's ability to spot talent?* I always thought I had pretty good ears, but it seemed I was out of step with the company when it came to some of these artists. I remember thinking, *If this was Berry Gordy, he would've signed these acts immediately!* But it wasn't just about musical taste. If the company wasn't going to sign acts that

I really believed in, that meant I didn't really have a voice. Plus, I felt like they were effectively taking money out of my pocket if we were going to pass on stuff that I thought was obviously hit material. I don't know what they were thinking, but they weren't thinking what I was thinking!

I was also feeling more and more out of the loop in terms of how the business was operated and where the money was going. As I mentioned, I'd signed over power of attorney at the start of the whole thing and had simply trusted Eddie to set it all up while I concentrated on writing and working in the recording studio. We had this lawyer named Frederick Patmon who represented us at Motown, and he was our partner in getting everything established with the new companies. We were each supposed to receive an equal share of the various businesses. I didn't care about the details. What I did care about, however, was making music and being compensated fairly for my work. That's why I left Motown. I understand that starting a new company requires investment, but I wasn't seeing anything from our new businesses, and I was starting to wonder if Patmon was looking out for my best interests. It all seemed very strange to me, and I was feeling more and more like I needed to get free to just do my own thing.

That era was a dark hour for me professionally. Though I was discouraged, I wouldn't allow myself to give up. I was determined to start looking for a way out. I always believe that there's another avenue to pursue if the one you're on isn't right. Sometimes, it can take some time to find it. A principle I've tried to embrace is to *believe and have faith, even when it's hard to see the fruits of your labor.* **Your dream can come true, but it never will if you give up. It's easy to believe and have faith when things are going well, but when you're in the midst of challenges is when your faith is tested. That's the time to double down and hang in there.**

I was certainly being tested in the early 1970s. In addition to my frustrations with the Hollands, I was facing a good bit of change in my personal life as well. I married my second wife, Daphne, in 1969 right after my divorce from Ann was finalized. Oddly enough, we slipped across the state line to Toledo, Ohio, where you could get married quickly without a lot of fanfare. That's the same place my mom and dad had gone to get married years before. Daphne and I met at a Sunset Strip nightclub called The Trip in 1967. That's fitting, because our relationship ultimately turned out to be a trip alright!

Daphne and I started seeing one another, and she moved in with me in Detroit around the same time we were getting our company off the ground. She was a beautiful and charming model, but what really attracted me to her was that I thought she was the kind of woman I should have on my arm. I allowed myself to be a little seduced by the idea that if you're going to be a big shot in the music industry, then you need to drive the right car, wear the right clothes, and have the right trophy wife by your side. Let me tell you, that's not the right foundation for a strong marriage partnership!

One thing Daphne and I were great at was fighting. She was a Los Angeles native and never wanted to move to Detroit to begin with. I think that difference in opinion about where to live created a foundation of resentment upon which the rest of our relationship was built. Almost as soon as she moved into my house in Detroit, Daphne was looking for a way to get back to California. Sometimes she'd return to the West Coast for months at a time. I subsidized her increasingly lavish lifestyle on the West Coast while I slept alone in our bed back home in Detroit. At least when she was gone, the house was quiet, and nobody was screaming. As time went on, and there wasn't any real money coming in from the company, things became strained for me financially. When I tried to rein in Daphne's spending a little bit, things between us got even more tense.

One night when Daphne was away, my doorbell rang. I could hear some commotion outside as my housekeeper answered the door. A moment later she called up the stairs, "Mr. Dozier, there's a man at the door who says he's your father. He's got some other men with him, too." I strained to hear what was going on outside and caught one of the voices. "Man, you're crazy. Your son don't live in no Palmer Woods." Somebody else chimed in, "We better get our black asses out of here before the police show up and throw us all in jail." Then I recognized one of the voices as my dad's: "It's OK, man. I'm telling you my *son* lives here." I had to laugh to myself at the scene I could hear going on out there. "Go ahead and let 'em into the den," I called downstairs. "Please offer 'em something to drink, and I'll be there in a couple of minutes."

When I got downstairs, I saw my father showing his drinking buddies around. "I told you this was my son's place," he was bragging as he pointed to the Gold records and the various awards on the wall. "Hey, Pop," I said. He spun around. "Lamont! There's my boy!" He came over and gave me a big hug. I could smell the liquor on his breath, and it was obvious he and his crew had been partying. As he introduced me to his friends, they all took off their hats and shifted around nervously. I could tell they felt like fish out of water, but my dad was grinning from ear to ear, and it felt good to know he was proud of me.

Unfortunately I had to pay an uncomfortable visit to my father not long after that. There was a woman he'd been staying with, and I got a call from her grown son. He told me, "Man, I don't know how to tell you this, but your father is abusing my mother and I need you to do something or I'm gonna hurt him." I had to go over there to try to talk to my dad, but he was drunk out of his mind. I said, "Listen, man, you can't be slapping this woman around like that. This guy was nice enough to call me before he came over here to kick your ass. He didn't have to do that. You can't be beating up this man's mother and not expect him to do something about it." My father was blabbering on saying, "I don't know why I do this" and all sorts of stuff, but there was no excuse for it. "You need to get your shit and move out," I told him. "You two weren't meant to be together, and even if you were, you don't treat anybody like that." He kind of nodded like he understood, but I finally left in disgust.

A couple of months later my dad stopped by my place again on a cloudy afternoon. He looked like he had something on his mind, so I invited him in to talk for a bit. As we settled down into a couple of oversized chairs in the den, he cleared his throat and shifted his gaze to an imaginary spot on the carpet. "I just wanted to come by to apologize," he said softly. "I know I haven't always done things right, and I haven't been a great father. I'm sorry for that." He looked up tentatively as if he was trying to gauge my reaction. I nodded slowly. "Nobody believes it when I say you're my son," he continued. "Our family is so proud of you, Lamont, and I just want to thank you for letting me be your father." I thought that was kind of a strange thing to say, as if I had any choice in the matter, but I knew he was trying to make amends in in his own way. "It's OK, Dad," I finally responded.

Shortly thereafter I got a phone call from my father's sister, Carrie. "Your dad's in a bad way," she said. "The doctors don't give him long." Two weeks later he was dead. He had cirrhosis of the liver from drinking corn liquor, bathtub gin, or whatever they called it. He was only fifty-one years old.

Though my father and I never had much of a relationship, his death got me thinking about what kind of man I wanted to be. I started reflecting on my own mortality and thinking about how we all eventually pass on from this world. We're not guaranteed a set number of days, and any day could be our last. I didn't want to put my energy into a marriage that wasn't meant to be or a business situation that wasn't in synch with my instincts as a creative person. Instead of inspiring me to cut loose and start fresh, however, it overwhelmed me and filled me with anxiety. I sank into a bit of depression. My tendency to avoid conflict even extended to facing down my own inner demons, and instead of my father's alcohol-related death at an early age prompting me to give up drinking, I kept turning to the bottle as a way to escape.

One night I was driving home drunk and crashed my car into a tree. The impact knocked the tree into some electrical wires, which fell down onto the car. I was too foggy to understand what was going on and was sitting there trying to figure out exactly what happened. Miraculously, Ron Dunbar happened to drive by at that moment and recognized my car. He pulled over. "Lamont," he yelled. "Don't move! You need to stay in the car while I get some help." I was too out of it to process what he was saying, so I opened the door, jumped out of the car, and stumbled over to him. There's no other way to explain why I didn't electrocute myself other than to say that the Master Muse wasn't done with me yet. Ron took me to the hospital to get checked out and then carried me home. Daphne was not amused. Before I could fall into bed to sleep it off, she decided we needed to yell at each other about it for a couple of hours.

My wife and I could barely stand one another, my business partners and I had very different ideas about what to invest in, and I was becoming a slave to the very thing that killed my father. I ended up developing agoraphobia, and it got to the point where any time I left the house I was terrified. It would take everything within me to go anywhere, and I experienced panic attacks on several occasions.

I was trying to cope with these feelings by myself, but I didn't have the tools to address what I was going through. Daphne finally convinced me to go see this expensive therapist, which I did for several months. I'd go every week, and he'd ask me all sorts of questions, but my crippling fears didn't seem to be getting any better. One day I was in a session with him and allowed myself to get really vulnerable. I was opening up to this guy in a major way, just pouring my heart out and going on and on. I was stretched out on the couch, and he was in his chair, just outside my peripheral vision. At some point I stopped talking to give him a chance to weigh in, but he was silent. Just as I was about to turn to make sure he was still there, the guy started snoring. I was paying this dude a *lot* of money to help me with my anxiety and agoraphobia, and he was sleeping while I bared my soul to him. I was so angry, I just got up and walked out.

I was absolutely fuming on the way home when something occurred to me. I wasn't anxious. Normally, my agoraphobia had me all twisted up about going out and driving around, but I'd gotten so pissed at the therapist that my usual fear hadn't kicked in. That was when I decided I'd had enough. I felt like I'd been used, abused, and messed over too many times, so when this guy checked out on me, something snapped. I decided I was done with letting fear and anxiety rule my life. I was finished with being a passive doormat. I was fed up with anxiety and agoraphobia, and if a therapist couldn't help me, I'd face it down myself. I'd been too quiet, too fearful, too passive, and too afraid of confrontation for too long. I wouldn't be victimized by anyone or any circumstances anymore. I wouldn't allow a fear of "rocking the boat" force me to stuff all those feelings down until I was hyperventilating. I was done. When that therapist fell asleep, I woke up!

Chapter Fifteen

SLIPPING AWAY

I originally signed with Motown because I wanted to be a singer, but Berry Gordy didn't need any more singers by the time I came along. He needed writers and producers. During my years at Hitsville, my thoughts about performing my own songs were pushed further and further onto the back burner until I was too overwhelmed and overworked to have the capacity to even entertain such thoughts. Once we had a chance to get ourselves established with the Hot Wax and Invictus labels, however, that old desire came creeping back in.

Not long after my encounter with the snoring psychiatrist, I went to see my Uncle James. I thought he might be able to give me some insight about what path I should take. James was always my top hype man, and I turned to him many times in my life when I needed a shot of encouragement. "I see you rising from the ashes," he told me. "Your power is in your music and your voice, and that's the music that will be your way forward. Focus on your first love, and it will take you where you want to be."

I decided I was going to start writing the best songs I could come up with, and I was going to find a way to not only write them but to produce them and sing them myself. As I said goodbye to anxiety and depression, I would open myself up to the muse to receive the songs that were intended to flow out of me. The music, I decided, was going to be my path to freedom.

This was the era when I came to understand one of my songwriting principles that's a little controversial to some people: *There's no such thing as writer's block.* **Instead of pulling back as a songwriter when I was facing obstacles, I decided to lean in. When I have the chance to talk to aspiring songwriters, I always tell them to stop feeding those lies about writer's block. Writer's block only exists in your mind, and if you tell yourself you have it, it will cripple your ability to function as a creative person. Sometimes you can't figure out what to do next, but that's not writer's block. If you tell yourself it is, you'll back off instead of plowing through and pushing forward. The answer to so-called writer's block is doing the work. If you press on, the answers you need will come through. You have to show the muses that you're capable and committed; then you'll get the answers you need. A higher power will come to your assistance when you're deliberate in your pursuit.**

That's exactly what I did in 1972, and it opened up a new opportunity when I recorded a handful of songs to issue as a solo artist. I figured if I could release a good showpiece for myself as an artist on one of our own labels, that would be a calling card for other labels that might want to sign me.

We issued "Don't Leave Me" on Invictus, but Eddie insisted we put it out under the name Holland-Dozier rather than releasing it under my name alone. He argued that, since Holland-Dozier-Holland had some degree of name recognition with the record-buying public, people would be more likely to resonate with it as something familiar. Though I resolved to change my life, that didn't mean I didn't face a few setbacks. In a moment of weakness, I went along to get along. I still think that's a great record, but the general public didn't necessarily know that was my voice on the lead vocal. Not that it mattered much anyway, since it never even hit the charts.

A few months later, Invictus put out "Why Can't We Be Lovers." This time the label read "Holland-Dozier" in large type with "featuring Lamont Dozier" printed in a smaller font beneath it. The song hit the *Billboard* charts in September and had climbed into the R&B Top 10 by Thanksgiving. That became my calling card. I finally had something I could quietly shop around to other labels in hopes of landing a new deal.

I continued to work on a few things for other artists, but I wasn't really invested in it. We recorded a Dionne Warwick album for Warner Bros. in 1972 that they released as *Just Being Myself* the following year. We wrote all but one of the songs and produced it in our studio, but it didn't really do much. As I like to say, in the music business, songs are king. If you don't have the right songs, you're not going to land the hits. In this case, the songs just weren't there. I know I certainly wasn't looking to give up my best material for other artists' projects since I had other plans for my own artist career.

By the end of 1972 I'd virtually disappeared from the office and the studio. I decided I'd do to the Hollands what we'd all done to Berry Gordy when we went on strike at Motown. I was reinvigorated by "Why Can't We Be Lovers," and songs started flowing out of me twenty-four hours a day, seven days a week. I couldn't have stopped them if I'd wanted to! But I wasn't turning these songs in as new compositions for Gold Forever Music. I was stockpiling them for myself.

Eddie was no dummy. It didn't take him long to figure out exactly what I was doing. He knew I was looking to establish my own thing, and he was likely hoping to talk me into staying. I wasn't going to get pinned down or tricked into compromising my vision. I was ready to do things for myself and to do them my way. A popular refrain around the company became "Where's Lamont?" I just couldn't be found. I was ducking and dodging the Hollands and their staff at every turn. They'd send people over to my house, but I just wouldn't answer the door.

I remember one day Brian showed up at my place. When I didn't answer, he started yelling, "Hey, Lamont! Come on, man, come to the door. I gotta tell you what's going on, man. We're working on a new distribution deal with Clive Davis and Columbia Records. It's gonna be big, man. I want to tell you all about it." I just waited for him to give up so I could go back to pounding out ideas on my piano.

My creative renaissance ushered in the clarity to see that there was no good reason for me and Daphne to stay together. She had been spending more and more time out in California, and I think we both knew our relationship was over. It's just that neither of us had said it yet. One day I got a call from my attorney, who was also based in Los Angeles. He said, "Lamont, I don't know how to tell you this, but Daphne and I are in love." I was quiet for a moment. I said, "Man, you've got a beautiful wife and children. Do you know what you're doing?" He said, "We can't help it, Lamont, we're in love." I said, "OK, man. Merry Christmas." He was kind of surprised. He said, "I thought you'd be upset. You don't mind?" I just kind of laughed. "Listen, man," I told him. "Investing in a relationship with Daphne is like buying oats for a dead horse. I'm done, so I hope it works out for you."

That was the "out" I'd been looking for. Soon after, I took Daphne out for a nice dinner. "Listen," I said. "You and I know that we were never meant for one another. We don't do anything but fight, and there's no chemistry between us. I think we both know it was time to go our separate ways long ago. The best thing we can do now is give each other the freedom to go start over." She agreed. There was no drama, and she was gone.

Now it was time to find another partner: a record label. Fortunately for me, the early 1970s was a period when many of the mainstream record companies were investing in expanding their roster of R&B acts. Soul music was big business, and everyone wanted their piece of the market share. In 1972 The Four Tops left Motown and signed with ABC/Dunhill. Their first two singles for their new label, "Keeper of the Castle" and "Ain't No Woman (Like the One I've Got)" became their first Top 10 pop singles since "Bernadette" five years earlier. That impressed me. I saw that the ABC brass was willing to put some muscle into helping Motown refugees evolve stylistically and commercially. On top of that, they purchased the historically black Duke and Peacock labels the following year, showing a real commitment to the genre.

In early 1973 ABC/Dunhill hired Otis Smith away from our labels to oversee the expansion of their R&B roster. Otis had actually worked for them previously before he became a vice president at our company. Like me, he had grown disillusioned and took an opportunity to return to the place where he'd previously thrived. Arleen Schesel, who had worked with Otis, left with him to become ABC/Dunhill's national promotion director for its R&B roster.

Arleen had been a real champion of "Why Can't We Be Lovers" when she was working for Invictus, but I later found out it could have been bigger. She called me one day once she was settled at ABC/Dunhill. "I thought that it would be only fair to tell you," she said, "that I was instructed to pull back on my promotion of your single when I was at Invictus. It could have been a much bigger pop hit if they'd let me keep working it, but my hands were tied." I guess it was obvious what I was trying to do, and everyone knew that a hit record would only ease my departure. Arleen really believed in me as a singer, so she made that call to let me know that she would still like to work with me. She encouraged Otis to sign me, and he eventually made an offer that included my own production company, the opportunity to work with my own stable of writers and producers, and a nice piece of money. Though I'd talked with some other labels, I decided to go with ABC/Dunhill. I knew Arleen and Otis, and it felt like the right fit.

The new deal meant I would relocate to Los Angeles, but it was going to be tricky to get out of town without the Hollands noticing. What wouldn't be tricky was putting together a team to take with me. A lot of people had grown really unhappy with the company. Paychecks were bouncing, and lawsuits had already begun. McKinley Jackson and Barney Perkins agreed to come with me. Popcorn Wylie came, too, though he opted to continue to live in Detroit and commute back and forth to Los Angeles. My brother Reggie, whom I'd put through audio engineering school and was becoming a reliable studio whiz in his own right, also came aboard as a recording engineer. At first, however, he stayed in Detroit as a decoy. If he was still at my house for a while, most people would assume I was still around, too. Once he did eventually head for the coast, my sister Norma and her husband stayed at my place so it would appear as if I might return at any time.

There was a guy named James Reddick who became like a personal assistant to me. He was from Detroit but had moved to Los Angeles, where he found a house for me to live in and became my information source and guide to L.A. He helped lay a lot of the groundwork so that things would go smoothly when I made my big move.

Just before we made our escape, Ronnie Dunbar dropped by the house. I knew he was on a reconnaissance mission for Eddie, and there was no hiding the trucks and boxes that were all over the place. Come to think of it, maybe it wasn't such a miracle that Ron "happened" to drive by that night when I crashed my car and nearly electrocuted myself on those power lines. Maybe he had been keeping tabs on me for a good while. At any rate, the door was open when he got to my house, so he strolled in. When he saw me, he stuck his hands in his pockets and tried to act nonchalant. "You moving, Lamont?" I shook my head. "No, man," I told him. "This is all the rest of Daphne's shit. I've got to send it all off to her in California. It's a pain, man." Ronnie wasn't buying that line for a second. "Eddie and Brian know you're not happy," he continued. "They suspected you'd be leaving town." I knew Ron would tell the Hollands whatever I told him, so I decided to send them on a wild goose chase. "Alright, man," I said. "I'll tell you what's going on, but can you keep a secret?" Ronnie nodded. "OK, I don't want Eddie and Brian to known, but I'm leaving town in a few weeks. I've been talking to RCA and Polydor, and they're both in a bidding war to sign me. I'll make my final decision in the next few days about which one of them I'm gonna go with."

In reality, I'd already signed the deal with ABC/Dunhill and was leaving the very next day to fly to the house I had already rented in Studio City, in Los Angeles's San Fernando Valley. They would never have imagined in a million years that I'd sign with

ABC/Dunhill. Otis Smith had left under strained conditions, and they probably assumed he hated all three of us. Of course Ronnie told the Hollands exactly what I'd said, which kept everyone busy chasing their tails for a little while. By the time they figured it out, I was already gone.

I boarded the plane to California with two cases of cassettes full of the songs that I'd been working on like a madman for the previous several months. Once the plane took off from Detroit, however, an old friend—actually, I should say an old enemy—came creeping up on me unexpectedly. It was a bumpy plane ride, and Mr. Agoraphobia decided to return. I'd taken the step of leaving the Hollands and leaving Detroit, but my anxiety had suddenly returned with a vengeance. I remember getting up several times during the flight to go vomit in the lavatory.

I thought I was leaving my fears in Detroit, but once I landed, I was finally able to leave them on the plane. I had to give myself a little pep talk: *OK, Lamont. You did it. You've come out here, and these folks at ABC/Dunhill have shown that they really believe in you. You can't let them think you're on shaky ground or anything. It's time to pull it together and show them you can deliver.* I got off that plane, and when my feet touched the California ground, I was a new man ready to start a new life.

I moved into my place on Dona Evita Drive, right off Laurel Canyon, and immediately felt like I was home. On one of the first days I was there, there was a knock on the door. Dusty Springfield was standing there with a plant. When I answered, she held it out and I took it in my hands. Then she just ran away! I guess she was shy and maybe had a little anxiety of her own. I recognized that kind of nervous behavior. It was probably really hard for her to come up to the house like that, so I really appreciated it. It was a very sweet gesture.

We went in the studio to start recording my new album pretty quickly after I got to Los Angeles. By the end of 1973 my debut ABC single "Trying to Hold on to My Woman" was making its way up the charts. The idea behind that song was that my friends might mock me for being henpecked, but I wasn't going to make the same mistakes I'd made in the past. I'd lost my woman before because I didn't treat her as good as I should have, but I wasn't going to let that happen again. I had a good woman now, and I was going to keep her! The song wasn't written about my own life per se, but it was kind of like those letters I wrote back when I was a kid and they called me the Candy Man. It was the kind of thing that women need to hear, but men aren't always the best at saying. I was trying to say it for all the guys out there who couldn't say it for themselves.

Apparently it really worked for one guy. One day I was sitting in my car at a red light in Los Angeles. This guy pulled up next to me and recognized me. He motioned for me to roll down my window. "Hey, man," he shouted. "I just want to tell you that your song 'Trying to Hold on to My Woman' helped me get back together with my wife when we were having some troubles. God bless you, man." I gave him a thumbs up just as the light changed, and he pulled off. That kind of thing is priceless. To write a song that people love hearing is great, but to feel like I helped save somebody's relationship? Man, that's fantastic!

There are different types of songwriters out there. Some are artist writers who are deeply confessional, while others are very commercially oriented. In either case, the songs that stand the test of time are the ones people can connect with on a personal level. I talk about writing songs from a place that moves you, but *the best songwriters know how to take personal feelings and translate them into universal experiences.* It always brings me joy when someone feels like one of my songs put words to something they

were going through. If you can start with that personal, passionate spark and then widen your message so that people can project their own experiences onto it, then you've achieved one of the building blocks of what it takes to be a special kind of writer.

I was fortunate enough to make that connection with "Trying to Hold on to My Woman." I guess plenty of other people felt the same way as that guy at the traffic light because the single reached the Top 5 on the R&B chart and climbed into the Top 15 on the pop chart, too. Of course, Arleen and her staff did a great job promoting the record. She basically continued her winning ways that she'd done on "Why Can't We Be Lovers," and I give her a lot of credit for helping me establish myself as a solo artist.

When the album was released, we called it *Out Here On My Own,* which was the name of the last song on the second side of the LP. Of course that title was also an important statement for me personally. I finally *was* out there on my own and doing my own thing. ABC put up a billboard advertising the album right across the street from the Hollands' studio in Detroit. They left it up for a couple of months, and that's when everybody in town saw that title and knew I was gone. Man, every time the Hollands looked out the window they had to see me!

If you look at the credits on that album, it shows that most of the songs were written by my personal assistant, James Reddick, and my arranger, McKinley Jackson. Of course I actually wrote all the songs by myself. It was the same situation as when we left Motown. I still had a publishing contract with Gold Forever Songs, so I had to create my own version of "Edythe Wayne." For some reason, I thought it looked better to have two names on there instead of just one. Though the two of us did work together, McKinley Jackson was listed as the album's producer, since I still had a production contract with the Hollands.

The following year, 1974, ABC/Dunhill released the second single from my debut album, "Fish Ain't Bitin.'" It started making its way up the charts but stalled out around number sixty. I hardly ever got political in my songs, but I criticized Richard Nixon in the lyrics of that one, and ABC received some kind of letter from the White House saying they should stop promoting a record that disparaged the president. ABC decided to take out an ad in *Cash Box* magazine that reprinted the full letter. You couldn't have asked for better publicity! Even though the single had basically died on its own, that ad revived interest in it. The disc jockeys started playing it more, and sales went through the roof. I was invited to perform it on *Soul Train*, and it ultimately became another Top 5 R&B hit. Richard Nixon saved my record. Thank you, Tricky Dick!

Unfortunately, I wasn't able to disentangle myself from Invictus without some complications. Following the success of *Out Here On My Own,* the Hollands released an unauthorized album called *Love and Beauty.* The cover falsely proclaimed it "the new Lamont Dozier album," creating the impression that it was the follow-up to my ABC debut. In reality, the LP was a cobbled-together collection of my Invictus singles, some instrumental mixes, a couple of stray recordings that had been left in the can, and some unfinished demos. Though I had songwriting and production contracts with the Hollands, I never had an artist contract with them. ABC sent a cease and desist letter to Columbia Records, which was distributing Invictus by then, but things only got nastier.

When I left the Hollands, I just walked away. In terms of what they were doing business-wise, I just cut the cord. By now you know that business never interested me, but I knew I needed a top-notch lawyer to get everything sorted out. I recruited William Krasilovsky, who was one of the best. He came on board and, following his direction in the early summer of 1974, we initiated a lawsuit against the Hollands for my share of the companies. I'd never received any money or any accounting when I was with them, and I felt like it was time to make it right. They then countersued, asserting that I'd breached my contracts. They even sued ABC for allegedly conspiring to drive their company into the ground by mining its people. That included McKinley Jackson, Freda Payne, Tony Newton, Angelo Bond, and others who came over to ABC because they weren't happy at Invictus. It seemed like everybody was suing everybody during that time.

As part of that whole legal drama, Krasilovsky filed a malpractice suit against Frederick Patmon, the attorney who was supposed to be our business partner in Invictus, Hot Wax, and the various associated companies. Patmon was dishonest in his dealings with me when everything was being established, and he ended up losing his license over it. He was suspended from practicing law for a long time and had to pay a hefty penalty. It was validating that the courts recognized that I'd been wronged, but that was only one piece of a multifaceted series of lawsuits that dragged on for a very long time.

I was locked in legal disputes with the Hollands for the better part of a decade, and we didn't even speak to each other during that time. In the end I was finally freed from all my contracts with the Hollands, but I had to forfeit my ownership share of Invictus, Hot Wax and our publishing companies to get completely disentangled. The whole thing was unpleasant, unfortunate, and very expensive. Sometimes it seems like the real winners of these prolonged legal showdowns are the attorneys. I'm a creator, not a fighter, so I just wanted to get everything resolved so I could get on with my life and various projects apart from Eddie and Brian.

Chapter Sixteen

I'M IN A DIFFERENT WORLD

One of the greatest honors of my career was getting voted
"number-one pop male vocalist for 1974" by *Billboard* magazine.
It was so gratifying to receive that kind of recognition for
something that I'd done on my own. While I was riding high
from that boost of encouragement, and while "Fish Ain't Bitin'"
was still climbing up the charts, ABC released my second album,
Black Bach, in May of 1975. By that point I was able to use my
own name on the songwriting credits again.

I'd always wanted to put out an album called *Black Bach* since
back in the Motown days. There was a saxophone player there who
told me, "Man, when you play those chords you come up with,
you sound like Bach." That was a huge compliment to me, "I can't
thank you enough for saying that, man," I told him. "Back when

I was a little guy, I'd sit on the piano bench listening to my Aunt Eula playing Bach's music and I just fell in love with it." He nodded. "Yeah," he responded, "well you were sure paying attention, man. You picked up on his spirit or something with those intricate chord voicings you use. I know you don't have any formal training, but you just naturally do things the way Bach would do."

Bach was the father of harmony, and I was always in awe of how much time he put into perfecting his craft. It wasn't about the money for guys like him. A lot of those legendary composers died impoverished, but they didn't care. They weren't looking for a buck; they were just obsessed with music. By declaring myself the "Black Bach," I wasn't trying to be arrogant. I was reclaiming my identity as someone who was madly and passionately in love with music. It wasn't about money or contracts or lawsuits or business or any of the rest of it. It was all about the love of the music.

I mentioned earlier that if you want to make it as a songwriter, you have to have a relentless work ethic. That's true, but there has to be something behind that work ethic if you want to fuel it for the long haul. In reality, someone can work really hard at something for a little while, but *to truly go the distance as a songwriter, you have to be completely consumed by it*. It has to be something that you're going to do even if you never make a dime at it. It has to come from deep inside you. It's almost as if you have to be chosen by the Master Muse. There have been times I've wished I could shake the all-consuming obsession, but God put this thing in me, and it's not going anywhere.

Black Bach yielded my third consecutive Top 5 R&B hit, "Let Me Start Tonite." It's a song about being good to your woman. I've always had an impulse to protect women, and I've tried to be an advocate for women in my music, but in real life my instinct to look out for women sometimes got me into some strange situations.

Though music drove a wedge between me and Ann when we were married, after she kicked me out of our home, she became increasingly preoccupied with maintaining a public image. She would refer to herself as "the first and only Mrs. Lamont Dozier." She enjoyed using my name and, in fact, long after we were divorced, she would host parties at the house I bought for her and my daughter, Michelle, making sure to get these soirées written up in the Detroit social columns as functions put on by "Mr. and Mrs. Lamont Dozier." I thought it was pretty weird. I didn't want to embarrass her in front of Michelle or cause a stink that would impact my daughter in any negative way, so I just ignored it and let it go.

Then, after we were separated in one instance and divorced in the other, Ann gave birth to two other children and gave them my last name. To date I have never had any kind of parental or personal relationship with either of them. Again, my instinct was to protect the feelings and reputations of others, but it created a delicate situation.

Though my personal life was complicated, I was very happy with my career in the mid-1970s. One of the great things about my deal with ABC/Dunhill was that I had the chance to produce albums for other artists. My primary focus was recording my own material, but I never lost my love for working with others in the studio. At first I produced some in-house projects for ABC/Dunhill, including Clarence Carter's *Real* LP in 1974, as well as an album called *Extra Sensory Perception* by Popcorn Wylie, who'd come with me when I left the Hollands.

Funny enough, I even made an album for Motown, thanks to my old friend Ty Hunter. When I left the Hollands, there was a lot of unrest happening around the company. The Glass House broke up in that same era and, ironically, Ty and Scherrie Payne ended up recording for Motown. Scherrie joined the post–Diana Ross Supremes after I recommended her to Mary Wilson, while Ty joined The Originals. They were kind of a male version of the The Andantes that appeared on a ton of Motown hits, including Jimmy Ruffin's "What Becomes of the Brokenhearted" and Stevie Wonder's "Yester-Me, Yester-You, Yesterday." By the early 1970s, they were having hits of their own, including "Baby, I'm For Real" and "The Bells," which Marvin Gaye produced. When singer C. P. Spencer departed in 1973, Ty took his place, and the group relocated to California. Thanks to Ty, I wrote and produced everything on The Originals' *California Sunset* album. We used the same crew that worked on *Black Bach,* and I think of those projects as unofficial companion pieces. It wasn't a big commercial hit, but I'm still very proud of that album.

In that same era, I did an album with Z. Z. Hill called *Keep On Lovin' You.* Neil Portnow was at United Artists at the time and called me to come over to work with Z. Z. The single "I Created a Monster" hit the R&B charts, and the album ended up selling pretty well. I don't know what kind of understanding Neil had with his boss, but I later found out that the album wasn't supposed to be a success. It was intended to be some kind of a write-off, and I overheard a conversation where Neil's boss was saying, "We're not supposed to be selling a bunch of goddamn records here! What do you guys think you're doing?" I couldn't believe my ears. That's when I figured out that sometimes some of these labels make more money with write-offs. That was a real eye-opener for me!

The following year I made an album with Margie Joseph for the Cotillion label called *Hear the Words, Feel the Feeling.* The single "Don't Turn the Lights Off" was a reworking of one of the songs I had recorded with The Originals. It hit the R&B chart and helped keep me in demand as a producer.

I was actually supposed to tour in support of my ABC albums.
I wanted to do it, but I just couldn't refuse all the people who
were coming around and asking me to produce albums for them.
I loved writing and being in the studio more than I loved hitting
the road and performing live.

After *Black Bach*, I recorded another album for ABC called
Prophecy, but it was never released. It wasn't that the company
didn't like it, but by the time it was finished, my ABC contract
was up, and I decided not to renew with them. Though I think
of that ABC period in very positive terms, I made the difficult
decision to accept an offer from Warner Bros. Records that I
couldn't refuse. Leaving ABC/Dunhill meant leaving *Prophecy* in
the can. It's too bad because it was a good album. I still listen to
it every now and then. Hopefully it'll see the light of day at some
point, but I had to let go of it at the time since I just couldn't
refuse the opportunity to go to Warner Bros. I'd always wanted
to record for Warners. Plus, they owned Atlantic by that point,
so maybe I subconsciously wanted to make an album for the
company that I'd blown it with when I sent my demanding letter
to Jerry Wexler back in my Romeos days!

The move to Warner Bros. coincided with the dawn of the
disco era, so I jumped on that bandwagon. My first album with
them was called *Right There,* and featured the single "Can't
Get Off Until the Feeling Stops," which is a record I always
liked. That was the biggest single I had in the US with Warner
Bros., but they had their sights set on a much wider reach
than I'd ever experienced in my career. They had me doing all
sorts of promotional trips that took me all over the world for
listening parties and banquets with champagne and the full royal
treatment. I think I even went to Poland on that first Warner
Bros. promotional trip, which was a totally new experience for
me. Warners was spending some serious money raising awareness

about Lamont Dozier the artist when I first signed with them, and it felt great to feel supported.

Probably the most memorable trip I took during the Warner Bros. years came after the release of my second album for them, *Peddlin' Music on the Side*. The single "Going Back to My Roots" wasn't a hit in the US, but it was a massive success in South Africa. The song wasn't inspired by Alex Haley's *Roots* but just emerged from a groove and a bass line that I'd come up with. The original lyric came about when I was visiting Detroit after I'd moved to Los Angeles, but the record was transformed into a nine-and-a-half minute African-themed opus thanks to a brainstorming session with South African trumpeter and arranger Hugh Masekela. The album was produced by Stewart Levine, who had a production company with Masekela, so Hugh and I got together in the studio and came up with some very cool concepts. We decided to put a secret message in the song, so he brought in a group of South African singers to chant in the African Yoruban dialect. This was at the height of Apartheid, when Nelson Mandela was still a political prisoner, so we put that message in there to encourage the people to stay strong and hold on.

The song really connected with the black population of South Africa, who got our message of hope loud and clear. A lot of artists were boycotting the country at the time due to the political situation, but when Mo Ostin at Warner Bros. called to ask if I would go down there, I knew it was the right thing to do. "I think it'd be great if you were to go and let the people know we're in their corner," he said. "It would be really fantastic to show them that Warner Bros. Records and the spirit of the American people are with them in their struggle." I quickly agreed and set out for what would be a truly eye-opening experience.

It took me twenty-seven hours and several plane changes to get from Los Angeles to Johannesburg. When I arrived, I came down the ramp from the plane to a sea of maybe 10,000 people. I assumed they were there to greet some politician or something and was completely shocked to discover they were there to welcome me. As I made my way through customs with the local Warner team, people were pressing in, just wanting to touch me. It was all pretty overwhelming! I'd had the "Tricky Dick" line in "Fish Ain't Bitin'," but I never thought of myself as a political artist. Now I was suddenly at the center of a movement!

Getting through customs was a little nerve-wracking. White guards with machine guns and no sense of humor pressed me about what my business was in their country. One particularly intimidating-looking official barked, "What are you doing down here, Mr. Dozier?" I tried to be as friendly as possible. "Well," I explained, "I'm a recording artist, and I have a record that I'm promoting." He cut me off. "Do you have a camera, sir?" I was confused. "A camera? Uh, no I didn't bring a camera." He jotted something down on a little notepad. "Are you writing anything? Are you a journalist?" I kind of chuckled. He didn't. "No," I replied quickly. "I'm no journalist. I'm just a singer." He scribbled another note. After what seemed like an eternity, they allowed me to proceed. The Warner representative explained that the authorities were suspicious that any Americans coming into the country were on a political mission. I guess that was true, because there were two cops who followed me around and watched me at a distance the entire time I was in the country. I had already been warned by my manager, "They've got microphones in all the buildings. Do not be critical of the government, or you'll be arrested."

When we left the airport, the local Warner Bros. staffers took me straight to a record store where they had an entire ceremony planned for me. It was unlike anything I'd ever experienced before or since. I stood in the middle of the store while people filed by. Someone was directing them, and they would simply come up, touch me, and move on without saying anything at all. It was a really eerie experience to have hundreds of people come by just to touch me, but that was their custom. It was their way of showing appreciation and respect. Later that night I appeared at a local club to sing the song, and the people just went nuts. The experience was deeply spiritual for me, and I could feel the love emanating from everyone in the place.

The following day I was taken to Soweto, where a local family served us lunch. These people had prepared a really nice table with fried chicken and vegetables and this massive spread. I wasn't really hungry, so I ate a few bites and left my plate. A moment later, one of the guys from Warners pulled me aside. "Lamont," he said, "It would be good if you could finish your food. These people prepared all this for us, and this is the equivalent of what they'd normally have in a month." I didn't know the reality of life in South Africa at the time, and when I think back now, I'm still overcome with emotion at the outpouring of love and generosity that they showed me. I rushed back over to that plate and ate every last bit of it. I sucked the chicken bones completely clean. Sometimes it's so easy to take our lives for granted, but when you're confronted with a different reality, it really opens your eyes.

I had never experienced the kind of love and respect that I received on that trip to South Africa. I was down there for ten days and got the chance to go on a safari and do all sorts of things I'd never had the chance to do before. It was a beautiful country, and it was spiritually reenergizing to be in the motherland from which all of humanity sprang.

As touched as I was by the good people I met there, I was constantly shocked by the racial injustice I saw. Even as a visiting American, I encountered some strange moments that underscored how much I took for granted. The new James Bond film, *The Spy Who Loved Me,* was playing when I was down there, and I decided I'd head over to the theater to check it out. As I was leaving the hotel, the bellhop stopped me. "Going out for the evening, Mr. Dozier?" I nodded. "Yeah," I said. "I'm gonna go check out that new James Bond movie." He smiled. "Actually, Mr. Dozier, we can have the film brought here so you can watch it in privacy." I wasn't picking up on the reason for his response. "Oh, no, that's OK," I said, "I don't want to cause any hassle for anyone." He finally had to tell me that I wouldn't be allowed in the theater as a black man. That shocked the hell out of me. As much as I loved the people I met on that trip, I was glad when I got back to America. I had a newfound appreciation for my freedoms in California.

I did one more album for Warner Bros. called *Bittersweet* that was produced by Frank Wilson. I loved working with Frank, and that's still one of my favorite albums. By that point I was in my late thirties and was conscious of staying on top of my game as an artist. I hired a personal trainer and set a goal of losing twenty pounds before embarking on another worldwide promotional tour. The music world was still fully caught up in the disco craze, and it was important to look and sound the part. The label released the funky dance track "Boogie Business" as a single. Like "Goin' Back to My Roots" before it, the song hit *Billboard*'s short-lived disco chart, but didn't break through on either the R&B or pop charts. Some of the other tracks on that album, including one called "I've Got it All with You," are still very special songs to me.

In the end, I recorded three albums for Warner Bros. I was disappointed that they didn't perform better commercially, particularly coming off the solid start I'd established at ABC. Joe Smith and Mo Ostin likely signed me at Warners because the company didn't have a particularly strong R&B roster in the early 1970s. Like most labels at the time, they were looking to beef up their black artist lineup to capitalize on the growing success of soul music. There's some really good stuff on those records, but I came along at a time when the company was still trying to get their R&B situation on firm footing. I think the albums likely would have performed better if Warner Bros. had been better established on the R&B front at the time. I ultimately ended up getting the rights back to the recordings from my Warner Bros. period, so maybe it's time to think about rereleasing some of that material once again.

Unfortunately, commercial success as an artist eluded me in the years right after my Warner Bros. deal was over. I was entering a period that would prove to be a real struggle for me professionally. On the upside, I would have the perfect partner beside me to help navigate some really turbulent times.

Chapter Seventeen

HEAVEN MUST HAVE SENT YOU

After Daphne and I divorced, I started dating around and spent time with several woman, including Scherrie Payne, who had been in The Glass House. I thought Scherrie was a really great singer, so when Mary Wilson was looking for someone to replace Jean Terrell in the Supremes in 1973, I suggested her.

Scherrie and her sister Freda used to go visit this guy named Reverend McGrew, who was kind of a psychic or spiritualist. They both raved about him, so when I was still with Warner Bros., I decided I'd go visit him to see if he had anything to say about my career direction. I made an appointment and, when the day came, I drove over to McGrew's apartment on Curson Avenue in Hancock Park and knocked on the door. He was wearing a long, flowing purple robe and held a lit candle in his hand. The guy was really an over-the-top flamboyant character, and I was a little amused by his dramatic flair. Still, he seemed like a nice person, and I thought he could be of some help, so I followed him through the dark apartment back to the table where he did his readings.

We settled down in our chairs, and I told him that I was trying to figure out what the future would hold for my career as an artist and songwriter. He told me all sorts of stuff about how great it was going to be and how much success I was going to have. I had no clue if he actually knew what he was talking about, but I sure liked the sound of it. After we finished talking about my music, I thought about Scherrie since she had referred me to McGrew in the first place. She and I weren't dating exclusively, but I wondered if there was any future in our little fling, so I asked about it. "You and Scherrie have a spiritual musical connection," he told me, "but that's not a relationship that's meant to be." He was quiet for a minute and I thought maybe that was all he was going to stay. Suddenly I was jolted as he began to speak quickly. "But I am seeing a girl who's gonna come into your life," McGrew continued." I raised my eyebrows. "It will happen around a year from now, and she's going to be a redhead." Intrigued, I leaned forward and rested my elbows on the table.

"Where am I going to meet this woman?" I asked him. "I'm not certain," he replied, "but she's the girl you're gonna really connect with. The two of you will marry and have three beautiful children." At that point I felt like what he was saying was completely out of synch with my feelings. "Man, you've gotta be kidding me," I said. "I've been married twice already, and I have a lot of qualms about going down that path another time." He nodded and closed his eyes. "This will be the last time," he said slowly. This is the person you're meant to be with forever."

I didn't know what to think as I drove home from McGrew's place. Scherrie and I continued to see one another, though she was traveling a lot. We were both dating other people, too, so that relationship ultimately kind of fizzled out. By the following year we'd completely gone our separate ways. I had a lot of respect for Scherrie, but I knew McGrew was right. That pairing just wasn't meant to be. I was working on a lot of projects in the mid-1970s, so I threw myself into the work. My artist career was going well, and I was on TV a good bit at the time on shows like *Dinah* and *American Bandstand*. Things were busy, and frankly, I kind of forgot all about what Reverend McGrew said about me meeting my soul mate.

In September of 1976 I was at Richard Perry's studio one night, working on some music I'd been hired to compose for a movie called *Fun with Dick and Jane,* starring George Segal and Jane Fonda. At some point a very attractive young redhead appeared in the control room. Someone was introducing her to the various people hanging around the studio. "And this," the host said, "is Lamont Dozier." The woman looked a little confused for a moment, as if she was expecting that Lamont Dozier looked very different than who she was seeing. "Oh, you're Lamont," she said as she extended her hand to introduce herself. She quickly recovered. "I'm Barbara Ullman," she continued. I work with Stanley Jaffe over at Columbia Pictures, and I just wanted to come by to say hello and say how thrilled we all are that you're working on the music for the film." I smiled. "Well, I'm very happy to be doing it."

"I have one of your albums at home that I really love," Barbara explained. "I'm the one who suggested they approach you about doing something for this project. I think it's going to be just the right fit." As she continued to talk about the film and the music, I felt a very strange feeling. My perception of my surroundings suddenly sharpened, as if I'd gone from watching a movie on a worn-out VHS tape to seeing it in digital high definition. Everything was brighter, clearer, and more focused. I don't know if there's really such a thing as love at first sight, but something had taken me over. I knew I wanted to be around this woman as much as humanly possible.

"Well, I don't want to interrupt your work," Barbara finally said. "It was a real pleasure to meet you, and I hope I'll see you again soon." We shook hands again, and she turned to go. It had been about a year since I'd gone to visit Reverend McGrew, but I suddenly remembered what he'd told me: "I see a girl who's gonna come into your life. It will happen around a year from now, and she's going to be a redhead."

I jumped up from my chair and ran out of the control room. I spotted Barbara reaching for the handle to pull the main studio door open and head out to the parking lot. By the time she'd gotten it open three inches, I was right behind her. I put my hand against the door, closing it firmly. She spun around quickly. "Hey," she laughed. "What's up?" I took a step back. "Are you coming back tomorrow night?" She smiled. "Maybe." With that, she pulled the door handle and disappeared into the night.

I couldn't stop thinking about Barbara. I called Columbia Pictures the next day and got her on the phone. "Hi, it's Lamont Dozier," I said. "I just wanted you to know I really enjoyed meting you last night, and I hope you'll come back again this evening. I also wanted to invite you to a barbecue at my house this Saturday afternoon, if you'd like to come." She was quiet for what seemed like a really long time, though it was probably only a couple of seconds. "I'll check my agenda book to see what's going on this weekend," she finally replied. "I'll tell you what. I'll come back by the studio tonight and we can talk about it then." I was thrilled when she showed up again that night. I was even more thrilled when she said she'd come to my barbecue on Saturday.

When my doorbell rang on Saturday, I felt a burst of excitement to get to spend more time with Barbara. I opened the door, and there she was, looking as radiant as ever. "Where is everybody?" she asked. I looked around, not sure what she meant. "It's just you and me," I smiled. Barbara laughed nervously. "I thought you were having a barbecue with a bunch of people. I thought this was a *gathering*." I was starting to worry I'd completely blown it already. "Uh, no," I stammered. "I'm a big fan of cooking and I just wanted to make some food for you to let you know how much I appreciate you thinking of me and suggesting me for the movie." She nodded slowly. "OK, yeah," she replied. "That sounds nice."

Once we got past that first little bit of awkwardness, Barbara and I had a great time. She was really easy to talk to and it was almost as if we'd known one another for years. We talked and laughed and shared stories with one another. "So, I have to tell you," Barbara said at one point, "I was being honest the other night when I said I had one of your albums and that it was my suggestion to have you work on the film, but I was kind of shocked when I first saw you. The album I have is *Love and Beauty*, and I always assumed that was Lamont Dozier on the front of the album. I laughed. "There's a close-up of the face of a *woman* on that record," I said. "You thought *that* was Lamont Dozier?" Barbara giggled. "I don't know. She had on those thick false eyelashes. I just thought Lamont Dozier was a cross-dresser or something, so I was surprised when I met you the other night." We had a good laugh about the case of mistaken identity.

After we ate, I took her to a Crusaders concert, and we came back and opened a bottle of wine. I felt like I could talk to her until the sun came up. "I'm fascinated by people who can write songs," Barbara said at one point. "I write lyrics and poems and things, and I wish I knew how to pair that stuff with music. You know that song 'You're So Vain' by Carly Simon? My boyfriend Brad is really infatuated with the idea that she wrote that about Warren Beatty. He's been kind of distant recently, and I think maybe if I could write him a song that would get his attention, you know?" I took a slow sip of wine and tried to act like my heart hadn't just sunk to the bottom of my stomach when she said the word "boyfriend." I nodded. "Yeah," I said, "music is a powerful thing."

Boyfriend or no boyfriend, I was smitten by Barbara Ullman. I wanted to be around her. We started hanging out together quite a bit—just as friends at first. I told her all about my failed relationships and she told me about her struggling romance with Brad. She really cared deeply for the guy and had thought they'd get married one day. He was her first love, but it seemed he wasn't as sure about the relationship as she was. She didn't live with him, and she was often suspicious about why he sometimes kept her at arm's length.

Barbara and I were having lunch together one afternoon, and I could see that she was distracted. "Something weird happened with Brad last night," she confessed when I asked what was bothering her. "I was over at his place off Coldwater Canyon, and we were watching TV. It was a nice night, so he had the front door open to let in the cool air. Suddenly, this young guy came through the door like he owned the place, but he stopped in his tracks when he spotted me. He looked me up and down, then glared at Brad. He pointed in my direction and said, 'What are you doing with *her?*' Brad jumped up and said, 'Hey, man, get out of here. We'll talk later!' So the guy took off. I asked him what in the hell that was all about and he was really nervous and shifty. He was obviously trying to cover something up."

I nodded. Yes, Barbara and I had gotten close. Yes, I was incredibly attracted to her, but at that point we were just friends, and I was determined to be a good friend. I set aside my own agenda in order to be the listening ear she needed. "What do you think it all meant?" I asked. She wrinkled up her nose, seemingly weighing if she wanted to tell me all the details. "OK," she sighed. "You're gonna think this is crazy, but I can't stop thinking about something this guy told me last year. Let me back up. I've got really curly hair, so I'm always looking for a stylist who can blow my hair straight. My friend Heidi works at this black hair salon, and last year she encouraged me to come in and see one of their stylists named Emory. While I was there Emory was telling me I should go visit this psychic named Reverend McGrew."

You can imagine I was pretty intrigued at that point! "Oh my God," I said. "I know McGrew. I've been to him myself. Did you end up going?" Barbara nodded. "Yeah," she said. "I just wanted to see what he had to say. I asked him if I was going to end up marrying Brad and he said, 'No. Brad is gay.' I laughed in his face. I told him I didn't believe that for a second. Reverend McGrew said, 'Brad will end up marrying a woman and having children with her, but he'll lead a double life. You won't end up with him.' After what happened last night, I can't stop thinking about what McGrew said. That guy that came in was sure acting weird. Brad made all sorts of excuses about it, but do you think he's actually gay? That would explain a lot about why I feel like he hasn't completely let me in."

"Barbara," I asked, "did Reverend McGrew say anything else to you about your future and who you will end up with, if it's not Brad?" She looked down at the table and started to fidget with the salt shaker. She nodded and drew in a deep breath. "Yes," Barbara responded. "He told me, 'You're going to meet someone who's really going to love you, and it's going to be incredible.'

He said it would be a black songwriter and that we'd have three beautiful children. I thought that sounded insane, so when I was leaving, I asked him sarcastically, 'So, when am I going to meet this black songwriter?' He looked me right in the eyes and said, 'In one year.' Well, guess what? It was September 26th when I first came to the studio to meet you. I got a really weird feeling that night, so I went home and checked my date book to see when it was last year that I'd visited with Reverend McGrew. It was September 25th."

"Barbara," I said. "Look at me. You're not meant to be with Brad. You're meant to be with me." I told her about my reading with Reverend McGrew and how he'd said I would meet a redheaded woman and have three children. "Don't you see? We're supposed to be together. There's a reason we met!"

We continued to see one another as friends, but that friendship was quickly evolving into something more. Barbara likes to say I took her on ninety dates before she even let me kiss her, and that's probably true! Everything unfolded very slowly, but our increasingly tight friendship blossomed into the deepest bond of love I'd ever experienced. She moved in with me in 1977, and we began a life together that did, in fact, produce three beautiful children later on down the road.

Earlier I mentioned the principle of being open to new opportunities as a writer and learning to say "yes" to new collaborations. I also encourage songwriters with a related concept: *Be open to all avenues for your songs.* **If someone wants you to write something for an independent film or a commercial or a web series, don't count it out just because you might think of yourself as only writing for your own albums as an artist. Writing songs for films was a new avenue for me in the 1970s. When those opportunities first began presenting themselves, I could have said, "No, that's not really the**

kind of thing I usually do." That would have been true, but had I not stretched myself, I would have missed out on some great opportunities. More importantly, I might have missed out on meeting Barbara!

Several years later when Barbara was on a phone call with Stevie Wonder and his then-manager, Rod McGrew, Barbara said, "Rod, are you by chance related to a guy who goes by the name of Reverend McGrew?" Rod said that he was his cousin, so Barbara told him all about how he'd predicted our meeting. Stevie was listening to all of this and said, "Rod, you never told me your cousin was a psychic!" Rod said, "Yeah, I never told you because I didn't think he was any good!" Maybe my meeting Barbara was the first thing he got right. In fairness, he did tell me we were going to have our own airplane and a bunch of other shit that never happened, so who knows? There's no denying, however, that something mystical was at work there, and that Barbara and I were meant to be together. I still get choked up thinking about it.

As our love blossomed, our relationship was not without its controversy. When we first got together, Barbara's parents were terrified that their nice Jewish daughter was getting together with a guy who had what her mother considered four strikes against him: I'd been divorced twice, I had children, I wasn't Jewish, and I was black. At one point, Barbara's mother pulled her aside for a heart-to-heart talk. "When you marry someone with baggage," she told Barbara, "their baggage becomes your baggage. I don't want that for you." Though they were protective of their little girl, Barbara's folks came around very quickly when they saw how in love we were. Plus, once I cooked one of my special meals for them, they were sold! In fact, they came to fill the roll in my life that Aunt Jenny and Uncle James had filled when I was a young man. They supported and championed us, treating me like the son they never had.

In 1979 Barbara and I discovered that she was pregnant. Learning that we were going to be parents together sparked a serious change in my life. While I was no longer battling the crippling anxiety I'd wrestled with back in Detroit, I put a lot of pressure on myself and internalized a good bit of stress from my career. Shortly after we received the good news about our first child together, I was taken to the emergency room at Cedars Sinai hospital with a severe nosebleed that resulted from extremely high blood pressure. I wasn't eating healthy food then, and I still drank from time to time to drown out the pressures I experienced from my work. I didn't smoke a lot, but I would probably finish a pack a week when I was drinking. Those habits, combined with the stress, were a recipe for disaster. My doctor at the time, Ray Weston, met us at the ER. He was deeply concerned for my well-being and wheeled my gurney around the hospital so I could see the people who were dying as the result of stroke or cardiac arrest. He wanted me to realize it was time to clean up my act. He implored me to stop drinking, to eat better, and to be faithful about taking my blood pressure medication. He checked me in to the hospital for three weeks so he could monitor me and make sure that when I walked out, everything was under control. Dr. Weston truly helped save my life.

In November, Barbara gave birth to a beautiful baby boy named Beau. Michelle and Andre were born at a time when fathers were kept out in the waiting area and out of the process, so being able to see my son the moment he came into the world was a really special experience for me. I went to all the classes and everything with Barbara in preparation for Beau's arrival, but nothing could have prepared me for the process of watching him emerge, have his umbilical cord cut, be washed off, and get placed under the lamps. It was just magical. I'll never forget when the nurses put him in my arms for the first time.

The responsibility of fatherhood changed something inside me at that point that I wasn't able to embrace the first two times I'd experienced it. I found myself quietly whispering to Beau the first time I gave him a bath at the hospital. "I've already thrown out the cigarettes," I told him. "And I've given up the alcohol. I'm going to be a healthy father and the kind of dad you deserve. I'm going to keep staying on top of my medication, and I'm going to be a role model for you, little man." I was flooded with this overwhelming sense of love that made me want to be the best parent I could possibly be. I wanted to be an involved father and to give Beau my undivided attention no matter how demanding my career might be.

Barbara and I married at a small ceremony in late 1980, and we had two more children together: Paris in 1984 and Desiree in 1988. I kept my promise that I made to Beau when he was a newborn, but the arrival of the other two was a chance for me to renew my commitment to my family each time. Those babies took care of me at least as much as I took care of them. They reminded me that I didn't need any unhealthy vices or anything in my life that might be detrimental to my own well-being or theirs. Love is a powerful thing. Whether it was setting aside the alcohol or getting my high blood pressure under control, I knew I needed to be around for my children.

When Barbara was pregnant with Paris, we had more time to prepare for his birth than we had when we found out she was pregnant with Beau. We converted the den in our house into a nursery. It had hardwood floors and a fireplace, but it was transformed with stuffed animals along the mantle, poking out of the fireplace, and all over the room. Because of Barbara's past problems with childbirth, we lined up a baby nurse to assist for a few weeks. She had a caesarean birth and needed bedrest again. The nurse, whose name was Gladys, was competent and loving, but she was an older black woman from a different time, and she said something one day that really touched a nerve with me. She off-handedly commented that black men make terrible fathers, and I fired her on the spot. Barbara was shocked at how quickly I acted, which was not typical for me. In fact, Barbara wasn't too happy because she really needed the help. Her mother wasn't able to step in because she was busy caring for Barbara's father at the time. I called my mother, who came out from Detroit to help us out for a couple of months. Maybe it was a little impulsive for me to let Gladys go so quickly, but my father wasn't a great dad, and what she said upset me. Words matter. Just because Gladys might have had or observed her own set of bad experiences didn't give her the right to lump all black fathers together. That's how people get the wrong information and the wrong thoughts. I was so committed to being a great dad that it really offended me. At least it proved to be a wonderful time for my mother to bond with Beau and Paris, and it was a blessing to have her in our home with my family.

My mom wasn't the only one who got a chance to come out from Detroit to visit us as Barbara and I were starting our family together. Back when Beau was still a baby, my older son, Andre, came out from Detroit to stay with us for a little while one summer. He was about thirteen at the time and loved to push Beau around in the stroller. He was an adventurous young guy, and he loved California. I bought him a bicycle, and it seemed like he rode that thing all over the city of Los Angeles. He kind of drove me crazy with worry taking that bike everywhere, but it was good to have him with us and spend some quality time together. It felt like things had really come together, and I was finally able to enjoy the kind of family life that I'd missed out on up to that point.

Of course becoming a family man meant a whole different kind of life for me. As it says in the Bible, the old had passed away and the new had come. On at least one occasion, though, the old Lamont came back to haunt me. We were all out at a restaurant as a family to celebrate my son Paris's birthday. All three of our children were there, and so were Barbara's parents. Suddenly, a woman that I didn't recognize appeared at the table. "Well, if isn't the Candy Man," she laughed. "Hey, Candy!" I didn't recognize this woman from Adam, but I knew that if she was aware of that name, then she knew me from somewhere. There I was in front of my family and my in-laws, thinking, *Oh, shit. Is this somebody I fooled around with back in the day or what? Maybe it was somebody I met when I was drinking or something.* I'm sure the look on my face was one of complete embarrassment. I was scrambling to get up from the table and pull this woman aside. "Look," I said to her, "I'm here with my wife and my family. Thanks for saying hello, but I'm going to get back to our gathering now." When I sat back down, my father-in-law couldn't stop laughing. I took a long sip of water and tried to act like nothing had happened.

As I looked around that table, though, I realized those were the people I most wanted to be with. My sons and daughter are all grown now, and Barbara and I have been together for more than four decades, but they're responsible for reorienting my priorities and truly transforming my life.

Chapter Eighteen
I JUST CAN'T WALK AWAY

Even as my artist career faltered a bit at Warner Bros., I stayed busy writing and producing for other artists. I recorded an album for Ben E. King in 1976 that included a single called "Somebody's Knocking." While that song was a new one, Ben ended up cutting three of the songs that I'd first recorded with The Originals on the *California Sunset* album. I think he really liked that Originals LP, and I had a great time working with him. I always really liked Ben's voice.

Another legendary voice I had the chance to work with the following year belonged to the great Aretha Franklin. Our paths had crossed plenty of times since we were both kids in Detroit, but when Aretha invited me to produce her *Sweet Passion* album in 1977, I jumped at the chance. Before our first meeting to discuss the album, I went through a bunch of demo tapes and pulled out some of my best unrecorded songs. When we got together, I played her the first one. She shook her head no, so I played the next one. Another no. This went on for five or six songs until Aretha finally said, "These are some good songs, Lamont, but you didn't write these specifically for me, did you? I had to admit that I hadn't. "But this is my top shelf stuff," I assured her. "I would only bring you the good stuff." She just smiled and adjusted one of her bracelets. "That's all fine and good," she quipped, "but you go home and you write some songs that are just for me. *Then* you come back and we'll listen to those." What was I gonna do? Aretha is the queen, after all! I did just what she asked and came up with a new batch of songs for the album. We recorded it at ABC Studios in Los Angeles, and though the album wasn't a big commercial success, working together on that project with an old childhood friend is still one of my most treasured experiences.

It seems like I was in the studio all the time in the late 1970s. I recorded an album for Lawrence Hilton-Jacobs, who was better known for playing Freddie "Boom Boom" Washington on the TV show *Welcome Back Kotter,* and I did another LP called *Clean* with former Motowner Edwin Starr, who is best known for his recording of the Norman Whitfield and Barrett Strong song "War."

I was busy, but times were changing once again, and not a lot of the things I was working on then really connected with the public in a meaningful way. In the early 1980s, times went from bad to worse from a financial perspective. There were still unresolved legal issues that hounded me, and I wasn't exactly burning up the charts with hit songs at the time. Then one day we got a knock on the door. Barbara opened it up and was greeted by a messenger with several boxes of financial documents and tax paperwork, as well as a letter from my business manager's office that they were basically quitting. They were paid five percent of my gross income, but I just wasn't making enough money for them to justify the amount of time it was taking to deal with my financial affairs.

Soon after, we were visited by an IRS agent. There were back taxes due, and a long series of ongoing problems with the taxman began. Barbara, who had just come off bedrest following complications from Beau's birth, jumped right in to try to get everything straightened out. She was juggling paperwork, accountants, and a new baby while I was in the studio trying to come up with something for a new deal so I could support my family. As money got tighter and tighter, it became difficult to meet all our financial obligations. Nobody could believe that I just didn't have money coming in, but then the bank foreclosed on us, and we lost our home.

Thank God for Barbara's parents, who really stepped in and helped us at our darkest hour. We needed a new place to stay, but we didn't have the money or the credit to get a place on our own. They loaned us money, paid my child support back in Detroit, and helped us lease a nice house on Stansbury Avenue in Sherman Oaks. It was a great place to raise our family, and my brother Reggie helped us convert the attic into a little hidden-away studio where I could record demos and things. When we rented the place, we had to use my in-laws' names, so we were supposed to be Leo and Sally Ullman. What we didn't know was that the landlord actually lived right across the street, so we had to keep up our identity as "the Ullmans" much more than we thought we would!

Having a landlord on your doorstep isn't a great situation, but having a *nosy* landlord just across the street is really irritating. This guy was always coming over to "check in" and make sure everything was OK with the house. One day the garage door was open, and Barbara was in there working on something. Of course Mr. Landlord spotted her and made his way across the street. Before she could disappear back into the house, he was standing in the garage looking at all these multitrack tapes that were labeled "Lamont Dozier" all over them. "What's all this?" he asked. Barbara had to think quick. "Oh, my husband dabbles in music a little bit as a hobby," she replied as nonchalantly as possible. That's the name he uses as a pseudonym. "Well, you better tell him to stick to his day job," the guy responded. "Everybody knows you can't make any money in music!"

During our time of financial struggle, I was trapped in a song publishing deal that I'd signed in 1977. The terms of the contract stipulated that I had to submit sixty-five wholly written songs to the publisher, and forty-five of them had to be commercially released. In other words, if I wrote a song with someone else, that would only count as half a song in tallying up the total. Even if I turned in five thousand songs, I'd still be stuck in the deal until forty-five of them were recorded by me or some other artist and released to the public.

Where my first two wives always saw my music as something they had to compete with for my attention, Barbara understood my drive and dedication. She had been a career woman, and she had a similar work ethic to mine. From the very start of our friendship, before we officially got together, she was questioning my manager or my lawyer about why they were or weren't doing this or that. She knew I was off in some other universe working on songs, so she made it a point to educate herself about the music business and become an advocate for me. She learned how to push me in the right way, and if it wasn't for Barbara, I might not have gotten myself back on track. It started in 1981 when we visited my attorney, Lee Phillips, to see if there was any way to get out of that bad publishing deal.

Lee studied the terms of the contract carefully, but it was ironclad. "I'm sorry, guys," he told us in his office one day, "but I just don't see any way out of this. It's just not possible." I might be conflict avoidant, but I'm also stubborn. "If there's no loophole," I said, "then I'll just have to get forty-five songs released." We walked out of Lee's office that day and I went into overdrive.

The next several months were a blur of work that far outpaced even what I'd done in my most hectic period at Motown. I wrote and recorded an independent album called *Lamont* for a little label called M&M Records. Ironically, I did the deal with Mike Roshkind, who was the Motown vice president who had tried to keep me at Hitsville by dividing and conquering the HDH team. In an odd twist of fate, we became friends after he left Motown and, in fact, he was the best man at my wedding to Barbara!

After the M&M project, I put together a really talented racially mixed group called Future Flight and secured them a deal with Capitol Records. I produced their self-titled album and wrote or co-wrote every song on the LP. I did the same thing with a group I assembled called Zingara, where I brought in different singers to perform on the various tracks. One of the songs, "Love's Calling," featured James Ingram on lead vocals, and it became a Top 30 R&B single. I was already dealing with enough craziness in the midst of trying to work my way out of my publishing contract, but there was additional drama surrounding Zingara that made it seem as if there were a negative cloud around it from the very start.

The album was released on Wheel Records, which I launched with a friend of mine named Rudy, who had access to some money through business partners he dealt with. After my very first meeting with Rudy, I came home to find a trail of blood that went all the way down my staircase and out the front door. This was right after Barbara had given birth to Beau, and we had a nurse who was staying with us for a little while. The nurse appeared in the entryway when she heard me come in. "Barbara's OK," she said as soon as she saw the look of shock on my face. "She's at the hospital, but she's OK." I found out that Barbara had hemorrhaged as the result of an injured vein in the vaginal wall that was caused by the obstetrician who delivered the baby. This was back in the days before we carried cell phones, and she wasn't able to reach me when I was away at the meeting. Barbara's parents and sister were out of town, so she called the doctor, who was in surgery at the time. An ambulance was called and, while she waited for medical help to arrive, Barbara was able to reach our dear friend Al Kasha.

Not only is Al an Oscar-winning songwriter, but he and his wife Ceil hosted a weekly Bible study at their Beverly Hills home that we attended regularly. We were very close with the Kashas, and Al made the long and winding drive up Laurel Canyon to our place in Studio City so he could meet the ambulance and follow Barbara to the hospital. What we didn't know at the time was that Al was suffering from agoraphobia. I know first-hand how crippling that can be, so I am forever grateful to Al for battling his fears to come help my wife. He was still at the hospital when I arrived to discover that Barbara had been rushed into emergency surgery. She was in the recovery room when I got there, where she received eight units of blood and plasma. I nearly lost the love of my life and the mother of my new son. I got down on my knees that night and thanked God that she made it through.

Though there's obviously no connection between Barbara's medical emergency and Zingara, the fact that I was away at that first Zingara meeting when it happened gave me a negative association with the project. But that was only the beginning of the saga. I mentioned that my business partner Rudy had some business associates that he brought into the deal as we set up

Wheel Records. In those days, you didn't really question where the money was coming from. Plus, I was so focused on getting Barbara back to good health and getting my songs released that I didn't really care!

After the Zingara album came out, Geffen Records approached us and wanted to buy out the group's contract. The investors didn't want to sell. I couldn't possibly imagine why they'd pass up such a great deal, but it soon came out that the financiers were cocaine smugglers, and they were using the label to launder money. The FBI was looking into them for all this stuff. I was pissed when this came to light. I called Rudy right away, "What are you doing, man? You're bringing these people to me that you know are involved in drugs?" Eventually, the owner and his wife got deported, and that was a scary time. Those weren't the kind of people I wanted to be mixed up with. In the meantime, Quincy Jones had heard the record and wanted to sign James Ingram. I didn't tell James what was going on, but I said he was free to leave. Of course, it all worked out really great for James and Quincy. Fortunately, I didn't experience any repercussions from any unsavory characters, and I managed to knock out a good chunk of my publisher's minimum delivery requirement with the album.

In addition to my independent album, the Future Flight release, and the Zingara LP, I did a one-off record for Columbia called *Working On You*. I had actually signed with Arista, but when my A&R man, Larkin Arnold, switched to Columbia, he took the project with him. It was too bad, because I thought it was a great album. Once it moved to a new label, however, it kind of got lost in the shuffle. One of the songs, "Cool Me Out," became a hit on the regional beach music scene in the Carolinas, but I didn't reach as many people as I'd hoped I would with that album.

One of my biggest career regrets happened around that time when I got a call from Irving Azoff. Barbara urged me to call him back but, for one reason or another, I never did get around to it. She knew he was one of the premier talent managers and power brokers in the music industry with an incredible roster of clients that included the Eagles, but I didn't make the call. Maybe I was just so focused on getting all those songs written and recorded in those days, but if I could go back in time and do something different, I would call Irving back! We did become friendly with one another years later, but we never really did do business together like we probably would have if I'd picked up the phone. At the time, though, I was in the midst of a feverish writing streak.

Even with the release of my Columbia album, I was still short a few records to fulfil my obligations. I called up everybody I'd ever met and asked them if they needed a song. I'd place a half song here and a whole song there. I contributed a couple of songs to Martha Reeves' *Gotta Keep Moving* album, for example, as well as several other projects until I finally got all forty-five songs released that I would need to free me from my publishing agreement. Lee Phillips was completely flabbergasted. He couldn't believe I'd actually done it. Not only had I done it, but I got it all knocked out within a few months.

The only problem is that the publisher still had to recoup $14,000 of the advance they'd paid me. Lee made an arrangement with Rob Dickens at Warner Chappell Music in the UK to advance me some money for a new administration deal that would kick in once I was officially out of my old one. That gave me the money I needed to get free. We were able to go in and say, "OK, here are your forty-five released songs, and here's the additional money." And that did it. I got out of the deal. After that, music publishing companies started changing the minimum delivery requirements in their contracts to limit how many songs on a single album could count toward fulfillment, and to limit the ability of independent releases to count toward the total. Because of me, they made it even more difficult for writers to get free from their contracts. They probably never assumed they'd need to enforce tighter restrictions, but they'd never come across anyone with my kind of determination before.

There's no substitute for talent when it comes to songwriting, but you have to have something more than talent: determination. I believe that *talent plus determination equals songwriting success*. You must have them both. You have to be prepared to kick the door down no matter how many doors are behind that one. You have to be stubborn. If somebody tells me I can't do something, I'll be determined to show them I can. You can do anything you make up your mind to do, and I'm living proof of that. I think some of the best songs of my career are in that batch that I created in defiance of the odds stacked against me. I may not be an aggressive personality type, but tell me I can't do something, and the challenge is on!

The timing turned out to be really good for starting fresh as a songwriter for the new decade. There was a bit of a Motown resurgence in popular culture at the time, which kicked into high gear when Phil Collins released a cover of "You Can't Hurry Love" in 1982. It went to number one on the UK chart and became a Top 10 single in the US, as well. The following year The Hollies scored a hit with a remake of "Stop! In the Name of Love." Soon after, the film *The Big Chill* was released, which was chock full of Motown songs and other hits from that era. The folks who had grown up on Motown were in their thirties and forties by then and were becoming nostalgic for the music of their youth.

I even briefly reunited with Eddie and Brian Holland in the early 1980s as the Motown revival was heating up. In

March of 1983 there was a taping for a television special called *Motown 25: Yesterday, Today, Forever.* It was shot in front of a live audience at the Pasadena Civic Auditorium and was designed as a concert to celebrate the legacy of Hitsville. That was the first time Eddie and Brian and I had a real conversation in many years. We chatted backstage for a while and discussed the idea of possibly working together again if the right project came along.

Soon after, the three of us were approached by Suzanne de Passe, who produced the *Motown 25* special. She had put together a team of partners that wanted to create a black-themed adaptation of *Oliver Twist* for Broadway called *Twist*. The Hollands and I agreed to do it and had a blast jumping into the project. We were able to set aside the disputes of the recent past, and we worked diligently together, just like we'd done in the old days. We came up with a handful of great songs that we were all really proud of. All was going well until we were presented with some funky paperwork asking us to sign over our publishing rights to the songs we created for the score. I was already in my new deal with Warner Chappell and couldn't have given over the publishing rights even if I'd wanted to! I ended up having to withdraw from the project. Since I was the "idea man," the Hollands withdrew as well, and the project fell apart.

Around that same time, the Four Tops returned to Motown for a comeback album. We thought it would be cool to reunite Holland-Dozier-Holland to write and produce the album, which was called *Back Where I Belong.* We had a great time doing it, but we ran into the same issue we'd run into over *Twist.* When the production paperwork came in, they asked us to sign over our publishing for all the songs on the album. I couldn't believe that, after everything we'd been through on that very issue, Motown would ask us to give up our publishing at that point in our careers. I wasn't in a position to do it, but even if I wasn't already in a publishing arrangement with

Warners, I wouldn't have considered it. As a result, Motown didn't really promote the album like they could have, and the whole thing sort of fizzled. We did manage to land a Top 40 R&B single with "I Just Can't Walk Away," but not much came of the big reunion of Holland-Dozier-Holland and Motown. I decided I wasn't ever going to work on any future projects where that publishing question came up, and I haven't to this day!

I did a few other things with the Hollands at the time. We wrote and produced for a couple of acts on Real World Records. Sterling Harrison was one of them, and Margo Michaels & Nitelite was the other. Brian and I also wrote an instrumental for Herb Alpert called "Blow Your Own Horn," which became the title track to one of his albums. We had a meeting at Herb's studio, and that title just came off the top of my head. It seemed so natural to me since he was a trumpet player. I couldn't believe nobody had ever suggested he do a song by that title! It was all just an organic off-the-cuff kind of thing. We cut the track, and then Herb took it and did what he does best. I had a great time reconnecting with Eddie and Brian outside a courtroom in that era, but I wasn't interested in getting back into an exclusive songwriting partnership.

That doesn't mean there was bad blood between me and the Hollands. By that point we'd been through enough drama together that I thought of them as family. Eddie and Brian had experienced their own share of business and legal entanglements, and I remember getting a particularly frightening visit one day after they'd been over at my house. The three of us were working on songs for *Twist* and the Four Tops record. They left after several hours of work and, within minutes, my doorbell rang. I thought one of the guys must have left something, so I flung the door open without asking who it was. Standing on my porch were two intimidating-looking FBI agents with dark suits and sunglasses.

They flashed badges and one of them said, "We're sorry to bother you, sir, but are the two men who just left your home Edward and Brian Holland?" Now, Eddie and Brian and I have had our differences over the years, but there's a bond of loyalty there that can't ever be broken. I had to think quick! "You know …" I scratched my head. "I can't remember what those fellas said their names were." The agent did not seem amused. "You're telling me you don't know who those men are, but you had them in your home?" he asked. "Yessir," I replied. "They were Jehovah's Witnesses. They knocked on my door and asked if I'd be interested in having a conversation about God, so I invited them in." The man nodded. "OK, sir," he replied. "Thank you for your time."

A few minutes later, the doorbell rang again. The Men in Black had returned. "Lamont Dozier," one of them said, "we have a search warrant to come into your home." They pushed past me and started poking around the house. I called my attorney, Lee Phillips, who got on the phone with one of the agents and convinced him he needed to speak with Robert Hinerfeld, a seasoned litigator from their firm, regarding their concerns. Soon after, they left, and I never heard anything more about it. My heart was in my throat when those men came into my house demanding information. I don't know what it was all about, but I still get nervous when I think of it!

I mentioned that I didn't want to exclusively work with the Hollands—or anyone for that matter—in the early 1980s. There were too many Motown fans, old and new, in the music industry who wanted to do all sorts of stuff, and I didn't want to limit myself. One of those fans was Pete Waterman, who, alongside Mike Stock and Matt Aitken, found huge success as the British songwriting and production team known as SAW. I'd never met him, but one day as his career was really getting going, Pete showed up and started knocking on the door of our rental house in Sherman Oaks. "Who is it?" I yelled through the door. "Hi, my name is Pete Waterman," he called back, "and I'm looking for Lamont Dozier," I didn't say anything. This was still in that period where things were kind of slow for me. Real slow, actually, so I didn't know if the guy on the other side of that door was some kind of bill collector or what. After a moment he spoke again: "I'm a songwriter and producer in London, actually," he said. "I've come to speak with you about perhaps coming over to the UK to work with some artists over there … . All expenses paid." I opened the door and invited him in.

As crazy as it sounds, we took him up on the offer. The English audience had always been good to me. The Northern Soul scene had latched onto "Why Can't We Be Lovers," and I felt like the fact that so much of the Motown renaissance was coming out of the UK could only be a good thing. Beau was still too young to have started grade school yet, so Barbara and I decided we'd move to London for six months to see if it would be a good opportunity.

During that era I recorded an album for the UK-based Demon label called *Bigger Than Life,* and I wrote stuff for some new acts that didn't really pan out for one reason or another. Finally, near the end of our time in London, Alison Moyet recorded a song of mine called "Invisible." It became a big hit for her and marked a turning point for me in terms of getting back on track financially.

The rest of the 1980s proved to be a phenomenal period for me as a songwriter. The interest in my classic songs was at an all-time high, with Sheena Easton hitting the charts with a remake of "Jimmy Mack" and British singer Kim Wilde topping the charts both at home and abroad with her interpretation of "You Keep Me Hanging On." As much as people were loving the old stuff, though, they were after me to write new songs, too.

Stewart Levine was a real champion of mine in that era. He'd produced "Goin' Back to My Roots" and the *Peddlin'*

Music on the Side album, and he always had a real appreciation for my songwriting style. He had produced everyone from Van Morrison to The Marshall Tucker Band to B.B. King, but after his production of "Up Where We Belong" became a massive hit in the early 1980s, he was in high demand. He moved over to London where, by that time, I had a flat of my own. I would spend several months each year in the UK, and Stewart and I really reconnected in that era.

When he was recruited to produce Boy George's first solo album following the breakup of his group Culture Club, Stewart brought me in as a writer. George couldn't come to the US as a result of drug and legal problems, so I flew to Montserrat to write and record at George Martin's Air Studios, back before it was destroyed by a volcano. Boy George and I co-wrote four songs that ended up on the album, including the title track, "Sold." The album was a big success in Europe, so Stewart starting tapping me for various projects, including a song called "You'll Never Know" for Boz Scaggs that became the B-side of his Top 40 single "Heart of Mine." I was feeling refreshed and reinvigorated. The songs were flowing freely as new opportunities were coming my way.

One of those opportunities emerged back in the US, after a meeting with some folks at Columbia Pictures in 1987. As I was departing, someone asked me, almost as an afterthought, "Hey, Lamont. Do you have a song for a new Bill Cosby movie?" Of course I said yes. I never say no, because you never know when something might be just the right pathway to a moment of success. "We've been looking for a song for this movie for six months," the guy told me, "but we can't find anything that sounds right." I smiled. "I'm sure I've got something," I assured him.

I went home and found a demo tape of a ballad called "Without You," which I sent to the studio. A couple days later, someone called me and said, "That's it! We love the song and want to use it for the closing credits of the film." My song was recorded as a duet by Peabo Bryson and Regina Bell, and I had a good feeling about it. In 1987 *The Cosby Show* was just about the biggest thing on television, and Cosby himself was a cultural phenomenon. How could it miss?

I found out how it could miss when Barbara and I went to see the movie, *Leonard Part 6,* on opening weekend. It was absolutely horrible. It was beyond horrible. By the time the closing credits came around, the theater was empty. Everybody had gotten up and walked out except for me and Barbara. Hell, I would have walked out, too, if I wasn't waiting to hear my song. Even though the movie was a complete stinker, Peabo and Regina did a nice job with the song. It ended up becoming a Top 15 hit on the R&B chart and a Top 10 hit on the Adult Contemporary chart, so at least something good came out of that film!

Several months later I got involved in making music for another film—*Buster,* staring Phil Collins—that would turn out to be a real career highlight. I first met Phil in 1985 when he stopped in L.A. for his massive *No Jacket Required* tour. It had been almost three years since he'd had his hit with "You Can't Hurry Love," and someone at Atlantic Records called and invited me to go to the show. It was a zoo backstage, where the label was lining up various people they wanted Phil to meet. When he got word that I was there, Phil came out of his dressing room and made his way over toward me. I reached out for a handshake, but he suddenly dropped to his knees and started bowing down to me. It was really cute, and I just started laughing. It felt good to know that one of the biggest pop stars in the world at the time was a fan of mine. I was a fan of his, too, and we instantly became friends.

A few weeks after we first met, Phil called me on the phone. "Lamont," he said, "I'm producing some stuff for Eric Clapton's new album here in L.A., and I'm hoping maybe you have some songs you could bring over." There were a couple of things I'd been working on for myself at the time, but I thought, *Hey, Eric Clapton's a big deal. I'd be happy to give him these songs!* I took them "Run" and "Hung Up on Your Love," and they recorded both of them. The album, *August,* was released in late 1986 and became Eric's best-selling solo project up to that point.

It was maybe a year later that Phil called again and told me he was working on *Buster,* which would be his acting debut. The movie was set in the 1960s, so they wanted music that had some of those classic elements. Phil was concentrating on his acting at the time, so he thought I could help him out on the music side. After reading the script, I sat down at the piano and started doing that thing I used to do back in the day at Motown. I ended up with a few songs, including "Two Hearts" and "Loco in Acapulco." I actually traveled down to Acapulco to personally play the songs for Phil while they were filming scenes down there. Somebody with the production company pulled me aside when I was on the set. "For the sake of promotional reasons," the guy told me, "it would be great to get Phil involved in the songs." I caught his drift and left plenty of space for Phil to contribute lyrics so we could become co-writers.

The Four Tops recorded "Loco in Acapulco" for the movie, which was a lot of fun. It felt good to go back in the studio with those guys once again, and it was just like the old days. We went right back to our tradition of eating ribs and everything. It was beautiful. Though that song didn't become a hit in the US, it was a Top 10 single in the UK, and the last real hit for them anywhere. It was also the last time I worked with the Tops, and I'll always treasure that moment that we got to reunite for one last victory lap together.

Phil recorded "Two Hearts" himself, and it climbed all the way to number one on the *Billboard* pop chart in the US. It also hit number one in Canada and Japan, plus it reached the Top 5 in countries all over the world. For whatever reason, it just blew up and seemed to resonate with people of different generations.

As had happened with the *Twist* musical and the Four Tops album a few years earlier, the question of song publishing came up once again when I worked on *Buster*. I had already determined I wasn't going to play that game anymore. In fact, I was told when I signed on for the project that I wouldn't receive a fee, but I would retain all my publishing and writer royalties. Later, one of the film's producers called wanting me to give my share of publishing to the production company. Barbara told her that wasn't going to happen, and the woman got nasty about it. We already knew the songs had been incorporated into the film, so Barbara said, "I think you should probably just take our songs out of the movie and get Phil to do some new ones for it because we are not giving you our publishing." She was furious, but of course there was nothing they could do about it. There was no way they were going to go back to Phil to have him write and record new songs and then synch the new material with the film. It would be hugely impractical, and Phil probably never would have agreed to it. When they saw we weren't going to budge, they had no choice but to proceed with the film as it was.

Barbara has always had my back and allows me to be the good guy when it comes time for a confrontation. She was mentored in the entertainment business by Jay Bernstein, who was a public relations genius and the godfather to our son, Beau. She learned well! Barbara knows how to pick our battles and how to look out for what's best for me in my career. The situation with the songs in *Buster* is just one example, and I'm so glad she stuck to her guns. We knew the songs were strong, but we never imagined just how successful they'd become. I was elated when "Two Hearts" got nominated for Best Original Song at the Golden Globe

Awards in 1989. I didn't think we'd win, but we ended up tying for first place with Carly Simon and her song "Let the River Run" from the movie *Working Girl*. It was really cool to go home that night as a Golden Globe–winning songwriter.

It was even cooler to get nominated for a Grammy Award for Best Song Written Specifically for a Motion Picture or for Television. I genuinely thought the award would go to the song "One Moment in Time," which Albert Hammond and John Bettis wrote for Whitney Houston to perform as the theme of the 1988 Summer Olympics. I was shocked when they announced me and Phil as the winners at the ceremony. Though I'd had quite a career up to that point, I'd actually never won a Grammy. It meant a lot to get that kind of recognition from the music industry for my work as a songwriter, especially considering I'd already been at it for almost thirty years at that point! On top of that, John Bettis, one of the writers of Whitney's song, sent me flowers and a note of congratulations the next day, which was really gracious.

That's a great survival tip in this business. There's enough negativity in this world, so you should always be happy for another person's success. *Don't waste your time being jealous or envious.* **There will always be someone out there who has something you don't, but why fixate on them instead of focusing on improving who you are? There's more than enough success to go around in this industry, so entertaining jealous thoughts is nothing but a waste of time. It won't do anything but eat at your insides and hamper your own creative flow. It saps your energy and holds you back from achieving your own goals. When others have a streak of good fortune, celebrate with those people—even if you consider them your "competition." They probably earned it and deserve it. Refuse to be**

swayed by negative thoughts and negative talk that only keeps you from fulfilling your destiny.

"Two Hearts" ended up winning nearly every award it was nominated for. The only one we missed was the Academy Award. We were nominated, but Carly Simon ended up going home with the Oscar that night. I didn't mind. I was just thrilled to be caught up in the validating whirlwind of the whole 1989 awards season.

The 1980s got off to a rocky start, but things had really turned around by the end. At some point during that string of success that started with Alison Moyet, I wrote a musical theater piece called *Angels* that I'm really proud of. Chuck Kaye at Warner Chappell was really excited about it and gave me a sizable advance so I could buy a new home for my family. By the time the "Two Hearts" thing took off, we were solidly back on our feet and really enjoying life.

The best part is that we were able to repay Barbara's parents for helping us out during those difficult years. We felt like paying them back what they'd loaned us wasn't enough. I wanted to give them an additional gift to let them know how much we appreciated them for really coming through for us when times were lean. We had accumulated 200,000 miles on American Airlines, so we sent them on a six-week trip to Europe and Israel. Barbara's cousin Beverly was a travel agent, so she was able to put together a first-class experience for them that was phenomenal. My father-in-law must have recorded the entire vacation with his handheld video camera, and I can't tell you how much joy it brought me to be able to give them that experience. As I would continue to learn in the coming years, there's nothing more important than family.

Chapter Nineteen

ANYTHING IS POSSIBLE

As the 1980s came to a close, I continued to find success with my music. I had met Mick Hucknall of Simply Red when he was writing songs for the band's *Men and Women* album. Stewart Levine had been working with them and suggested that the two of us get together. Mick came to L.A., and we ended up writing four songs. The first two, "Infidelity" and "Suffer," went on the *Men and Women* album, and "Infidelity" became a Top 40 hit in the UK. The other two, "You've Got It" and "Turn It Up," went on the band's 1989 album, *A New Flame*. "You've Got It" was released as a single and hit the Top 10 on the Adult Contemporary charts in the US. The album included the group's cover of the old Harold Melvin & The Blue Notes hit

"If You Don't Know Me by Now," which was a huge single for Simply Red. As a result, the album sold very well, earning Gold status in the US and multi-Platinum status in the UK.

Soon after, I got the chance to work with one of the most successful artists of the late 1980s. Debbie Gibson was just sixteen years old when her debut album, *Out of the Blue,* was released in 1987. She came right out of the gate with four consecutive Top 5 singles, including the chart-topping hit "Foolish Beat." What's amazing is that Debbie wrote everything by herself on that album and the follow-up album, *Electric Youth*—which also spawned a number-one hit with "Lost in Your Eyes." Both albums were multi-Platinum smashes in the US, so when somebody at Atlantic Records suggested that Debbie collaborate with me for her third album in 1990, I thought it would be a great opportunity.

Debbie was still a teenager, and I was pushing fifty when we began work on the album that would become *Anything Is Possible,* but I really respected her drive and work ethic. I went out to New York for a couple of weeks for that project, and we worked really hard. We collaborated on four songs that ended up on the album, including the title track, which became a Top 30 single on the pop chart. Even though *Anything Is Possible* was certified Gold, it wasn't as big as her first two releases. The teen craze in pop music was fading at the time, and though Debbie was twenty when the album came out, it wasn't easy for her to make the transition to adulthood in the eyes of the public. I really liked working with her and had hoped for bigger things for that album. But you never know. A lot of this business is about throwing stuff against the wall and praying that something sticks.

Around the same time I was working with contemporary artists like Mike Hucknall and Debbie, I was continuing to have success with cover versions of the old Motown songs. "This Old Heart of Mine" had been an Isley Brothers hit back in 1966. When Rod

Stewart covered it in 1975, it was a Top 5 single in the UK, though it didn't perform very well on the US charts. Then he rerecorded it with Ronald Isley as a duet, hitting the Top 10 on the US pop chart and number one on the adult contemporary chart in 1990.

It was great to see my name in the charts for both current and classic compositions. Thanks, in part, to my elevated profile as a multi-decade-spanning songwriter, I was offered the chance to make a new album as an artist for Atlantic Records. *Inside Seduction* was released in 1991. In the US, Atlantic released "Love in the Rain" as the single. I remember when I first met with Doug Morris at the label to play him some demos that I'd been working on. He listened through the first song with his eyes closed. The second song was "Love in the Rain," and he continued to listen with his eyes closed through the first chorus. Suddenly, his eyes snapped open and he sat straight up in his chair. Then he reached over and shut off the tape. I thought, *Oh boy, he really hates this stuff. I guess I wasted a couple of hours of the day coming over here for this meeting.* Doug stood up and said, "Lamont, I've heard all I need to hear." *Here we go,* I thought. But then he extended his hand. "You've got a deal." Knowing how much Doug loved the song, I wasn't surprised that Atlantic wanted to release it as a single. It hit the R&B charts, though it would be my last charting single as an artist. At least so far!

One really cool aspect of the *Inside Seduction* album is that my friends Eric Clapton and Phil Collins appeared—playing guitar and drums, respectively—and Phil sang harmonies on "The Quiet's Too Loud," which was issued as a single in the UK. Phil and I wrote and produced the song together, and we even made a video for it, which was a first for me.

That concept of the quiet being too loud is true for me when it comes to songwriting. I need a little TV or background noise to write because the silence gets in the way of my process. That's not true for every writer. Some

**need complete solitude and silence. Others do their best
work while driving in the car. Still others seem to thrive
when they're engaged in another activity like cooking,
bicycling, or shopping at the grocery store. There's no
secret formula that works for everyone, but if you're serious
about songwriting, you need to *understand what kind of
environment you need to do your best work, and then make sure you
intentionally create that environment for yourself on a regular basis.***

Around the time my Atlantic album was released, we were at
home one evening when the phone rang. My daughter Desiree,
who was still pretty young at the time, picked up the receiver.
"Hello, Dozier residence," she said. "Hello there," the voice on the
other end responded. "May I please speak to Lamont?" Desiree,
sounding like a responsible little adult, replied, "May I ask who's
speaking?" The caller answered, "Yes, this is Aretha Franklin."
Desiree let out a laugh. "Uh, yeah, OK. Sure." She rolled her eyes.
"Like this is *really* Aretha Franklin!" When I heard that I grabbed
the phone as quick as I could. Fortunately the Queen of Soul had
a good sense of humor. She was calling to ask if I'd be interested
in opening up the shows on her tour, but I wasn't interested in
touring at that point, opting to do some promotional trips instead.

Just before I completed the *Inside Seduction* album, I stopped
in Chicago, where I got a chance to visit with my son Andre. He
was a really smart guy, so I was thrilled to be able to send him
to Michigan State, where he got a degree in finance. He also
became fluent in French since Dozier is a French name. After
graduation he landed a job as a credit analyst at Chicago's LaSalle
National Bank, and his mother had all sorts of plans that he'd
one day become the first black president of the United States. We
got together for lunch when I was in town and then went and
listened to the new album together. I hadn't seen him in quite a
while, but we had a great time catching up.

When I was about to leave town a couple of days later, Andre came by my hotel. We visited for a bit until it was time for me to head to the airport. As we were parting ways, he hailed a cab. "Do you take a taxi everywhere you go?" I asked him before he slid into the backseat. "Yeah, but it's cool," he smiled. "I don't mind it." I laughed. "Man, I gotta get you a car. I'm gonna take care of that so you've got your own ride." He gave me a hug and jumped in the taxi. I turned to walk away, but a really strange feeling came over me. I came back out of the lobby to see if Andre was still there. I wanted to take another look at him for some reason, but he was gone.

A couple of weeks later, I was driving down the freeway on the way to a meeting at MCA Records. Suddenly I felt terribly sick and pulled the car over to the shoulder. I called Barbara. "Honey, something's wrong with me," I told her. "I can barely breathe. I feel terrible—like maybe I'm having a heart attack or something. It's like my body is shutting down." That, of course, really scared her. "Do you need me to call an ambulance?" she asked. "No, not yet," I said. "Let me just gather myself for a minute to see if it passes." I ended up sitting there for about fifteen minutes, but then I began to feel better. I went on to the meeting and managed to get through it. I was still feeling a little weak afterward, so I came home and got in bed.

The phone rang about an hour later. It was my mother. "I have some really bad news," she said. "Andre's dead." I felt like someone had punched me in the stomach. I nearly passed out. "What? That doesn't make sense," I stammered. "What are you talking about?" My mother was crying on the other end of the line. "It was a heart attack," she said. "It was really sudden." Andre was only twenty-four years old. There's no way to describe the feeling of losing a child if you haven't experienced it. I later discovered that he passed away around the same time

I was feeling so sick on the side of the freeway. I've always been sensitive in that way. If something is wrong with someone I love, I have the ability to pick up on it in a physical way. I guess I'm in tune in that way, but I get these feelings that come over me sometimes, and I know that it means someone I love is suffering.

I was devastated when I realized I wouldn't be able to attend Andre's funeral back in Detroit. I literally couldn't visit Michigan without fear of being arrested because my first wife, Ann, had lied about me failing to pay child support. When Daphne and I married, Ann pretty well left us alone, but I think that's because Daphne and I never had children together. I mentioned that Ann thought of herself as the one-and-only Mrs. Lamont Dozier— even long after we were divorced—and the idea of me having children with anyone else really sent her into a tailspin. In fact, when Barbara got pregnant with our son Beau, Ann made all sorts of threats about what she would do if Barbara and I got married. Once that happened, things became very difficult between her and me.

One time Ann brought Michelle and her other children to Los Angeles for a visit and offered to bring Andre along, too, since they all lived in Detroit. Andre's mother, Hattie, entrusted him to Ann's care, but, when they landed at LAX, she abandoned Andre at the airport. He was only nine years old at the time, but thank God a kind stranger helped him call Hattie from a pay phone, who then called us to alert us to go pick him up.

Maybe Ann considered it some kind of retaliation for my marrying Barbara, but she reported that I was a deadbeat who hadn't ever paid child support, and though I had actually *overpaid*, she made it appear as if I hadn't. I ended up losing my driver's license in California over the whole thing, and there was a warrant out for my arrest in Michigan. If we ever wanted to visit family in Detroit, we would have to fly into Canada and then my mother, siblings, aunts and everybody would have to come across the bridge to see us. That went on for years and years.

Finally, Barbara went to Detroit and spent the day in the family law courtroom to scout out an attorney who could potentially help us with our case. She saw a guy named David Findling, who seemed like a smart and tough lawyer. After the hearing, Barbara followed him out into the hallway. "Excuse me," she said. "I was really impressed with how you defended your client in the courtroom. Obviously she's a woman, but do you ever represent men?" He nodded. "Sure, I represent men," he told her. Barbara filled him in on my situation. "Before I can represent your husband," he told her, "I'll need to speak with him directly." David and I were on the phone the very next day. I explained that I'd been paying everything I was supposed to pay and had the canceled checks to prove it. David was shocked that I'd been paying Ann directly rather than via a receivership, and he got down to business right away to get to the bottom of what was going on.

As it turned out, Ann had a friend who worked in the government and that person was destroying the evidence of payment. That's why it appeared in the system that I hadn't actually been paying. I'm so glad I kept those returned checks! There was a hearing and, when the judge found out that Ann had been gaming the system, he threatened to throw her in jail. She wound up getting off with a stern warning, but the good news was that my name was finally cleared. After years of turmoil, we were able to put that dark chapter behind us. Once it was resolved, it was like the sun came out. A huge weight was lifted.

Unfortunately, we were still in the middle of all that drama when Andre passed away, so I had to stay home. Hattie was so distraught over Andre's death that Barbara had to claim his body in Chicago. She even cleaned out his apartment, which Hattie was just too shattered to face. Andre was Hattie's only child, and she was just a basket case. That's not the kind of thing you can ever get over, and I know Hattie still suffers from that loss to this day. I was so grateful that Barbara was there to step up to the plate to take care of things.

I was really touched by the outpouring of love and support from my friends. Eric Clapton lost his four-year-old son Conor that same year in a terrible accident, and he wrote me a deeply moving letter. I knew that he really understood the pain of losing a child. His words were encouraging during that terrible time. Going through that experience is something I wouldn't wish on my worst enemy, if I had an enemy, and I'm still haunted by it to this day.

I never spoke about it to anyone, but after Andre died, I sank into a deep depression that lasted nearly ten years. I could still write at the piano and go out a bit socially when I had to, but none of it was easy. I felt guilty, thinking maybe I could have somehow prevented Andre's death, but of course I couldn't have. Those feelings mixed with regret for not being able to spend as much time with him as I would have liked kind of blindsided me. I retreated into a shell of sadness and became increasingly disengaged with the day-to-day raising of our children. My younger children, Paris and Desiree, suffered as a result of my inability to spend a lot of time with them. I yearned to connect, but depression is a powerfully destructive force. Barbara ended up shouldering most of that responsibility while being there for me, too. It was a long and winding path out of that dark tunnel of depression, but the love of my music and the love of my family eventually brought balance back into my life.

Chapter Twenty

REFLECTIONS

Any songwriter who has a significant amount of success eventually becomes institutionalized in some way and starts getting formally recognized for their achievements in the past. There's no greater honor than to be lauded for your contributions to your industry, and that's what began happening in the late 1980s when Eddie and Brian and I started receiving various awards for our body of work.

I had the surreal experience of being inducted into the Songwriters Hall of Fame in 1988, right in the middle of my fresh wave of success. Eddie and Brian and I went to New York for the ceremony, where we performed "How Sweet It Is (To be Loved by You)" and "Baby I Need Your Loving." Mary Wilson was on hand to sing a few of our songs, too, and it was a great evening.

I invited my entire family to come to the induction banquet, including my mother, my brothers and sisters, and my Aunt Jenny and Uncle James, who had been so supportive of my musical interests when I was a kid. When we went up on the stage to accept our award, I thought about all those times when I was starting out, and my mother would say, "Lamont, you need to just get a job and forget about all this music stuff. There ain't no future in it." When I gave my acceptance speech, I said, "Maybe now my mother will stop buggin' me about gettin' a job up at Ford's." The whole family got a big kick out of that. I felt particularly honored for being acknowledged by the Hall of Fame, because the honor came from the songwriting community. It's the ultimate validation to be recognized as part of America's grand songwriting tradition that goes back to the Gershwins, Irving Berlin, Cole Porter, and all the greats.

A couple of years later, we were inducted into the Rock & Roll Hall of Fame alongside Hank Ballard, Louis Armstrong, The Four Tops, The Kinks, The Platters, Simon & Garfunkel, The Who, Bobby Darin, The Four Seasons, Charlie Christian, Ma Rainey, and the songwriting team of Gerry Goffin and Carole King. Diana Ross gave the induction speech for us at the ceremony and joined The Four Tops onstage for the all-star jam at the end of the evening to sing "I Can't Help Myself." It was another great night of feeling the love from the music industry.

The recognition and outpouring of respect has continued ever since. The Recording Academy honored us with the National Trustees Award as part of the 1998 Grammy ceremony. Then, in 2002, I was given the President's Lifetime Achievement Award by the National Music Publishers Association. The following year, BMI honored Eddie, Brian, and me with the highly prestigious BMI Icon award, which recognized our "unique and indelible influence on generations of music makers." In 2007 I received the Thornton Legacy Award from the University of Southern

California's Thornton School of Music. In 2009 the Songwriters Hall of Fame acknowledged us once again with their highest honor when we were selected as the recipients of its annual Johnny Mercer award. The designation goes to a writer or writing team that's already been inducted into the Hall of Fame to recognize the most outstanding work among the world's songwriting luminaries. It has been bestowed on people like Harold Arlen, Sammy Cahn, Stephen Sondheim, Leiber & Stoller, and other legends, so that one really floored me.

I remember there was a luncheon to celebrate the Johnny Mercer Award and Stephen Schwartz got up to speak. Stephen is an incredible composer and lyricist who has written a ton of stuff, including *Godspell* and *Wicked*. He said, "I wouldn't be standing here if it wasn't for Holland-Dozier-Holland. The first time I heard their work it made me realize what I wanted to do with my life." Now that brought tears to my eyes!

I have been deeply touched by each of these honors, and I don't take any of them for granted. In fact, I get kind of emotional when I think about the way Eddie and Brian and I have been appreciated for our contributions to the music world. The only downside I can think of to getting a lifetime achievement award is that I'm not done living yet! Hopefully I've got a lot of life and a lot of songs left in me. Getting recognized for your body of work can have the effect of linking you primarily with the past, no matter how great the stuff might be that you're creating in the present. I am immensely proud of the classic songs, but I know the Master Muse has more songs for me, and I'm definitely not interested in hanging it up yet.

As I mentioned, Barbara is not just my wife, she's also my business partner. We're a team, and she's great at handling all the practical stuff when I'm off in the creative stratosphere. She's always been like a firefighter who can anticipate business problems and put out the fires before they get out of hand. She's also got great instincts in terms of strategizing for my career. In the early 2000s, we realized that if people wanted the old stuff, then we'd give them the old stuff—but with a new twist. We formed our own label together called Hithouse Records and put out an album called *An American Original*. I recorded a bunch of Holland-Dozier-Holland classics from the heyday, but I presented them the way many of them were originally conceived: as slow lovelorn ballads. It was how the songs sounded before Brian and I sped them up to make them radio friendly, and people really responded to hearing them in a more intimate presentation. I even earned a Grammy nomination for Best Traditional R&B Vocal Album for that project, which meant a lot to me— especially considering I never received a Grammy nomination for any of those songs the first time around!

I've since recorded a couple of more albums that revisit and reinterpret some of the classic material: *Reflections Of* in 2004 and *Reimagination* in 2018. It's been really gratifying to see how much people appreciate hearing these songs in their original, though less familiar, form.

An even greater thrill is to have seen my children develop their own musical interests. When my son Beau was still a small child, he became fascinated by anything musical. He would crawl around and then pull himself up to touch my recording equipment in an effort to figure out how it all worked. As he grew, he came home from elementary school one day and said, "Hey, Dad, they were playing this song on the bus today. I don't know if you know it or not." He went over to the piano and started playing it. He was probably around nine or ten, and just started plucking out this melody as if it was the most natural thing in the world. He'd never had a lesson, but he had a natural ear for it. My son Paris was the same way.

As they got a little older, both boys got into hip-hop. They gave me insight into some of the new music that was coming along for their generation, and that became part of my continuing education. I gave them the space to discover their own music and do their own thing, and I think I wound up learning at least as much about music from them as they taught me. Since I was always in my home studio, we created a small portable studio setup in each of the boys' rooms. They began experimenting and trying different things, and I was always eager to hear what they were coming up with. Beau and Paris created music that was different from one another and different from what I do, and I loved to see them soaking it all up and expressing themselves in their own ways.

Once I was able to emerge from the fog of depression that descended on me after Andre died, Barbara and I really enjoyed raising our family. I wanted them to have the absolute best opportunities, so all three of our children attended a fashionable but strict private school called the Buckley School in Sherman Oaks. Through the school we met some really great people and became close friends with the parents of quite a few of our children's friends. We always enjoyed attending birthday and holiday parties, and Barbara and I both got involved in the school meetings, recitals, and various activities.

One of the couples we became friendly with was Robert and Kris Kardashian, whom we met at a Buckley School parent night when Beau was in the nursery class. Robert had been a big fan of my ABC Dunhill albums, and we bonded instantly. We've always had a wonderful time at the Kardashian family's annual Christmas Eve celebration, which we've attended for almost forty years now. Even after Robert and Kris split up, they managed to be one of the most beautiful models for healthy co-parenting that I've ever seen. Bruce Jenner was a phenomenal second father to the Kardashian kids that he helped raise, and we've always appreciated our relationship with the whole family.

When he was in high school, Beau made a cassette with recordings of his original songs. It was just something he recorded in his room, and he wasn't trying to shop it to record companies or anything. He gave a copy to Kim Kardashian, who really liked the songs and ended up playing it for her friend Allison Azoff. Allison is Irving Azoff's daughter, and she told her dad how much she loved it. Irving ended up calling the house one day to say he was interested in having a meeting about signing Beau. This time we called him back! Irving did wind up doing a deal while Beau was still a teenager, which gave him a great start in the music business. I was really proud that he did it all on his own without asking me to pull any strings.

While Beau was working on music in his room from a young age, Paris was in the next room making music of his own. He was doing some experimental stuff that was a hybrid of punk and hip-hop. Beau was best friends with Kahbran White growing up, who is the son of Maurice White of Earth, Wind & Fire. Thanks to our boys being close, Barbara and I became close with Maurice and his wife Marilyn. Kahbran was interning for Rob Cavallo at Disney's Hollywood Records in the early 2000s and ended up playing Paris's rough demos for him. They signed Paris as an artist, but then September 11th happened. Paris's stuff was really edgy for a Disney company anyway, but the whole tone changed after the attacks, and the Disney folks were hesitant to go in a direction that was outside the boundaries of their typical tween-oriented fare. The timing wasn't right, but it was great to see others recognizing my son's talent.

At the time, some people assumed that Beau and Paris got record deals as a result of having the last name Dozier, but nothing could be further from the truth. I intentionally stayed out of it so they could make their own way and develop their own musical perspectives. Both boys worked their butts off for years writing, recording, and fine-tuning their songs in their bedrooms until they each came up with something that was fresh and original. When you're the child of someone who's successful in the music industry, there are always haters out there who want to tear you down. As a result, Beau and Paris had to work twice as hard to prove themselves. As it turned out, neither of them got an album released from those early deals, and it was truly heartbreaking. I think it probably hurt me as badly as it did them. To see your kids not get something they worked so hard for is gut-wrenching as a parent, but they never gave up, and they both continued to find their own way in this world.

Beau continued to pursue his music and has written and produced for a long list of artists that includes Boyz II Men, JoJo, Avant, Tiffany Evans, Backstreet Boys, Vanessa Hudgens, Fifth Harmony, Nelly, and others. He is one of the best songwriters, programmers, and producers in contemporary music, and his gifts for melody, lyrics, and song structure blow me away. We've worked on many songs together, and it's always a thrilling experience. Not only does Beau have special gifts of his own, but he also has a real eye for talent. He works for *American Idol* and spends part of the year traveling all over the country to audition people who want to be contestants on the show. He has great instincts and a great ear for that kind of thing.

Paris still writes, produces, and does musical theater. I have collaborated with him on productions for the Chicago Children's Theatre and the Children's Theatre Company in Minneapolis that earned rave reviews. Paris is one the most brilliant lyricists I've ever worked worth, but he ultimately decided to reinvent himself professionally. He moved out of state and went back to school to work on his master's degree. He's preparing to enter a doctorate program to earn a PhD in psychology and has maintained a 4.0 grade point average while juggling various musical and other creative projects. I'm amazed at his energy level and his work ethic.

My daughter Desiree is a really great writer and creative person in her own right, but she didn't have a desire to pursue music professionally like the boys did. She's similar to them, however, in how hard she worked in school. Desiree went to the Annenberg School for Communication and Journalism at the University of Southern California where she really excelled. Though she applied to several schools, USC was her first choice. She went through four rounds of interviews during the admissions process and really sweated it out waiting to hear if she'd been accepted. Even though she had already been admitted to several other schools, she had her sights set on USC. She knew what she wanted, and I wasn't surprised when she made it because she has always applied herself in academics, sports, the arts, or any other challenge anyone could put in front of her. If it sounds like I'm bragging, I am! Today Desiree works as a director of communications, social media, and public relations. She's beautiful like her mother, but she has a more introspective personality that reminds me of myself. She has a deep sense of loyalty and integrity, and I can't wait to give her the wedding of her dreams and walk her down the aisle when the time is right. She is such an amazing young woman. Her middle name is actually Starr, which is appropriate because she's such a beautiful and bright star in my life.

I was really excited when Desiree decided to go to USC because I had already gotten involved in their Thornton School of Music through Chris Sampson, who is the founding director of their Popular Music Program. As an artist in residence professor, I was part of helping them put that program together, and I discovered that I draw a lot of energy and inspiration from working with students who love music and are hungry to learn their craft.

Working with college kids keeps me young. The music world has changed so much since I first started out, but the heart of it never changes, and that heart is a great song. No matter what genre or era you're talking about, if you don't have a great song, then you aren't going to move people. It's harder than ever before for a young writer to carve out a living these days, but if you've got it in your blood, there's no way to shake it. For a lot of us, writing songs is like a fire burning through our bones. It's not a question of *if* we're going to do it, but *how* we're going to do it.

As I look back now over my sixty-plus years as a songwriter, singer, and producer, I feel really gratified by where I am today. All the drama and the lawsuits with Berry Gordy and the Hollands have been settled. It took a long time, and it caused a lot of pain for a lot of people. Even after all the court battles and bad blood, I still love Berry Gordy. There's no denying his talent or his place in music history. What Berry and Holland-Dozier-Holland accomplished together is a musical legacy that nobody can deny. I went through times of feeling bitter and angry, but holding on to those feelings doesn't hurt anyone but me. At some point I accepted that Motown was Berry Gordy's ballgame. It was his bat, his ball, his glove, and his playing field. At the end of the day, his basic philosophy was "bring me the hits." Within that framework he gave us the room to develop and express ourselves as writers and producers. When I think about that catalog that Brian and Eddie and I were able to put together for that decade or so we were together, it kind of boggles my mind. What a special thing to be a part of! As I look back on the 1960s now, I don't think about contracts, damaged relationships, or legal disputes. I think about the music.

When Eddie and Brian and I received our star on the Hollywood Walk of Fame in 2015, Berry was there to make the presentation. We laughed together and we reflected on what we'd all created. There was a luncheon afterward, and Stevie Wonder sat down at a piano in the banquet room. He was there for two or three hours and practically played the entire catalog of Holland-Dozier-Holland songs. To bask in that kind of love and respect gave me such warm feelings about Motown and all the frustrations and disputes kind of melted away.

In February of 2019, CBS filmed a television special called *Motown 60: A Grammy Celebration*. Brian and Eddie and I were on hand, as were Berry, Smokey, Diana Ross, Stevie, Martha Reeves, and other Hitsville veterans. There were also newer artists like Pentatonix, Ciara, and John Legend on hand to pay tribute to the music we'd made in that tiny little studio on West Grand Boulevard. Before the taping for the main show, the producers got some of us together in a nearby hotel banquet room to shoot a segment about Motown songwriters. Valerie Simpson sat at the piano while Smokey Robinson, Mickey Stevenson, Brian, Eddie, and I gathered around her to swap stories and sing little bits of one another's songs. The segment was cut down to a fairly brief moment for the broadcast, but that little reunion of Motown writers reminded me what it was all about. Take away the elements of celebrity, ego, money, contracts, conflicts, legal clashes, and interpersonal conflicts, and you're left with a body of work that has touched the hearts of countless fans. The songs. That's all that matters now.

We all have our problems, we all have our failings, and we all have our demons. I made the decision, however, to look for the positive in people. From my father to my ex-wives to unscrupulous music industry executives, I've been through my fair share of pain and hurt, and I know I've probably caused

unintentional pain in the lives of others from time to time. I
choose not to dwell on the negative but to focus on what I
can control, which is my own attitude and outlook. No matter
what life throws at you, there's a lesson that can be applied that
will lead to improvement. I believe in karma, so I don't look for
payback anymore. The Master Muse will take care of all that stuff.
That's in his hands, and it isn't my place to worry about it.

I've reached a place in my life where I've achieved the balance
I sought for a long time. I am as passionately in love with my
music as I've always been, but I also recognize that nothing can
take the place of family. I have a wonderful wife and children,
who are so important to me. I'm blessed to have my brother
Reggie and my sisters, who are back in Detroit. I sadly lost my
mother back in 2007, but I have so many wonderful aunts, uncles,
nieces, nephews, and cousins—not to mention Barbara's sister
Sheryl, who is like another blood relative to me. I feel so blessed
to have these beautiful people in my life. One the greatest joys
for me now is being around my granddaughter, Dawson Soleil
Dozier. Dawson is Beau's daughter and is my first grandchild. My
son Paris and his wife Sandra are expecting a baby boy very soon,
and I couldn't be more excited. Grandchildren are a whole new
form of love, and there's nothing better!

**I'll leave you with one last lesson that has become my
mantra for both songwriting and life:** *I don't say I have bad
days anymore. I have good days and I have learning days.* **When
things aren't going right, there's always something to
be learned from the experience. There's a way to grow
and improve. I've shared plenty of tips and principles
with you, but the truth is that I think of myself less as
a teacher and more as a student. I'm a lifelong learner
when it comes to songwriting but also when it comes to
being a musician, producer, husband, father, grandfather,**

and friend. The day any of us thinks we've got nothing left to learn is the day we've lost touch with reality. Sometimes I experience disappointments or I get a piece of bad news, but I choose to trust that I will be shaped and molded on that "learning day" to become a better version of myself. To live up to your full potential, you have to approach writing and life with humble awe.

As for my future, I guess it's in the hands of the Master Muse to decide when to turn off the flow of song ideas that I've been blessed enough to receive for all these years. It doesn't seem that time is coming in the near future, though. I still write several hours a day, seven days a week. You can usually find me at my piano every morning by 10 AM. I work for a while and then take a break to watch TV and clear my head before returning to the piano in the midafternoon. I still write about twenty songs a month. Not every one of them is completely finished, but they're all at least eighty percent complete. Sometimes you have to give them a little breathing room to know which ones are worth finishing.

If I start a song on a Monday, I might work on it for two or three days in a row. Then I'll leave it alone for a few days and come back to it the following Monday with a fresh mind. Sometimes I'll come back and say, *Hey, that's a good start!* Other times I'll think, *Boy, that's a piece of shit!* I need that perspective, and the song needs the time to simmer and marinate. It's just like cooking. You can't rush it if you want the flavors to emerge. The song will ultimately tell me what it wants, so I just have to have the patience to let it unfold and the personal integrity to set aside my ego and be honest about what is and isn't good. It's a dance I've been doing for more than sixty years, and one I hope I'll still be doing for many years to come. In the meantime, if you need me, I'll be at my piano trying to get around myself.

LAMONT'S GUIDING PRINCIPLES OF SONGWRITING

Though I sprinkled various nuggets and observations about songwriting throughout the book, I'm listing them here again for easy reference. As noted, these are not "songwriting rules" so much as a set of guiding principles that I've relied on in my career as a writer. The number next to each principle refers to the chapter of the book in which it appears.

1. *Don't take something that belongs to someone else unless you have their permission.* Before I can ever consider a song finished, I have to make sure that I'm not unintentionally lifting someone else's idea. The same principle applies

to unintentional "borrowing" as well as sampling and
building off someone else's work.

2. *You need to have a point of view that informs what you want
    to say.* Know who your audience is and what values you
    want to transmit through your lyrics. Nobody else can
    decide that for you, but if you want to be a great writer,
    it's crucial that you understand your own perspective and
    how you can best communicate it.

3A. *If you want to write songs that move people, you have to write
    from a place that moves you.* You need to find an emotional
    connection to your subject. If it doesn't resonate with
    you, it's probably not going to resonate with someone
    else, either. In that respect, all songwriting is personal.
    You've got to be willing to put your own heart on the
    line if you want to touch the hearts of your listeners.

3B. *Ideas are all around us if we keep an ear out for them.* If
    you want to be a great songwriter, you've got to absorb
    conversations, books, movies, TV shows, and art. You've
    got to experience the world with open ears and eyes to
    pick up on those universal truths that others might miss if
    they're not paying close attention. Being a songwriter is a
    way of life. And that way is all about observation.

4A. *Think about what you're trying to communicate before you
    throw down the first line or idea that comes to your mind.* Let
    the song reveal itself to you. Marinate in the idea so that
    it can properly emerge. There's no set amount of time that
    will take. Some songs come in a rush like a freight train,
    but others want to be chased for a while. You've got to be

mentally prepared to spend the time it takes to get a song to where it needs to land.

4B. *You must educate yourself about the business. Then, once you've educated yourself, you've got to be realistic.* If you want to live the life of a songwriter, read some reputable books about how the music business works. Or consider taking a class or two. Then, ask good questions and draw from the wisdom of those who have gone before.

5. *You have to recognize what's beyond your control.* You can write a song, record it, release it, find success with it, and sometimes something can still go awry. There are certain things that are just out of our hands. It's important to be diligent to control what you can control. Beyond that, you have to release the songs into the wild and trust that the right thing is going to happen.

6. *It's crucial to be open to new situations.* When you're starting out as a writer, there will be opportunities to collaborate with different people, and I always encourage newer writers to get in the habit of saying "yes." Some of those encounters will lead to nothing, but you never know who you'll click with or where a particular collaboration will lead you down the road. Be open to experiment and try new things.

7. *Be flexible enough to change your ideas when it's appropriate to do so.* I'm not saying that writers should compromise their vision or change things on a whim, but I am saying there are situations where we must avoid being rigid in order for the song to emerge as what it was meant to be in the first place. Never become so rigid that you're not willing

to at least consider changes that will tip the scale to help the song earn the attention it deserves.

8A. *Never count out a possible opportunity.* Sometimes our minds want to jump right to the reasons something might not work instead of considering how we can make something possible. I try to live my life and pursue my writing career in such a way that I hope for the best outcome rather than restrain myself with negative "what-ifs." Don't decide that someone will probably give you a "no" and miss out on an opportunity for them to give you a "yes!"

8B. *If you want to find success, surround yourself with the right people.* This business is about knowing what you do best and then surrounding yourself with the right people who know how to complement your talents. Nobody is an island, and the right combination of people will not only serve your skills but will also give you a sense of artistic community and encouragement to make you better at the important piece that you bring to the puzzle.

9A. *Always put the song ahead of your ego.* Sometimes you think a song should be one way, but that song will tell you if it's meant to be something else entirely. Don't fight it! It's a delicate balance to pursue your vision while having the humility to be willing to let the Master Muse guide you along the right route.

9B. *Do your best work, enjoy your successes, and don't get stuck in the paralysis of overanalysis.* If you don't let go of your songs and let them be done when they're done, then self-doubt can eat at you and ultimately destroy your creative impulses.

10A. *You can have the success you dream about, but you've got to have a relentless work ethic.* To truly "make it" you have to want it bad enough and be willing to put in the sweat equity. If you want to succeed, you can't play around at your career because there are other people out there dedicating their lives to it, and they'll beat you out every time.

10B. *It might be a cliché, but you meet the same folks on the way up that you meet on the way down, so always treat others the way you want to be treated.* You never know where life's circumstances will take you or who you might need help from in the future. I've always tried to steer clear of the drama and the backbiting and the politics that come along with the dirty business of music. It's easy to get sucked into it, but if you want to do it right, don't forget about the Golden Rule that you learned back in kindergarten or Sunday school.

11. *Know when to break your own rules.* The better you know the rules, the wiser you are about when and how to break them. Soak up all the songwriting wisdom you can as you dedicate yourself to the craft, but recognize that there's occasionally a time and place to set it all aside and pursue something outside the box.

12. *You have to be true to yourself.* People will come and go from your life. Seasons will change. Fashions and fads will ebb and flow. Different people will want different things

from you at different times, but you have to have a strong sense of self in order to stay grounded and centered.

13. *Know when to push the envelope.* The flip side of that coin is knowing when not to push the envelope. It usually isn't a good idea to write about something that's going to make your audience uncomfortable simply for the sake of making them uncomfortable. But there's also something to be said for writing songs that might leave people a bit unsettled for the sake of making them think or moving them emotionally. You can't make a gimmick out of that kind of thing, but a few well-timed envelope pushes usually make for a more interesting songwriter.

14. *Believe and have faith, even when it's hard to see the fruits of your labor.* Your dream can come true, but it never will if you give up. It's easy to believe and have faith when things are going well, but when you're in the midst of challenges is when your faith is tested. That's the time to double down and hang in there.

15A. *There's no such thing as writer's block.* Stop feeding those lies about writer's block. Writer's block only exists in your mind, and if you tell yourself you have it, it will cripple your ability to function as a creative person. The answer to so-called writer's block is doing the work. If you press on, the answers you need will come through. You have to show the muses that you're capable and committed, then you'll get the answers you need.

15B. *The best songwriters know how to take personal feelings and translate them into universal experiences.* If you can start with that personal, passionate spark and then widen your message so that people can project their own experiences onto it, then you've achieved one of the building blocks of what it takes to be a special kind of writer.

16. *To truly go the distance as a songwriter you have to be completely consumed by it.* It has to be something that you're going to do even if you never make a dime at it. It has to come from deep inside you. It's almost as if you have to be chosen by the Master Muse.

17. *Be open to all avenues for your songs.* If someone wants you to write something for an independent film or a commercial or a web series, don't count it out just because you might think of yourself as only writing for your own albums as an artist. Writing songs for films was a new avenue for me in the 1970s. When those opportunities first began presenting themselves, I could have said, "No, that's not really the kind of thing I usually do." That would have been true, but had I not stretched myself, I would have missed out on some great opportunities. More importantly, I might have missed out on meeting Barbara!

18A. *Talent plus determination equals songwriting success.* You must have them both. You have to be prepared to kick the door down no matter how many doors are behind that one. You have to be stubborn. You can do anything you make up your mind to do. Tell me I can't do something, and the challenge is on!

18B. *Don't waste your time being jealous or envious.* There's more than enough success to go around in this industry,

so entertaining jealous thoughts is nothing but a waste
of time. It won't do anything but eat at your insides and
hamper your own creative flow. When others have a streak
of good fortune, celebrate with those people—even if you
consider them your "competition." Refuse to be swayed
by negative thoughts and negative talk that only keeps
you from fulfilling your destiny.

19. *Understand what kind of environment you need to do your
best work, and then make sure you intentionally create that
environment for yourself on a regular basis.* There's no secret
formula that works for everyone, but if you're serious,
you'll figure out works best for you and make sure to put
it in practice.

20. *There are no bad days. There are good days and there are
learning days.* When things aren't going right, there's
always something to be learned from the experience.
There's a way to grow and improve. To live up to your
full potential, you have to approach writing and life with
humble awe.

LIST OF LAMONT'S CHARTING SINGLES AS A SONGWRITER

Following is a complete list of Lamont's nationally charting singles organized according to the year each first charted. The entries appear in the following format: artist, song title, writer credit, record label, release number, charting position, and chart name.

If a song charted multiple times, all charting versions are listed under the initial entry. The years of the subsequent charting versions are included in parentheses. Additionally, some entries include a noncomprehensive sampling of notable cover versions. The following abbreviations are used:

R&B =   *Billboard* Rhythm & Blues chart (US)
HOT =   *Billboard* Hot 100 (pop) chart (US)
AC =   *Billboard* Adult Contemporary chart (US)
CTRY =   *Billboard* Hot Country Singles chart (US)
UK =   UK Singles Chart
HDH =   Holland-Dozier-Holland

★ All entries through 1972 were written with Eddie Holland and Brian Holland unless otherwise noted. All entries from 1973 onward were written by Lamont Dozier solo unless otherwise noted.

1962

The Marvelettes—"Someday, Someway"
(with Fred Gorman, Brian Holland)
Tamla 54065—#8 R&B

The Marvelettes—"Strange I Know"
(with Fred Gorman, Brian Holland)
Tamla 54072—#10 R&B / #49 HOT

1963

Martha & The Vandellas—"Come and Get These Memories"
Gordy 7014—#6 R&B / #29 HOT
Notable cover versions: Fontella Bass, Bette Midler, Laura Nyro, The Supremes

The Marvelettes—"Locking Up My Heart"
Tamla 54077—#25 R&B / #44 HOT

The Marvelettes—"Forever" (with Fred Gorman, Brian Holland)
Tamla 54077—#24 R&B / #78 HOT
        Baby Washington & Don Gardner—Master 5 9103—#30 R&B / #119 HOT (1973)
Notable cover versions: Marvin Gaye, Martha & The Vandellas, Carla Thomas

Martha & The Vandellas—"Heat Wave"
Gordy 7022—#1 R&B / #4 HOT
        Linda Ronstadt—Asylum 45282—#5 HOT / #19 AC (1975)

Notable cover versions: Cilla Black, Lou Christie, Phil Collins, Human Nature and Martha Reeves, The Jam, Lulu, Joan Osborne, Dusty Springfield, The Supremes, The Who

The Miracles—"Mickey's Monkey" (with Brian Holland)
Tamla 54083—#3 R&B / #8 HOT
Notable cover versions: Lou Christie, The Hollies, Martha & The Vandellas, Mother's Finest, Smokey Robinson, The Young Rascals

Mary Wells—"You Lost the Sweetest Boy"
Motown 1048—#10 R&B / #22 HOT
Notable cover version: Dusty Springfield

Marvin Gaye—"Can I Get a Witness"
Tamla 54087—#3 R&B / #22 HOT
    Lee Michaels—A&M 1303—#39 HOT (1971)
    Sam Brown—A&M 509—#15 UK (1989)
Notable cover versions: The Buckinghams, Commodores, Z. Z. Hill, Lulu, The Rolling Stones, Dusty Springfield, The Supremes, The Temptations, Earl Van Dyke and the Soul Brothers, Stevie Wonder

Martha & The Vandellas—"Quicksand"
Gordy 7025—#7 R&B / #8 HOT

The Miracles—"I Gotta Dance to Keep From Crying"
Tamla 54089—#17 R&B / #35 HOT

The Supremes—"When the Lovelight Starts Shining Through His Eyes"
Motown 1051—#2 R&B / #23 HOT
    Boones—Motown 1334—#25 AC (1975)
Notable cover versions: Debby Boone, Bonnie Pointer, Dusty Springfield, The Zombies

Eddie Holland—"Leaving Here"
Motown 1052—#27 R&B / #76 HOT
    The Birds—Decca 12140—#45 UK (1965)
Notable cover versions: The Isley Brothers, Motorhead, Pearl Jam, The Who

1964

Martha & The Vandellas—"Live Wire"
Gordy 7027—#11 R&B / #42 HOT

The Supremes—"Run, Run, Run"
Motown 1054—#22 R&B / #93 HOT

Marvin Gaye—"You're a Wonderful One"
Tamla 54093—#3 R&B / #15 HOT
Notable cover versions: Don Bryant, Art Garfunkel

Martha & The Vandellas—"In My Lonely Room"
Gordy 7031—#6 R&B / #44 HOT
Notable cover versions: Phil Collins, Diana Ross & The Supremes

Eddie Holland—"Just Ain't Enough Love"
Motown 1058—#31 R&B / #54 HOT
Notable cover versions: The Isley Brothers

The Supremes—"Where Did Our Love Go"
Motown 1060—#1 R&B / #1 HOT / #3 UK
   Donnie Elbert—All Platinum 2330—#6 R&B / #15 HOT (1971)
   J. Geils Band—Atlantic 3320—#68 HOT (1976)
   The Manhattan Transfer—Atlantic 11182—#40 UK (1978)
Notable cover versions: The J. Geils Band, Little Anthony and the Imperials,
Manhattan Transfer, The New Christy Minstrels, Marie Osmond, The
Pussycat Dolls, Rare Earth, Soft Cell, Spice Girls, Ringo Starr

The Four Tops—"Baby I Need Your Loving"
Motown 1062—#4 R&B / #11 HOT
   Johnny Rivers—Imperial 66227—#3 HOT (1967)
   O.C. Smith—Columbia 45206—#30 R&B / #52 HOT /
#21 AC (1970)
   E.D. Wofford—MC/Curb 5012—#77 CTRY (1978)
   Eric Carmen—Arista 0384—#62 HOT / #30 AC (1979)
   Carl Carlton—RCA 13313—#17 R&B / #103 HOT (1982)

Notable cover versions: Blue Swede, Carl Carlton, Eric Carmen, Paul Carrack, Lou Christie, Marvin Gaye & Tammi Terrell, Human Nature, La Toya Jackson, Gladys Knight & The Pips, Lulu, Michael McDonald, Gene Pitney, Johnny Rivers, Mitch Ryder & The Detroit Wheels, O.C. Smith, Phoebe Snow, Lisa Stansfield, The Supremes, Was (Not Was), Kim Weston and Marvin Gaye

Eddie Holland—"Candy to Me"
Motown 1063—#29 R&B / #58 HOT

Marvin Gaye—"Baby Don't You Do It"
Tamla 54101—#14 R&B / #27 HOT
       The Band (as "Don't Do It")—Capitol 3433—#32 HOT (1972)
Notable cover versions: Humble Pie, The Isley Brothers, Nicolette Larson, The Small Faces, The Wailers, The Who, Stevie Wonder

The Supremes—"Baby Love"
Motown 1066—#1 R&B / #1 HOT / #1 UK
       Joni Lee—MCA 40592—#62 CTRY (1976)
       Honey Bane—Zonophone 19—#58 UK (1981)
Notable cover versions: Emma Bunton, Erasure, La Toya Jackson, The Mothers of Invention, Donny Osmond, Diana Ross, Shalamar

The Supremes—"Come See About Me"
Motown 1068—#2 R&B / #1 HOT / #27 UK
       Nella Dodds—Wand 167—#74 HOT (1964)
       Jr. Walker & The All Stars—Soul 35041—#8 R&B / #24 HOT (1967)
       Mitch Ryder—New Voice 828—#113 HOT (1967)
Notable cover versions: Afghan Whigs, Dave "Baby" Cortez, Nella Dodds, The Ikettes, Gladys Knight and the Pips, Martina McBride, Tracy Nelson, The Newbeats, The Originals, Freda Payne, Bonnie Pointer, Martha Reeves, Mitch Ryder and the Detroit Wheels, Neil Sedaka featuring Mary Wilson, Earl Van Dyke and the Soul Brothers, Jr. Walker and The All Stars, Rita Wilson

Marvin Gaye—"How Sweet It Is (To Be Loved By You)"
Tamla 54107—#3 R&B / #6 HOT / #49 UK
      Jr. Walker & The All Stars—Soul 35024—#3 R&B / #18 HOT / #22 UK (1966)
      James Taylor—Warner 8109—#5 HOT / #1 AC (1975)
Notable cover versions: Michael Buble, The Captain & Tennille, Dave "Baby" Cortez, The Elgins, Jerry Garcia Band, The Grateful Dead, The Isley Brothers, Brenda Lee, Marilyn McCoo and Billy Davis, Jr., Human Nature, Michael McDonald, Joan Osborne, Kenny Rogers, Sam & Dave, Dinah Shore, Take 6, Earl Van Dyke and the Soul Brothers, Joe Williams

The Four Tops—"Without The One You Love (Life's Not Worth While)"
Motown 1069—#17 R&B / #43 HOT
Notable cover version: The Supremes and The Four Tops

The Supremes—"Stop! In the Name of Love"
Motown 1074—#2 R&B / #1 HOT / #7 UK (1964) / #62 UK (1989 reissue)
      Margie Joseph—Volt 4056—#38 R&B / #96 HOT (1971)
      The Hollies—Atlantic 89819—#29 HOT / #8 AC (1983)
      Glee Cast (in a medley with "Free Your Mind")—Fox album track—#38 HOT (2010)
Notable cover versions: The California Raisins, Barbara Dickson, Leif Garrett, Gloria Gaynor, The Hollies, Human Nature, The Isley Brothers, Jonathan King, La Toya Jackson, The New Christy Minstrels, Gene Pitney, Billy Preston, Rare Earth, Johnny Rivers, Kim Weston

1965

Martha & The Vandellas—"Nowhere to Run"
Gordy 7039—#5 R&B / #8 HOT / #26 UK
      Nu Generation (as "Nowhere to Run 2000")—Concept 16—#66 UK (2000)
Notable cover versions: Phil Collins, Grand Funk, The Isley Brothers, Michael McDonald, Laura Nyro and LaBelle, Esther Phillips, Bonnie Pointer, Dusty Springfield, Tower of Power, Wild Cherry

The Supremes—"Back In My Arms Again"
Motown 1075—#1 R&B / #1 HOT / #40 UK
> Genya Ravan—20th Century 2374—#92 HOT (1978)
> Cynthia Manley—Atlantic 89920—#109 HOT (1983)
> High Inergy—Gordy 1688—#105 HOT (1983)

Notable cover versions: Michael Bolton, Fanny, The Forrester Sisters, The Jam, Nicolette Larson

The Four Tops—"I Can't Help Myself (Sugar Pie Honey Bunch)"
Motown 1076—#1 R&B / #1 HOT / #23 UK (1965) / #10 UK (1970)
> The Magnificent Men (as part of "Sweet Soul Medley—Part 1")—#90 HOT (1967)
> Donnie Elbert—Avco 4587—#14 R&B / #22 HOT / #11 UK (1972)
> Price Mitchell & Jerri Kelly—GRT 016—#65 CTRY (1974)
> Bonnie Pointer—Motown 1478—#42 R&B / #40 HOT (1979)
> Trisha Lynn—Oak 1083—#65 CTRY (1989)
> Billy Hill—Reprise 22746—#58 CTRY (1989)

Notable cover versions: Phil Collins and Paul Young, Jimi Hendrix featuring Curtis Knight, Human Nature, La Toya Jackson, Taj Mahal, Martha and the Vandellas, Dolly Parton, Bonnie Pointer, Johnny Rivers, Kid Rock, Shalamar, The Supremes, The Temptations and The Four Tops, Irma Thomas, Earl Van Dyke and the Soul Brothers, Bobby Vee

The Supremes—"Nothing But Heartaches"
Motown 1080—#6 R&B / #11 HOT

The Four Tops—"It's the Same Old Song"
Motown 1081—#2 R&B / #5 HOT / #34 UK
> Jonathan King (under the name The Weathermen)—B&C 139—#19 UK (1971)
> KC & The Sunshine Band—T.K. 1028—#30 R&B / #35 HOT / #47 UK (1978)

Notable cover versions: Boyz II Men, Phil Collins and Paul Young, Human Nature, Iron and Wine, Johnny Rivers, Rod Stewart, The Supremes, Bobby Vee, Wild Cherry

Martha & The Vandellas—"Love (Makes Me Do Foolish Things)"
Gordy 7045—#22 R&B / #70 HOT
Notable cover versions: Diana Ross and the Supremes

Kim Weston—"Take Me In Your Arms (Rock Me a Little While)"
Gordy 7046—#4 R&B / #50 HOT
      The Isley Brothers—Tamla 54164—#22 R&B / #121 HOT (1968)
      The Doobie Brothers—Warner 8092—#11 HOT / #29 UK (1975)
Notable cover versions: Blood, Sweat and Tears; Phil Collins; Jermaine Jackson

The Supremes—"I Hear a Symphony"
Motown 1083—#2 R&B / #1 HOT / #39 UK
Notable cover versions: Booker T. & The M.G.s, The Isley Brothers, The Jackson 5, Quincy Jones, KC and the Sunshine Band, Wayne Newton, Diana Ross, The Temptations, The Ventures, Stevie Wonder

The Four Tops—"Something About You"
Motown 1084—#9 R&B / #19 HOT
      LeBlanc & Carr—Big Tree 16092—#48 HOT (1977)
Notable cover versions: Cilla Black, Phil Collins, Dave Edmunds, The Grass Roots, Quincy Jones, Coco Montoya

The Supremes—"My World Is Empty Without You"
Motown 1089—#10 R&B / #5 HOT
      Jose Feliciano—RCA Victor 9714—#87 HOT (1969)
Notable cover versions: Afghan Whigs, The Andantes, Vikki Carr, Jose Feliciano, Margie Joseph, The Miracles, The Originals, Della Reese, Mary Wells, Stevie Wonder

1966

The Elgins—"Darling Baby"
V.I.P. 25029-A—#4 R&B / #72 HOT
      Jackie Moore—Atlantic 2861—#22 R&B / #106 HOT (1972)

The Elgins—"Put Yourself in My Place"
V.I.P. 25029-B—#92 HOT / #28 UK (1971 reissue)
      The Isley Brothers—Tamla Motown 708—#13 UK (1969)
Notable cover versions: The Hollies, The Supremes

The Four Tops—"Shake Me, Wake Me (When It's Over)"
Motown 1090—#5 R&B / #18 HOT
Notable cover versions: Shaun Cassidy, Barbra Streisand, The Supremes,
Al Wilson

The Isley Brothers—"This Old Heart of Mine (Is Weak For You)"
Tamla 54128—#6 R&B / #12 HOT / #47 UK (1966) / #3 UK (1968)
      Tammi Terrell—Motown 1138—#31 R&B / #67 HOT
      Rod Stewart—Warner 8170—#83 HOT / #4 UK (1976)
      Rod Stewart with Ronald Isley—Warner 19983—#10 HOT /
#1 AC / #51 UK (1990)
Notable cover versions: Boyzone, Lou Christie, The Contours,
Shalamar, The Supremes, Bettye Swann, Tammi Terrell, The Temptations,
Wild Cherry, The Zombies

Kim Weston—"Helpless"
Gordy 7050—#13 R&B / #56 HOT
      Tracey Ullman—Stiff 211—#61 UK (1984)
Notable cover versions: The Four Tops, The Manhattan Transfer

Jr. Walker & The All Stars—"(I'm A) Road Runner"
Soul 35015—#4 R&B / #20 HOT / #12 UK (1969)
Notable cover versions: King Curtis, Fleetwood Mac, Peter Frampton,
Jerry Garcia Band, Humble Pie, Dr. Feelgood, Steppenwolf, James
Taylor, Trombone Shorty, Geno Washington and the Ram Jam Band,
Paul Weller

The Supremes—"Love Is Like an Itching in My Heart"
Motown 1094—#7 R&B / #9 HOT
      Good Girls—Motown 2013—#10 R&B (1990)

Notable cover versions: Nona Hendryx, Diana Ross, Shalamar, Paul Young

The Isley Brothers—"I Guess I'll Always Love You"
Tamla 54135—#31 R&B / #61 HOT / #45 UK (1966) / #11 UK (1969)
Notable cover versions: The Supremes

The Supremes—"You Can't Hurry Love"
Motown 1097—#1 R&B / #1 HOT / #3 UK
        Phil Collins—Atlantic 89933—#10 HOT / #9 AC / #1 UK
(1982)
        Dixie Chicks—Columbia album track—#60 CTRY (1999)
Notable cover versions: Boyzone, The California Raisins, The Four
Tops, Human Nature, The Jackson 5, Melanie, Bette Midler, Graham
Parker, Diana Ross, Stray Cats

Marvin Gaye—"Little Darling, I Need You"
Tamla 54138—#10 R&B / #47 HOT / #50 UK
        The Doobie Brothers—Warner 8404—#48 HOT (1977)

The Four Tops—"Reach Out I'll Be There"
Motown 1098—#1 R&B / #1 HOT / #1 UK (1966) / #11 UK
(1988 remix)
        Merrilee Rush (as "Reach Out")—AGP 107—#79 HOT (1968)
        Diana Ross—Motown 1194—#17 R&B / #29 HOT / #16
AC (1971)
        Gloria Gaynor—MGM 14790—#56 R&B / #60 HOT / #14
UK (1975)
        Michael Bolton—Columbia 74798—#73 HOT / #8 AC /
#37 UK (1992)
        Michael McDonald—Motown album track—#12 AC (2004)
Notable cover versions: Average White Band, Michael Bolton, Boyz II
Men, Boyzone, Petula Clark, Joey Dee and the Starliters, Gloria Gaynor,
Genesis, The Hollies, Thelma Houston, Human League, Gerald Levert,
Thelma Houston, The Jackson 5, Michael McDonald, Eddie Money, The
New Christy Minstrels, Rare Earth, Diana Ross, Narada Michael Walden

The Elgins—"Heaven Must Have Sent You"
V.I.P. 25037—#9 R&B / #50 HOT / #3 UK (1971 reissue)
        Bonnie Pointer—Motown 1459—#52 R&B / #11 HOT /

#43 AC (1979)
Notable cover versions: Marvin Gaye, Lulu, Johnny Mathis and Deniece
Williams, Bonnie Pointer, Diana Ross and the Supremes

Chris Clark—"Love's Gone Bad"
V.I.P. 25038—#41 R&B / #105 HOT
Notable cover versions: The Jackson 5, Michael Jackson

Martha & The Vandellas—"I'm Ready for Love"
Gordy 7056—#2 R&B / #9 HOT / #22 UK
Notable cover versions: The Four Tops, Bettye LaVette, Barbara
Mitchell, June Pointer, The Temptations

The Supremes—"You Keep Me Hangin' On"
Motown 1101—#1 R&B / #1 HOT / #8 UK
        Vanilla Fudge—Atco 6495—#67 HOT / #8 UK (1967)
        Vanilla Fudge—Atco 6590—#6 HOT (1968)
        Wilson Pickett—Atlantic 2682—#16 R&B / #92 HOT
(1969)
        Jackie DeShannon (as medley with "Hurt So Bad")—Imperial
66452—#96 HOT (1970)
        Kim Wilde—MCA 53024—#1 HOT / #30 AC (1987)
        Glee Cast—Fox album track—#123 HOT (2009)
Notable cover versions: Booker T. & The M.G.s, The Box Tops, Phil
Collins, Aretha Franklin, Human Nature, Tom Jones, KC and the
Sunshine Band, Madness, Hugh Masekela, Reba McEntire, Melanie,
Lisa Stansfield, Rod Stewart, Jackie Wilson

The Miracles—"(Come 'Round Here) I'm the One You Need"
Tamla 54140—#4 R&B / #17 HOT / #45 UK (1966), #13 UK
(1971)
Notable cover versions: The Cowsills, The Jackson 5

The Four Tops—"Standing in the Shadows of Love"
Motown 1102—#2 R&B / #6 HOT / #6 UK
Notable cover versions: Phil Collins, Daryl Hall & John Oates, The
Jackson 5, Rod Stewart, The Ventures, Barry White

1967

The Supremes—"Love is Here and Now You're Gone"
Motown 1103—#1 R&B / #1 HOT / #17 UK
Notable cover versions: Phil Collins, Doris Duke, Michael Jackson, The Lettermen, Rare Earth

Martha & The Vandellas—"Jimmy Mack"
Gordy 7058—#1 R&B / #10 HOT / #21 UK
  Sheena Easton—EMI America 8309—#65 HOT (1986)
Notable cover versions: Animal Collective, Phil Collins, Sheena Easton, Bettye LaVette, Laura Nyro and LaBelle, Bonnie Pointer

Ike & Tina Turner—"A Love Like Yours (Don't Come Knocking Every Day)"
A&M—#16 UK
This song originally appeared as the B-side of Martha & The Vandellas' "Heat Wave" single. Though Ike & Tina Turner had the only charting version, it was also covered by The Animals, Juice Newton, Harry Nilsson and Cher, Manfred Mann, Dusty Springfield, Kim Weston, and others.

The Four Tops—"Bernadette"
Motown 1104—#3 R&B / #4 HOT / #8 UK
Notable cover version: Funkadelic

The Supremes—"The Happening"
Motown 1107—#12 R&B / #1 HOT / #6 UK
  Herb Alpert—A&M 860—#32 HOT / #4 AC (1967)
Notable cover version: Trini Lopez

The Four Tops—"7 Rooms of Gloom"
Motown 1110-B—#10 R&B / #14 HOT / #12 UK
Notable cover versions: Blondie, Pat Benatar

The Four Tops—"I'll Turn to Stone"
Motown 1110-B—#50 R&B / #76 HOT
Notable cover versions: Jackie DeShannon, Barbara Randolph, The Supremes

Marvin Gaye—"Your Unchanging Love"
Tamla 54153—#7 R&B / #33 HOT

The Supremes—"Reflections"
Motown 1111—#4 R&B / #2 HOT / #5 UK
Notable cover versions: The Four Tops, The Jackson 5, The Lettermen, Michael McDonald, Leo Sayer, The Temptations, Luther Vandross

The Four Tops—"You Keep Running Away"
Motown 1113—#7 R&B / #19 HOT / #26 UK
Notable cover versions: Chuck Jackson, The Messengers

Barbara Randolph—"I Got a Feeling"
Soul 35038—#116 HOT
The original version was recorded by The Four Tops and later covered by Barbara Randolph, Lisa Stansfield, and others.

The Supremes—"In and Out of Love"
Motown 1116—#16 R&B / #9 HOT / #13 UK
Notable cover version: The Les Baxter Singers & Orchestra

1968

The Supremes—"Forever Came Today"
Motown 1122—#17 R&B / #28 HOT / #28 UK
        The Jackson 5—Motown 1356—#6 R&B / #60 HOT
(1975)
Notable cover versions: Commodores, The Jackson 5, Shalamar

The Four Tops—"I'm in a Different World"
Motown 1132—#23 R&B / #51 HOT / #27 UK

1969

The Honey Cone—"While You're Out Looking For Sugar?"
(HDH with Ronald Dunbar)
Hot Wax 6901—#26 R&B / #62 HOT
Notable cover version: Joss Stone

The Flaming Ember—"Mind, Body and Soul"
(HDH with Ronald Dunbar)
Hot Wax 6902—#26 HOT

The Glass House—"Crumbs Off the Table"
(HDH with Ronald Dunbar)
Invictus 9071—#7 R&B / #59 HOT
        Laura Lee—Hot Wax 7210—#40 R&B / #107 HOT (1972)
Notable cover versions: Laura Lee, Dusty Springfield

The Honey Cone—"Girls It Ain't Easy"
(HDH with Ronald Dunbar)
Hot Wax 6903—#8 R&B / #68 HOT

100 Proof (Aged in Soul)—"Too Many Cooks (Spoil the Soup)"
(HDH with Ronald Dunbar, Angelo Bond)
Hot Wax 6904—#24 R&B / #94 HOT

1970

Chairmen of the Board—"Give Me Just a Little More Time"
(HDH with Ronald Dunbar)
Invictus 9074—#8 R&B / #3 HOT / #3 UK
Notable cover versions: Doc Severinsen, Kylie Minogue

The Flaming Ember—"Shades of Green"
(HDH with Ronald Dunbar)
Hot Wax 6907—#88 HOT

Freda Payne—"Band of Gold"
(HDH with Ronald Dunbar)
Invictus 9075—#20 R&B / #3 HOT / #1 UK
        Charly McClain—Epic 04423—#22 CTRY (1984)
Notable cover versions: Afghan Whigs, Belinda Carlisle, Kimberly
Locke, Sylvester, Bonnie Tyler

The Honey Cone—"Take Me With You" (HDH with Ronald Dunbar)
Hot Wax 7001—#28 R&B / #108 HOT

Chairmen of the Board—"(You've Got Me) Dangling on a String"
(HDH with Ronald Dunbar, General Johnson)
Invictus 9078—#19 R&B / #39 HOT / #5 UK
> Donny Osmond—Polydor/Kolob 14417—#109 HOT

The Flaming Ember—"Westbound #9"
(HDH with Ronald Dunbar, Daphne Dumas)
Hot Wax 7003—#15 R&B / #24 HOT

Chairmen of the Board—"Everything's Tuesday"
(HDH with Ronald Dunbar, Daphne Dumas)
Invictus 9079—#14 R&B / #38 HOT / #12 UK

Freda Payne—"Deeper & Deeper"
(HDH with Ronald Dunbar, Norma Toney)
Invictus 9080—#9 R&B / #24 HOT / #33 UK

The Honey Cone—"When Will It End"
(HDH with Ronald Dunbar)
Hot Wax 7005—#117 HOT

The Glass House—"Stealing Moments From Another Woman's Life"
(with Brian Holland)
Invictus 9082—#42 R&B / #121 HOT

1971

Freda Payne—"Cherish What is Dear to You (While It's Near to You)"
(with Brian Holland, Angelo Bond)
Invictus 9085—#11 R&B / #44 HOT / #46 UK
Notable cover version: The Blossoms

Chairmen of the Board—"Chairman of the Board"
(with Brian Holland)
Invictus 9086—#10 R&B / #42 HOT / #48 UK

The Flaming Ember—"Stop the World and Let Me Off"
(HDH with Ronald Dunbar, Angelo Bond)
Hot Wax 7010—#43 R&B / #101 HOT

Chairmen of the Board—"Hanging On (To a Memory)"
(HDH with Ronald Dunbar, Daphne Dumas)
Invictus 9089—#28 R&B / #111 HOT
Notable cover version: The Style Council

The Glass House—"Look What We've Done to Love"
(HDH with Ronald Dunbar)
Invictus 9097—#31 R&B / #101 HOT

Chairmen of the Board—"Try On My Love for Size"
(with Brian Holland)
Invictus 9099—#48 R&B / #103 HOT / #20 UK

Freda Payne—"You Brought the Joy"
(with Brian Holland)
Invictus 9100—#21 R&B / #52 HOT

Freda Payne—"The Road We Didn't Take"
(with Brian Holland, Daphne Dumas)
Invictus 9109—#100 HOT

1972

Honey Cone—"The Day I Found Myself"
(HDH with Ronald Dunbar, General Johnson)
Hot Wax 7113—#8 R&B / #23 HOT

The Politicians—"Free Your Mind"
Hot Wax 7114—#33 R&B / #110 HOT

Holland-Dozier, featuring Lamont Dozier—"Why Can't We Be Lovers"
Invictus 9125—#9 R&B / #57 HOT
Notable cover version: Jr. Walker & The All Stars

Laura Lee—"If You Can Beat Me Rockin' (You Can Have My Chair)"
(with Brian Holland, Ronald Dunbar)
Hot Wax 7207—#31 R&B / #65 HOT

Holland-Dozier, featuring Lamont Dozier—"Don't Leave Me Starvin" For Your Love (Part 1)"
Invictus 9133—#13 R&B / #52 HOT
Notable cover version: Laura Lee

★ **Note: From this point forward, all songs written by Lamont Dozier solo, unless otherwise noted.**

1973

Holland-Dozier, featuring Brian Holland—"Slipping Away"
(with Brian and Eddie Holland)
Invictus 1253—#46 R&B

Holland-Dozier, featuring Lamont Dozier—"New Breed Kinda Woman"
(HDH with Richard Wylie)
Invictus 1254—#61 R&B

Lamont Dozier—"Trying to Hold On to My Woman"
ABC 11407—#4 R&B / #15 HOT

1974

R. Dean Taylor—"There's a Ghost in My House"
(HDH with R. Dean Taylor)
V.I.P.—#3 UK
        The Fall—Beggar's Banquet 187—#30 UK (1987)
Notable cover version: Graham Parker

Lamont Dozier—"Fish Ain't Bitin'"
ABC 11438—#4 R&B / #26 HOT

Lamont Dozier—"Let Me Start Tonite"
ABC 12044—#4 R&B / #87 HOT

1975

Lamont Dozier—"All Cried Out"
ABC 12076—#41 R&B / #101 HOT

Z. Z. Hill—"I Created a Monster"
United Artists 631—#40 R&B / #109 HOT

1976

Margie Joseph—"Hear the Words, Feel the Feeling"
(with McKinley Jackson)
Cotillion 44201—#18 R&B

Lamont Dozier—"Can't Get Off Until the Feeling Stops"
Warner 8240—#89 R&B

1977

Shalamar—"Uptown Festival"
Soul Train 10885—#10 R&B / #25 HOT
Note: medley includes "I Can't Help Myself," Stop! In the Name of Love," and "It's the Same Old Song"

1982

Lamont Dozier—"Shout About It"
(with Gary Rotter and Sy Goraieb)
M&M 502—#61 R&B

1983

The Four Tops—"I Just Can't Walk Away"
(HDH)
Motown 1706—#36 R&B / #71 HOT / #18 AC / #95 UK

1985

Alison Moyet—"Invisible"
Columbia 04781—#31 HOT / #21 UK

1987

Simply Red—"Infidelity"
(with Mick Hucknall)
#31 UK

1988

Peabo Bryson & Regina Belle—"Without You"
Elektra 69426—#14 R&B / #8 AC / #89 HOT / #85 UK

Phil Collins—"Two Hearts"
(with Phil Collins)
Atlantic 88980—#1 HOT / #1 AC / #6 UK

1989

The Four Tops—"Loco in Acapulco"
(with Phil Collins)
Arista 111 850—#7 UK

Simply Red—"You've Got It"
(with Mick Hucknall)
Elektra 69269—#7 AC / #46 UK

1990

Debbie Gibson—"Anything is Possible"
(with Debbie Gibson)
Atlantic 87793—#26 HOT / #48 AC / #51 UK

1991

Lamont Dozier—"Love in the Rain"
Atlantic 87687—#60 R&B

2005

Joss Stone—"Spoiled"
(with Beau Dozier and Joss Stone)
Relentless 16—#32 UK

Usher—"Throwback"
(HDH and Richard Wylie sample with Richard Butler, Justin Smith, Patrick Smith)
LaFace album track—#20 R&B / #114 HOT
Samples "You're Gonna Need Me," Dionne Warwick (1973)

2006

Fantasia with Big Boi—"Hood Boy"
(HDH sample with Johnta Austin, Frank DeVol, Antwan Patton)
J Records album track—#21 R&B / #103 HOT
Samples "The Happening," The Supremes (1967)

2008

Lil Wayne—"Gossip"
(HDH sample with Dwayne Carter and Nicholas Warwar)
Cash Money album track—#114 HOT
Samples "Stop in the Name of Love," Margie Joseph (1971)

2010

Marsha Ambrosius—"Far Away"
(HDH sample with Marsha Ambrosius, Sterling Simms, and Justin Smith)
J Records album track—#3 R&B / #74 HOT
Samples "You Keep Me Hangin' On," The Supremes (1966)

LIST OF LAMONT
DOZIER SOLO ALBUMS

Following is a complete list of Lamont's solo albums in order
of release. The entries appear in the following format: album
title, date, record label, release number, charting position on the
Billboard R&B album chart (if applicable), and list of song titles.

Out Here On My Own **(1973)**
ABC Records—ABCX-804 / #11 R&B
Breaking Out All Over
Don't Want Nobody to Come Between Us
Let Me Make Love to You
Fish Ain't Bitin'

Interlude
Trying to Hold On to My Woman
Take Off Your Make Up
Out Here On My Own

Black Bach (1974)
ABC Records—ABCD-839 / #27 R&B
Why Can't We Be Lovers
Thank You for The Dream
All Cried Out
I Wanna Be with You
Let Me Start Tonite
Put Out My Fire
Shine
Rose
Blue Sky, Sliver Bird

Love and Beauty (1974)
Invictus Records—KZ 33134
Why Can't We Be Lovers
Don't Stop Playing Our Song
If You Don't Want to Be in My Life
The Picture Will Never Change
Don't Leave Me
Don't Leave Me (Instrumental)
New Breed Kinda Woman
Enough of Your Love
Slipping Away
★ Note: Unauthorized nonofficial album of previously released
recordings, demos, and instrumentals

Right There (1976)
Warner Bros. Records—BS 2929 / #59 R&B
Prophecy
It's the Same Old Song
Right There
Jump Right On In
Grooving On A Natural High
I Can't Get Off
My Baby's Got A Good Eye
With A Little Bit of Mending
Wild Frame of Mind
Ain't Never Loved Nobody
Joy

Peddlin' Music on the Side (1977)
Warner Bros. Records—BS 3039 / #59 R&B
Sight For Sore Eyes
What Am I Going to Do About You (Girl)
Break the Ice
Tear Down the Walls
Going Back to My Roots
Family
Peddling Music On The Side

Bittersweet (1979)
Warner Bros. Records—BSK 3282
I Got it All with You
We're Just Here to Feel Good
Fly Away Little Bird Song
Boogie Business
True Love is Bittersweet
Tough Act to Follow
Let Your Love Run Free
Love Me to the Max

Lamont (1981)
M&M Records—104AE
You Oughta Be in Pictures
Ain't Never Had it So Good
I Ain't Playing
I See You
The Pressure is On
Shout About It
Locked Into You
Ain't No Way
Help is On the Way

Working On You (1981)
Columbia Records—ARC 37129
Cool Me Out
Why (Ain't My Love Enough)
Nobody Told Me
Too Little Too Long
Playing For Keeps
Interlude
(You've Got Me) Wired Up
Starting Over
Working on You
Chained to Your Heart
You Made Me a Believer

Bigger Than Life (1983)
Demon Records—FIEND 12
Bigger Than Life
Right Where I Wanna Be
On the One
Round Trip Ticket
Love Wars
Call the Wagon
Nowhere to Go but Up
Second Wind
Scarlett O'Hara
Hero of My Heart
★ Note: UK release

Inside Seduction (1991)
Atlantic Records—7 82228 / #28 R&B
Feeling Each Other Out
Love in The Rain
That Ain't Me
Inside Seduction
What Chew Doing
The Vibe
The Quiet's Too Loud
Attitude Up
I Wanna Hold You Forever
No Comment
When We're Together
Pure Heaven

An American Original (2002)
Hithouse Records 8 2436200022 1
Where Did Our Love Go
This Old Heart of Mine
(Love Is Like A) Heatwave
Stop! In the Name of Love
My World Is Empty Without You
I Hear a Symphony
Baby I Need Your Lovin'
Baby Love
I Can't Help Myself (Sugar Pie, Honey Bunch)
How Sweet It Is (To Be Loved By You)
Reach Out, I'll Be There
Reflections

Reflections Of (2004)
Jam Right Entertainment—54633 / #74 R&B
I Hear A Symphony (R&B Remix)
Where Did Our Love Go
This Old Heart of Mine
(Love Is Like A) Heatwave
Stop! In the Name of Love
My World Is Empty Without You
I Hear A Symphony
Baby I Need Your Lovin'
Baby Love
I Can't Help Myself (Sugar Pie, Honey Bunch)
How Sweet It Is (To Be Loved By You)
Reach Out, I'll Be There
Reflections
I Hear a Symphony (Dance Remix)
★ Note: Grammy-nominated album

Reimagination **(2018)**
V2 Records—VVNL329552
Supremes Medley: Where Did Our Love Go, Stop in the Name of
Love, Come See About Me, Baby Love (featuring Graham Nash)
How Sweet It Is (To Be Loved by You) (featuring Gregory Porter)
Reach Out, I'll Be There (featuring Jo Harman)
You Keep Me Hanging On (featuring Rumer)
Reflections (featuring Justin Currie)
I Can't Help Myself (Sugar Pie, Honey Bunch)
This Old Heart of Mine (Is Weak for You) / My World Is Empty
Without You (featuring Cliff Richard)
In My Lonely Room (featuring Todd Rundgren)
Take Me in Your Arms (Rock Me a Little While) (featuring
Marc Cohn)
(Love Is Like A) Heat Wave / Nowhere to Run (featuring
Jo Harman)
Baby I Need Your Loving (featuring Lee Ann Womack)
Bernadette

ACKNOWLEDGMENTS

The process of writing this book required a lot of looking back. As I think about all the people who have come in and out of my life over the years, I'm filled with gratitude for those who shaped me, encouraged me, challenged me, supported me, and loved me.

Though I wrote about them already, I can't say enough about my wonderful family. I have nothing but gratitude for my brother Reggie and my sisters Laretta, Zel, and Norma. If it weren't for family, and especially the support of my Aunt Jenny and Uncle James, I don't think I would be the man I am today. Though she was a little skeptical about the music thing at first, my mother made sacrifices for our family that set each of us on a solid path. I am truly grateful for her influence.

I thank the Master Muse for Barbara, my beautiful partner in all things and the mother of our wonderful children, Beau, Paris, and Desiree. Barbara's parents, Leo and Sally, and her sister Sheryl became a second family to me and my life is richer for having them in it.

Truly loyal friends are hard to come by, and our family has been graced with some really special ones. They don't come any better than Stephanie Crane. She and Barbara have been best friends since they were in high school together. The daughter of Harry Crane, who created *The Honeymooners*, Stephanie followed in her dad's footsteps. She's a wonderful writer, but an even more wonderful supporter of Barbara, me, and our whole family.

Tracy and John Avildsen are Desiree's godparents, and Barbara and I are their daughter Bridget's godparents. John, who was an Oscar-winning director, would film all our family holidays and birthday parties. Sadly, after a battle with pancreatic cancer, he passed away on my birthday in 2017. His loss is huge, and I miss him greatly. Tracy, who is a talented actress, remains a loyal friend to our entire family, and we all value her faithfulness.

Two of my entertainment attorneys, Daniel Stuart and Lynn Quarterman, have worked with Barbara and me, as well as with Beau and Paris, for more than twenty years. I am so grateful to have them in my corner. Not only have they made sure that my legal paperwork is sound, but they are also trusted personal friends.

Another amazing friend in our lives is Jeff Scheftel. And I can't forget Lisa Margolis, who took the photo of me on the front of the book.

I've been with BMI from the very beginning of my music career and have worked with some truly amazing people there over the years. Frances Preston, Barbara Cane, Del Bryant, Linda Livingston, Charlie Feldman, Fred Cannon, Phil Graham, Alison Smith, Mike O'Neill, and the entire BMI staff are now part of my extended family.

I also have to thank the music industry colleagues who have become dear friends, including Jon Platt, Tom Sturges, Andrea Torchia Alford, Jo-Ann Geffen, Jeremy Geffen, Richard Davis, Eric Gardner, Chris Sampson, Fred Mollin, and especially Evan Lamberg for looking out for me over the years.

One of the truly enriching experiences in recent years is the time I spent serving the Recording Academy as a Trustee, a Governor, and a member of the Grammy board. Serving alongside fellow music professionals as an advocate for our industry is an opportunity I treasure. I'll always especially value my time chairing the Advocacy Committee when we walked Capitol Hill to lobby our elected officials to stick up for the rights and protections of musicians and songwriters. Thanks to all those who joined me and to everyone who fights hard on behalf of music creators everywhere.

I want to thank my co-author, Scott B. Bomar, for coming to me with the idea to write my book for BMG, and for being the most incredible collaborator and writer I could ever imagine. Scott, you've been such a blessing to me. Thank you.

Thank you, as well, to the Funk Brothers and all the musicians and recording artists who made me look good throughout my career. And thanks to Bill Brendle, a fabulous orchestrator and arranger I've been working with for the last twenty years.

I also have to thank my brothers, Eddie and Brian Holland, whom I love like family. We might have had our differences over the years, but we created a special body of work together. In the end, I'm really glad we all found each other on West Grand Boulevard all those years ago.

Finally, thank you to Berry Gordy for taking me under your wing at Motown and giving me the freedom to soar. I will always love you.

INDEX

Note: *p* before a number indicates a photograph.

308